D1566515

Hamlin Garland

and the Critics

An Annotated Bibliography

Hamlin Garland
and the Critics
An Annotated Bibliography

by
Jackson R. Bryer
and
Eugene Harding
with the assistance of
Robert A. Rees

The Whitston Publishing Company
Incorporated
Troy, New York
1973

International Standard Book Number 0-87875-020-7
Library of Congress Catalog Card Number 75-183300
Copyright 1973 by Jackson R. Bryer and Eugene Harding
Printed in the United States of America

PREFACE

The long life and literary career of Hannibal Hamlin Garland was one of great variety, considerable controversy, and many paradoxes. His first work, published as the last decade of the nineteenth century began, was hailed as the herald of a new realistic movement in American fiction. His last books, which appeared as a nation all too aware realistically of the seriousness of its financial and political ills was preparing for its second World War in twenty-five years, were largely dismissed as the work of a reactionary eccentric. In between, Hamlin Garland had highly successful careers as a lecturer on literary topics, as a vocal and influential spokesman for Henry George's single-tax policies, as the author of romantic novels, as an elder statesman of American letters who rose to a position of great prominence in the American Academy of Arts and Letters, and as a Pulitzer Prize-winning author of autobiographical volumes upon which his reputation as a writer will most likely most securely rest.

The sheer length of Garland's life and the amount of work he produced, as well as the number of lecture appearances he made throughout the United States, have made the task of achieving any measure of completeness in this bibliography virtually impossible. Many local newspaper interviews and articles have doubtlessly gone unlocated. The library of the University of Southern California has a large collection of newspaper clippings about Garland, and we have been fortunate in having access to this file; but many of these items could neither be identified nor verified and thus could not be listed. They do, however, exist in the collection at Southern California, and we urge the interested student/scholar to consult the complete collection as a supplement to our bibliography.

Somewhat paradoxically we have discovered in our work on Garland that the amount of substantial and worthwhile comment on his work is relatively small. Although he was remembered by the many editorial writers who felt moved to eulogize him in 1940 as the Dean of American Letters, one can almost count on the fingers of two hands the critically valuable contributions on Garland in books and periodicals. For this reason principally, we have tended to include in this bibliography almost anything and everything on Garland which we found. We have not anticipated the use to which our list will be put; nor have we consciously excluded any sort of item, save for the most ephemeral biographical squibs in American literature anthologies and biographical dictionaries.

The basic arrangement of the bibliography is chronological. In this way, we have attempted to demonstrate the fluctuations of Garland's critical reputation as well as the various stages of his career. We have observed this kind of arrangement in the first two sections of the bibliography, reviews and periodicals, but not in the third, books, because most of the comment about Garland in books is grouped within the last twenty or thirty years.

In order to facilitate our task of annotation, we have adopted certain abbreviations. In most instances, we have abbreviated Garland's name to HG or G; New York as a place of publication has been shortened to NY. In addition, we have established abbreviations for the titles of many of Garland's books. A list of these is included following this Preface. The spelling of words such as *Coolly (Coulé, Coulee)* and *theater (theatre)* varies according to their spelling in the text cited or to which reference is made.

The preparation of this bibliography would not have been possible without the help of many persons. In an earlier, somewhat shorter, form, it appeared in the Fall 1970 and Spring 1971 issues of *American Literary Realism*, whose editor, Clayton L. Eichelberger, and his associates were responsible for much of whatever value this final version posesses. Others who contributed significantly were Joseph M. DeFalco, William T. Lenehan, Robert Venuti, Stephen Sirota, and Mrs. Joanne Giza.

Jackson W. Bryer
College Park, Maryland
May, 1973

ABBREVIATIONS

AMERICAN INDIAN	BOOKS OF THE AMERICAN INDIAN
BACK-TRAILERS	BACK-TRAILERS FROM THE MIDDLE BORDER
BOY LIFE	BOY LIFE ON THE PRAIRIE
BURIED CROSSES	THE MYSTERY OF THE BURIED CROSSES
CI	CRUMBLING IDOLS
CAPTAIN	THE CAPTAIN OF THE GRAY-HORSE TROOP
CAVANAUGH	CAVANAUGH
COMPANIONS	COMPANIONS ON THE TRAIL
CONTEMPORARIES	MY FRIENDLY CONTEMPORARIES
DAUGHTER	A DAUGHTER OF THE MIDDLE BORDER
EAGLE' HEART	THE EAGLE'S HEART
FOLKS	PRAIRIE FOLKS
FORESTER'S DAUGHTER	THE FORESTER'S DAUGHTER
FORTY YEARS	FORTY YEARS OF PSYCHIC RESEARCH
GOLDSEEKERS	THE TRAIL OF THE GOLD-SEEKERS
GRANT	ULYSSES S. GRANT
HESPER	HESPER
HIGH TRAILS	THEY OF THE HIGH TRAILS
IMPRESSIONS	IMPRESSIONS OF IMPRESSION-ISM
JASON EDWARDS	JASON EDWARDS
JOYS	JOYS OF THE TRAIL
LONG TRAIL	THE LONG TRAIL
MTR	MAIN-TRAVELLED ROADS
MEMBER	A MEMBER OF THE THIRD HOUSE (novel)
"MEMBER"	"A MEMBER OF THE THIRD HOUSE" (drama)
"MILLER"	"MILLER OF BOSKOBEL" (drama)
MONEY MAGIC	MONEY MAGIC
MOUNTAIN LOVERS	HER MOUNTAIN LOVER
NEIGHBORS	AFTERNOON NEIGHBORS

TABLE OF CONTENTS

v

A. REVIEWS OF BOOKS BY HAMLIN GARLAND

A1. *"MTR."* Chicago *Tribune*, 13 Jun 1891, p. 12.
    Review of *MTR*. HG's stories "have attracted notice
by their Tolstoian boldness, plain speaking, and accurate
observation." His "pictures and incidents of toil...are
surely wonderfully touching and suggestive." "'Mrs.
Ripley's Trip'" is unexcelled, in its way, by anything in
our home grown literature of homely things."

A2. "Pictures of Western-Farm Life." *America*, 6 (18 Jun 1891),
    332-333.
    Review of *MTR*. Reviewer protests that, though G's
realistic pictures are probably accurate, he does seem to
dwell too much on the seamy side of life. G's stories are
powerful but "inexpressibly sad." Several stories are
briefly summarized; and the review concludes, "for power,
truth and pathos it would be difficult to find six stories by
another American author which would bear comparison with
these."

A3. "Summer Reading/Novels and Short Stories." N.Y. *Daily
    Tribune*, 28 Jun 1891, p. 14.
    Brief review of *MTR*. "Every one of the stories is ex-
cellent, and they are fit to be compared with the best continental work of the same kind."

A4. Flower, B. O. "A Vivid Picture of the Lights and Shadows
    of Western Farm Life." *Arena*, 4 (Aug 1891), xvii-xxiii.
    Review of *MTR*. It is "one of the most valuable con-
tributions to distinctive American literature which has
appeared in many years." "With the boldness of Tolstoi,
with the originality in treatment of Ibsen, and with a wealth
of tenderness, love, and humanity far exceeding either,

Mr. G has...given [us] a work destined, I believe, to hold a
permanent place in our literature, and to be one of the
most characteristic and valued contributions of the new
school known as Impressionists." HG is to be praised
for presenting the "truth" about the Western farmer.
[Each story is briefly described and commented on.]
There are, however, "positive defects" in the volume.
They arise principally from HG's "enthusiastic accep-
tation of the tenets of realism or literalism." Flower
wishes that "our author had dealt somewhat more spar-
ingly with dirt, grime, and perspiration." But, despite
these small imperfections, *MTR* "should find a place in
the library of every thoughtful person who is interested
in the welfare of the great toiling masses."

A5. Harte, W. B. "About Books." *New England Magazine*, 10
(Aug 1891), 3-9.
Review of *MTR* (4-7). Stories in the volume are "as
realistic as anything written by Ibsen; but at the same
time, they have a more dramatic quality, and are besides
relieved with an undercurrent of humor, which makes the
realism, true realism." Though G is socially concerned,
he never preaches in his art. His stories are written with
"deep conviction." Overall, this is an extremely enthusiastic review.

A6. "Four Novels." *Nation*, 53 (13 Aug 1891), 125.
Review of *MTR* (125). "Mr. G writes with the pen of
uncompromising realism." "There is no doubt that power
of observation and of rendering the results with exactness
is disclosed in these stories; but they lose by a succes-
sive reading. Descriptions of the same uninviting interiors,
the same birds and insects ... finally produce an impression
of monotony and mannerism."

A7. [Howells, William Dean]. "Editor's Study." *Harper's*, 83
(Sep 1891), 638-642.
Review of *MTR* (639-640). HG "has a certain harshness
and bluntness, an indifference to the more delicate charms
of style," but he "has a fine courage to leave a fact with the
reader, ungarnished and unvarnished." "Under the Lion's
Paw" is "a lesson in political economy, as well as a

tragedy of the darkest cast''; ''Return of a Private''
is ''a satire of the keenest edge, as well as a tender
and mournful idyl''; ''Up the Coulé'' is ''a tremendous
situation'' and ''the allegory of the whole world's
civilization''; ''Mrs. Ripley's Trip'' has ''a delicate
touch, like that of Mrs. Wilkins.'' *MTR* is a ''work of
art'' and ''of fine art,'' though ''the material will strike
many gentilities as coarse and common.''

A8. ''Reviews.'' *Saturday Review* (London), 73 (23 Jan 1892),
     97-110.
     Review of *MTR* (103). Very brief review which praises
     the book for its realistic pictures of the West.

A9. ''Books of the Day.'' *Arena*, 5 (Feb 1892), xxix-xli.
     Review of *Jason Edwards* (xxix-xxxiii). After an-
     nouncing that he knows of ''no American writer who pre-
     sents real life as vivdly and powerfully as Mr. G,'' the
     reviewer harangues dilettante and genteel literature,
     which stands in contrast to the realism of HG, an author
     who seeks truth and reform. ''Mr. G's new novel is very
     strong; so vividly are many scenes presented that the
     reader for days cannot erase the mental pictures. And
     this strength . . . comes not from any tricks or inventions
     of the author; it depends on his absolute fidelity to truth
     or reality.''
     ''Unlike most works which deal with social problems
     in story form, this work is nowhere dull for it does not
     preach; it pictures facts, presenting them so vividly that
     the interest is sustained from cover to cover. It is also
     a work of great interest from a literary point of view and
     this of course gives it an added value.''

A10. ''The Short Story.'' *Atlantic*, 69 (Feb 1892), 261-270.
     Review of *MTR* (266). HG's earnestness is to be com-
     mended, but it is difficult to accept the totally grim
     pictures of life in the West that he paints. HG ''in his
     enthusiasm for Mr. Howells . . . has married Russian de-
     spair and French realism.'' Nevertheless, he ''may be
     telling the truth. If he is, the sum of human grief and
     suffering is still greater than we had supposed. Mean-
     while, writing is writing, and Mr. G must accept and take

3

to heart the warning that monotony is the danger of the
earnest man.''

A11. ''Recent Publications.'' New Orleans *Daily Picayune*, 28
Feb 1892, p. 11.
Brief review of *Jason Edwards*. ''The wealthy and
cultured one-tenth [of the world] ...does not know how
the poor and struggling nine-tenths live, and such works
as this, which bears the impress of truth upon its face,
will enlighten them if they care to know.''

A12. Matthews, Brander. ''American Fiction Again.'' *Cosmopolitan*, 12 (Mar 1892), 636-640.
Review of *MTR* (638-639). Matthews praises HG's
realism, his attempt to say something about real men
and women, but laments the crudeness in his style. HG
is the first writer to bring the West to the reading public,
but he is often too pessimistic: ''This note of pessimism,
heard now and again in these virile tales, is the only
thing about them which is not American.''

A13. ''Recent Fiction.'' *Overland*, 2d S, 19 (Mar 1892), 330-333.
Review of *MTR* (332). In these stories ''The Man with
a Hoe theme is translated into terms of American life.''
But the harshness of the stories is only one side of the
truth. ''Mr. G would doubtless disclaim any intention of
showing the whole truth in his stories, and put them forward only as dashes of shadow to modify the general
picture of rural life in literature.''

A14. ''Four New Novels.'' N.Y. *Times*, 20 Mar 1892, p. 19.
Review of *Jason Edwards*. HG's ''style is clear and
robust, and he presents a true picture of one of the sad-
der phases of American life.''

A15. ''Three Books of Stories.'' N.Y. *Times*, 17 Apr 1892, p. 19.
Review of *Member*. ''Mr. G is crude at times, for he
tells of the Octopus, reaching 'into every man's pocket.' ''
The novel ''may serve to show how much corruption there
is and act as a warning.''

A16. Flower, B. O. ''Books of the Day.'' *Arena*, 5 (May 1892),
xxxiii-xlvii.

Review of *Member* (xl-xliii). HG's descriptions are "powerful, thrilling, and vivid," even when he deals with the East as he does here. The "dramatic intensity ...thrills the reader" at times. [Flower uses the review as a platform for the expression of his own opinions on corruption and government.]

A17. "The New Books." *Review of Reviews* (American), 5 (May 1892), 499-503.
Very brief review of *Member* (503). HG "writes in breezy, forceful familiarity with the vernacular of the average Western American."

A18. "Fiction." *Literary World*, 23 (7 May 1892), 165-167.
Brief review of *Member* (166). HG "presents real life untouched by poetry or beauty of any kind," and his story "has a very wholesome moral."

A19. "More Novels." *Nation*, 54 (12 May 1892), 362-363.
Review of *Member* (362-363). The book is "a righteous effort to bring to judgment the political trickster and all his works," but HG's style and manner are deficient.

A20. "Briefer Notices." *Public Opinion*, 13 (14 May 1892), 146-147.
Very brief review of *Member* (147). "The book is not agreeable, because it has so many evil characters who indulge in coarse language and profanity; but the plot holds the attention quite steadily. It is written in a terse, forcible style."

A21. "Romance in Dakota." Brooklyn *Daily Eagle*, 24 Jul 1892, p. 17.
Review of *Norsk*. The work is "unsurpassed as a picture of the civilized man at once co-operating with and fighting bountiful but savage nature." There is "nothing in story telling literature to excel the naturalness, pathos, humor and homelike interest with which the little foreigner Elga's development is traced." The only blemish in the story is that "the dialect becomes, as in so many clever American stories, needlessly trashy."

A22. Payne, William Morton. "Recent Books of Fiction." *Dial*,
13 (Aug 1892), 101-105.
Review of *Member* (102-103). "If Mr. HG continues to
produce works as strong as *Member*, he will make himself
a distinct literary force." In the book, "his expression
taking the form of a compactly knit and strikingly dramatic narrative, he holds the attention almost breathless,
and leaves the reader no opportunity to reflect upon his
faults of style."

A23. "Tales by Balzac and Others." N.Y. *Times*, 7 Aug 1892,
p. 19.
Review of *Norsk*. This "little romance" can make one
both "laugh and cry."

A24. "Fiction." *Literary World*, 23 (27 Aug 1892), 294-296.
Brief review of *Norsk* (294). The "whole story" is
"charmingly poetic. The characters are well drawn and
vivid, but it is the manner in which the story is told that
gives the value to Mr. G's book."

A25. "Recent Publications." New Orleans *Daily Picayune*, 4
Sept 1892, I, 7.
Review of *Spoil*. Reviewer suggests that, contrary to
G's own claims, he seems to know nothing about the Mid-
West. The style of *Spoil* is awkward and thus the book is
"heavy, unlikely and slanderous."

A26. "The World of Books." N.Y. *World*, 18 Sep 1892, p. 28.
Review of *Spoil*. Book is a "wholesome sample of the
realistic style of writing." Reviewer calls G a genius
and compares end of *Spoil* to Dickens' *Great Expectations*.

A27. Flower, B. O. "Books of the Day." *Arena*, 6 (Oct 1892),
xli-lv.
Review of *Spoil* (xli-xlvi). The book's strength lies in
the "marvelous fidelity with which life is portrayed";
it would not be "an exaggeration to claim that *Spoil* is
the greatest story of life in the Northwest that has ever
been written, and the most faithful picture of conditions
as they exist in this section which has yet appeared in
American literature."

A28. Habberton, John. "All the Books." *Godey's*, 125 (Oct 1892),
       403-410.
       Brief reviews of *Norsk* and *Jason Edwards* (408). Re-
       viewer finds "little imagination" in *Norsk*, but a lot of
       romance and photographic fidelity to the western scene.
       The review of *Jason Edwards* is mostly plot summary.

A29. "New Books." *Literary Northwest*, 2 (Oct 1892), 61-65.
       Brief review of *MTR* (62-63). "Mr. G unites as writers
       seldom do, truth and art. The children can read and enjoy
       his stories; the philosopher can spend his life in the solu-
       tion of the problems suggested."

A30. "The New Books." *Review of Reviews* (American), 6 (Oct
       1892), 366-372.
       Very brief review of *Spoil* (372). It is "G's best novel
       thus far."

A31. "Novels and Short Stories." *Book Buyer*, 9 (Oct 1892), 381-
       382.
       Brief review of *Norsk* (381). "On the whole, the story
       is one of the best pieces of work that Mr. G has done."

A32. "Recent Novels." *Nation*, 55 (6 Oct 1892), 262-264.
       Brief review of *Norsk* and *Spoil* (262). The quality of
       HG's realism is "bludgeonlike" and takes away all the
       charm from his work--what little charm exists. HG's
       facts are always true; but "facts do not make art," and
       there is a certain carelessness in the workmanship.

A33. Flower, B. O. "Books of the Day/Some Notable Reformative
       Works of Fiction." *Arena*, 6 (Nov 1892), lxii-lxv.
       Brief review of *Member* (lxiv). The novel unmasks
       corruption in government and corporations. It is a
       "powerful dramatic story which teaches a great truth."

A34. "Recent Fiction." *Critic*, NS 18 (5 Nov 1892), 248-250.
       Brief review of *Spoil*. "There is a tremendous flavor of
       the wild West about everything here, but however interest-
       ing it may be as an agency for the development of a great
       country, it is hardly profitable as a theme for literature."

A35. "New Novels/By American and Foreign Authors." N.Y.
Daily Tribune, 13 Nov 1892, p. 14.
Review of *Spoil* and *Norsk*. *Spoil* is "trite"; its characters "are in no respect interesting or attractive"; and
"the shadows are too black; the compensations are too
generally ignored; the coarseness and roughness of grain
are put too much in evidence."
There are "pretty and pathetic things" in *Norsk* but
also "a hardness and an exaggerated realism which are
dangerous traits in a young writer.... Mr. G has apparently to learn that even in new settlements and under dis-
couraging conditions there remains enough spring in human
life to make it need, seek and find amusement; and that in
the hewing out of independence there are occasional lei-
sure, recreation and even festivity."

A36. Habberton, John. "All the Books." *Godey's*, 125 (Dec 1892),
641-650.
Review of *Member* (644). Brief plot summary reflecting
G's accurate picture of government corruption.

A37. Payne, William Morton. "Recent American Fiction." *Dial*,
14 (16 Feb 1893), 112-115.
Brief review of *Spoil* (114). HG "is a vigorous writer,
acutely conscious of a mission and a message, but his
work is sadly defective in both structure and expression." He employs "the methods of a realism now much
in vogue, but with little imaginative coloring, and still
less insight into the deeps of human character."

A38. Flower, B. O. "Books of the Day." *Arena*, 7 (Apr. 1893),
i-xxi.
Review of *Folks* (xiii-xiv). This powerfully written
book of stories forms a companion volume to *MTR*. "The
Sociable at Dudley's" is "a wonderful piece of realism."
"There is a real historical value in ... [HG's] work,
greater than that of anyone who has heretofore essayed to
portray life in the Northwest."

A39. Reid, Mary J. "Book Reviews." *Literary Northwest*, 2 (Apr
1893), 428-434.

8

Review of *Folks* (431). More than any other American
writer, HG resembles Turgenev. "If one would know what
life upon a Dakota farm is in all its bitterness, pathos
and sweetness, read" *Folks.*

A40. "Recent Fiction." *Nation,* 56 (1 Jun 1893), 408.
Review of *Folks.* Although HG's work is realistic,
"the novelty of the region which he is introducing to
literature is not sufficient of itself to maintain one's
interest." HG should deal more with "the hearts of
his prairie folk" and less with his settings.

A41. "New Books and Reprints." *Saturday Review* (London), 76
(15 July 1893), 82-84.
Very brief review of *Folks* (83). Characters are "presented with admirable force and not without humour."

A42. "Our Library Table." *Athenaeum,* No. 3439 (23 Sep 1893),
416-417.
Review of *Folks* (416). Compared to the works of Bret
Harte, the stories lack "charm." They "are more useful
as pictures of Western life in America under certain conditions than valuable as literature."

A43. "Songs." Boston *Evening Transcript,* 4 Dec 1893, p. 6.
Advance review of *Songs.* "When . . . [HG] theorizes
least he is of course most an artist. And although his
disdain of forms occasionally appears with startling
distinctness, in the main he sinks notion in emotion in
Songs and with refreshing and often delicious naturalness
sings of the life and nature that he knows best of all."

A44. Monroe, Lucy. "Chicago Letter." *Critic,* NS 20 (9 Dec
1893), 384.
Mention of and praise for *Songs*: "In spite of their rough-
nesses and occasional discords," HG's verses "have the
fragrance of the soil; they catch the color of cloud shadows on tasselled grain, they have the terrible freedom
of the wide fields . . . ; they have even the loneliness of
the prairies and their crushing absorption of man in nature."

A45. "A Western Image-Breaker." N.Y. *Daily Tribune*, 20 May
    1894, p. 14.
    Review of *CI*. "The trouble with Mr. G is that while
    he is a young man of good natural powers, his intellec-
    tual training has been scanty and defective. Matters that
    were trite when his great-grandfather was a little boy he
    advances as new discoveries; his unbalanced enthusi-
    asms leave him unable to see the just relations of things.
    With the zeal of a new convert he starts out to subdue all
    the world to some very old theories; with short-sighted
    fanaticism he makes some minor and yet unsettled ques-
    tions of art and letters the essential articles of a creed."

A46. C. "Some Recent American Verse." *Poet-Lore*, 6 (Jun 1894),
    204-213.
    Review of *Songs* (204-205). The "breeziness and fresh-
    ness of the great Western prairies" breathe through these
    verses. HG knows nature and has good choice of imagery.
    His real strength in poetry is most visible when he deals
    with some "homely incident." "Growing Old" and "The
    Farmer's Wife" illustrate that common touch.

A47. "CI." *Literary World*, 25 (2 Jun 1894), 164-165.
    Review. "All that Mr. G says of the virtues of origin-
    ality and truth to nature is but the thousandth repetition
    of propositions that are dangerously near to platitudes
    for any well-read person." HG "studiously avoids spe-
    cific facts. They would easily make an end of his soph-
    omoric rhetoric...."

A48. "Mr. HG's Essays." *Independent*, 46 (21 Jun 1894), 801.
    Review of *CI*. "Mr. G has a delightful genius, a rich,
    honest nature; but he is impatient because in fifteen
    minutes or thereabout he cannot convince the world that
    the classics are a set of stolid sphinxes and that all that
    art needs at present to make it flame like a sunrise is
    simply to turn loose upon it a prime lot of Western boys
    and girls who have been happily steered free of collegi-
    ate influences and classical reading." "We do not find
    Mr. G a clear reasoner; he does not seem to be familiar
    with the history of literatures; he evidently speaks from
    his emotional centers, not from rich treasures of know-

ledge;...but we feel with a thrill of welcome the genuine
American spirit flashing out of all his unscientific, ill-
digested and critically ineffectual struggles toward voicing the meaning of literary art.''

A49. ''On Various Topics.'' *Book Buyer*, 11 (Jul 1894), 307-309.
Brief review of *CI* (308). HG's essays ''seem a trifle
hysterical to the reader who lives in the chill of Atlantic
fogs.''

A50. Hale, Edward E., Jr. ''Signs of Life in Literature.'' *Dial*,
17 (1 Jul 1894), 11-13.
Review of *CI* (11-12). Nothing HG says is really new.
''He takes Walt Whitman's thesis as to a native literature,
looks at in the light of the experience of the last twenty-
five years, and puts forth the whole thing as his own prophecy for the future.''

A51. [Review of *CI*]. *Nation*, 59 (19 Jul 1894), 53.
''The practice of most men is notoriously better than
the worst of their dogmas, and Mr. G will not be found an
exception to the rule.'' HG should reassess his ideas on
culture.

A52. ''*CI*.'' *Critic*, NS 22 (15 Sep 1894), 169.
Review. ''The East is naturally proud of the West, even
when she is somewhat boisterous and self-asserting, as an
old athlete is proud of the hard knocks he gets from the
lad whom he has taught to box; but there is a limit to patience.'' [Generally biased, unfavorable review.]

A53. ''Poetry and Verse.'' *Critic*, NS 22 (20 Oct 1894), 257.
Review of *Songs*. HG ''confounds the raw material of
poetry with the finished product; his realism often lacks
the charm that feeling alone can give.'' ''Pictorial,
rather than musical, Mr. G's verse too often suffers from
Whitmanity.''

A54. Flower, B. O. ''Some Important New Books.'' *Arena*, 10
(Nov 1894), xvi-xxxvi.
Review of *CI* (xvi-xviii). HG is ''profoundly human and
genuinely sympathetic,'' more so than Ibsen, with whom

he is compared. Flower praises the poetic quality of
HG's work and singles out "The Return of a Private" in
MTR and "A Branch Road" as being "highly poetical"
in parts. *Spoil* is truthful and vivid.

A55. "Literature of Today." Chicago *Times-Herald*, 7 Dec 1895,
pp. 10-11.
Review of *Rose* (10). "Of the simplicity, the honesty
and the unblinking candor of the book, too much cannot
be said in praise. It is candor that causes one to wince,
and much of it is unnecessarily brutal, as Mr. G, if he
were a woman, would know; but not one word is super-
fluous from the author's standpoint...."

A56. "Recent Publications." New Orleans *Daily Picayune*, 23
Dec 1895, p. 9.
Review of *Rose*. Very brief plot summary, which con-
cludes by saying that it is a "readable tale."

A57. F., E. "Realism Run Mad." Providence *Sunday Journal*, 29
Dec 1895, II, 13.
Review of *Rose*. HG is of no consequence and has
never written any "literature." He is too concerned with
sex, and his style is like that of a police report. The
reviewer summarizes *Rose*, pointing out its shortcomings
and HG's obsessions. [A scathing attack on HG, Howells,
and realism.]

A58. "New Books." Philadelphia *Press*, 5 Jan 1896, III, 28.
Review of *Rose*. HG has failed in the novel: "it lacks
substance, style and interest." It is realistic after the
manner of Howells, but so many of Howells' imitators
have made realism distasteful. HG has used "filth in
the making of fiction." Some passages in the novel
could not be quoted in a newspaper. HG can't write better stories than he has in the past, and none worse than
Rose.

A59. "Wisconsin Folks." N.Y. *Times*, 5 Jan 1896, p. 31.
Review of *Rose*. "The book can hardly be called morbid and unwholesome, for it lacks the artistic power to be
thus dignified; but Mr. G's modernity is depressing, and

his fancied originality is merely a bad case of atavism
as Mr. Howells would call it." HG's "style is not good,
his vocabulary is neither rich nor pure, but he has splendid faith in himself, and we trust he is in the enjoyment
of the good health he prates so much about."

A60. "Among the New Books." Cincinnati *Commerical Gazette*,
12 Jan 1896, p. 23.
Review of *Rose*. Destined to be the "book of the season." *Rose* is realistic but contains perhaps too much
detail. The heroine is "wonderfully sketched all the way,"
and readers will enjoy watching her grow up.

A61. Trent, W. P. "Mr. G's New Novel." *Bookman* (NY), 2
(Feb 1896), 512-514.
Review of *Rose*. "It is almost needless to say that
Mr. G's latest story is frankly realistic; it is a pleasure
to add that it is well written, strong, and in the main
wholesome." HG will be a great writer, but he needs
work on characterization. He is a writer much like
Thomas Hardy.

A62. Payne, William Morton. "Recent Fiction." *Dial*, 20 (1 Feb
1896), 76-81.
Review of *Rose* (80). The title of the novel "is a most
uncompromising title, and seems to symbolize an unnecessarily stern insistence upon the particular form of realism
or veritism of which Mr. HG has so often made himself so
outspoken and unamiable a prophet." The novel itself is
"characterized by several noticeable defects, such as an
obtrusive didacticism, a repulsive lack of reticence concerning those details of the sex problem that it should be
the first principle of wholesome art to avoid, and a style
that is often slovenly." But in the creation of the character Rose "Mr. G has achieved his success."

A63. "Literature." *Independent*, 48 (6 Feb 1896), 188-190.
Review of *Rose* (189). The novel is "strikingly un-
equal." The early chapters "are flagrantly low in their
purpose, and just miss being obscene in some of their
gross allusions .... Obviously wrought in imitation of
Flaubert and Zola and Tolstoi, the book falls far short

13

of its models and rings with a cheap, gruff and shallow
rusticity. It has no style, no fascination, no beauty.
Evidently Mr. G looks upon beauty as inimical to truth.''
The picture of the Middle West ''is about as true as the
picture of a woman with a cancer on her face would be
true to the feminine countenance of our country.'' ''The
story has its fine points, its flashes of true and strong
description, its occasional gleams of dramatic fire, and
its scattered leaves of natural beauty; but the whole is
hopelessly rough, uncouth, swaggering in its attitudes,
plebeian in its taste and vulgar in its meaning.''

A64. [Review of *Rose*]. *Critic*, NS 25 (8 Feb 1896), 89.
Rose reflects the influence of Zola and Howells. It is
sustained by its ''hearty, vivid, flesh-and-blood realism,
which makes it readable even to those who disapprove
most conscientiously of many things in it.'' In comparison
with Hardy's *Jude The Obscure*, *Rose* ''leaves a more dis-
agreeable taste in the mouth . . . . Mr. G's word 'sexmaniac'
is barbarous enough; but the continual dwelling on (we
had almost said gloating over) the thing is far worse.''
Rose lacks style.

A65. ''The Midland Book Table.'' *Midland Monthly*, 5 (Mar 1896),
285-288.
Review of *Rose* (285). ''There is in this latest novel
of Mr. G even more suggestion of power than was to be
found in *MTR*. Rose is by far the best heroine this artist
has yet pictured.'' There is ''purpose'' in the novel; ''but
it is suggested, not forced. It is made subordinate to the
author's artistic sense.''

A66. Howells, William Dean. ''Life and Letters.'' *Harper's Weekly*,
40 (7 Mar 1896), 223.
Review of *Rose*. ''The scheme'' of the novel ''has apparently been so dear to the author, the lesson he wished
to convey has seemed so important, that he has somewhat
sacrificed the free movement of his characters to them''
at times. At other times, ''there is a frankness in his portrayal of the rustic conditions which Rose springs from,
very uncommon in our fiction, and there is an acknowledg-
ment of facts and influences usually blinked.'' But ''along

with this valuable truth there is a strain of sentimentality which discredits it." Howells also remains un-
convinced that a person, man or woman, can live down
his past; so he cannot accept Rose on HG's terms.
Finally, Rose is "less interesting and charming...
in her Chicago phase than in her student avatar in
Madison." The parts of the book dealing with university life are "a contribution to literature" and "alone
would justify the being of the book."

A67. "Recent Fiction/Some Fancy and Some Realism." N.Y.
Daily Tribune, 19 Apr 1896, p. 26.
    Review of *Rose*. HG's "style is turgid, strained and
forced; his psychology materialistic and vicious. Life
to him is a series of purely physical and physiological
sensations, more or less closely indentified with sex.
One may search his pages in vain for a glimpse of pure
spiritual emotion--there is not one."

A68. "Recent Fiction." *Review of Reviews* (American), 13
(May 1896), 627-631.
    Review of *Rose* (627). Although Rose's "life in the
town of Madison and collegiate work in the university
are passed over quite too sketchily," G has "given us
a strong, clear picture of certain phases of life in the
Northwest." G "is more successful in the short story
than in the novel; nevertheless his work gives every
promise of growing riper and better in the future."

A69. "Fiction." *Saturday Review* (London), 83 (30 Jan 1897),
128-129.
    Brief review of *Rose* (128): "Some may object to the
extreme outspokenness on subjects of sex. There is,
perhaps, a little too much of it; but one can see the
necessity for it in most instances, and the general tone
of the book is by no means objectionable, though subjects are now and then touched upon which even contemporary fiction usually avoids."

A70. "New Fiction." *Saturday Review* (London), 83 (29 May
1897), 615-616.

Review of *Rose*, which is "a good book, in spite of its being written in American, in which language 'plead' (presumably pronounced 'pled') is the past tense of 'plead,' " because it "gives us a fresh notion of Amercan life, and of country life in Wisconsin, of city life in Chicago, and it shows American woman from her own point of view."

A71. "New Novels." *Athenaeum*, No. 3643 (21 Aug 1897), 252-253.

Review of *Rose* (253). Although the novel is "more robust and less imitative" than most American novels, and although Rose is "a fine creature," who is "described with some care," her portrait "is not very successful" because "one fails to get any vivid idea of the girl." HG "has much to learn in the matter of style," and he has "not yet shaken himself free from Americanisms." The end of the book seems "tame," but possibly Mr. G himself "intends to imply that the end is commonplace, that woman's highest aim is marriage, and that even a poetess reaches a sublime goal if she succeeds in marrying a good, honest sort of fellow."

A72. "Recent Publications." New Orleans *Daily Picayune*, 22 Aug 1897, II, 24.

Review of *Wayside*. This is G's most charming book. High praise for the first story in the collection, "A Preacher's Love Story."

A73. "Fiction." *Saturday Review* (London), 85 (12 Mar 1898), 368-370.

Brief review of *Wayside* (370). Tales are "worth reading," although none are "quite so good or so new" as *Rose*.

A74. "Mr. G's Writings." *Critic*, NS 29 (26 Mar 1898), 213.

Brief review of *Jason Edwards, Member, Spoil, Wayside*. HG is an interesting figure in literature not so much for his artistic worth, "though that is not small," but because "he has so exhaustively set forth his discontent with all kinds of human conditions as to make himself a very satisfactory mouthpiece for the dissatisfied." One finds in HG's work a growing optimism. "We can hardly ask writers to be more complaisant than life, but we certainly have the right to complain when they depict existence as even more depressing than it has pleased Providence to make it."

A75. "American Fiction." *Athenaeum*, No. 3675 (2 Apr 1898), 434.

Review of *Wayside*. The novel is not as good as *Rose* because there is too much "affectation" and self-consciousness. However, it is interesting because it deals with rural areas not well-known.

A76. "Books of the Week." *Outlook*, 58 (16 Apr 1898), 979-982.

Brief review of *Sweetwater* (979-980). "One is always impressed by Mr. G's obvious sincerity, but it cannot be said that this story is an illustration of that kind of fiction to which Mr. G himself has given the name of veritism."

A77. "Recent Novels." *Spectator*, 81 (16 Jul 1898), 88-89.

Review of *Jason Edwards* (88-89). HG is a person "who entertains strong views on social and industrial questions, but he is not an aggressive partisan, and most readers will regard his story in the light of an effective illustration of the fact that failure can often be far more heroic than success." The last section of the novel is "a charming sketch of the rigours and romance of life on a Dakota prairie."

A78. "Novel Notes." *Bookman* (London), 14 (Aug 1898), 138-141.

Brief review of *Jason Edwards* and *Norsk* (138). "Never in American fiction has the life of the workers been so sternly pictured" as in *Jason*. It is "the saddest [tale] that has ever come across the Atlantic to us." *Norsk* is "of more cheerful tenour and reminds us of the best days of Bret Harte."

A79. "Recent Fiction." *Saturday Review* (London), 86 (1 Oct 1898), 447-449.

Brief review of *Jason Edwards* and *Norsk* (448). Latter is the better of the two, for "we have the true touch and feeling necessary for the perfect picture, and we find ourselves keenly following it through to the end, never wearying"; but all of G's books "always merit serious attention," for he writes "with strength and force."

A80. "Books of the Week." *Outlook*, 60 (29 Oct 1898), 536-544.
Review of *Grant* (539-540). Basically descriptive.

A81. "HG's Life of Grant." N.Y. *Times Saturday Review of Books*, 29 Oct 1898, p. 715.
Review of *Grant*. The reviewer praises *Grant* for its scholarly research and addition of numerous new facts concerning Grant's life as well as its "lucid and charming style." HG's work, especially his objectivity, wins laudatory comment.

A82. Monroe, Lucy. "Chicago Items." *Book News*, 17 (Nov 1898), 126-128.
Review of *Grant* (126). Although "it is undeniable that a bit of hero-worship has crept into the book" and although "as a human document the work would have been more accurate if [HG] had dealt less tenderly with the warrior's early weakness," the narrative "is simple," and it is "a life of Grant reduced to its essential elements."

A83. Williams, Talcott. "With the New Books." *Book News*, 17 (Nov 1898), 117-118.
Brief review of *Grant* (118). "There is some want of grasp and comprehension due to Mr. G's lack of general knowledge and education, but there is in circulation no better book for those who have grown up since the war."

A84. "Final Notes." *Book Buyer*, 17 (Dec 1898), 482-493.
Very brief descriptive mention of *Grant* (484).

A85. "The Season's Books." *Outlook*, 62 (3 Dec 1898), 875-884.
Brief review of *Grant* (878). "This is a plain, homely, straight-forward account . . . a successful endeavor to tell the story at first hand, to fill in the background of actual conditions, and to let the man stand forth in his strength and his faults without any attempt to heighten the one or to soften the other."

A86. "Briefs on New Books." *Dial*, 26 (1 Jan 1899), 23-25.
Brief review of *Grant* (25). Highly laudatory review
commends the thoroughness of HG's work.

A87. "Biography and Gossip." *Critic*, NS 31 (Mar 1899), 257-260.
Review of *Grant* (257-258). "If the author has dwelt
upon the strong points of Grant's character, he has made
no attempt to gloss over the weak ones," and this impartiality is praiseworthy. [High praise for HG's work.]

A88. "Books of the Week." *Outlook*, 62 (13 May 1899), 128-132.
Brief note (129) announcing that *Rose* has been issued
in a new edition by Macmillan.

A89. "G's Journey to the Klondike." N.Y. *Times Saturday Review
of Books*, 10 Jun 1899, p. 384.
Review of *Goldseekers*. Although "the quality of Mr.
G's descriptive writing is not much above the average of
daily newspaper correspondence," the book is "readable,"
despite HG's "deficient" sense of humor. The "unini-
tiated reader" will be both puzzled and amused by HG's
verses, although some of them "would pass muster with
much of the magazine verse of the present hour."

A90. "Books of the Week." *Outlook*, 62 (24 Jun 1899), 442-447.
Brief review of *Goldseekers* (446). "Whatever Mr. G
writes has the stamp of his own abounding personality,
has a style which is attracting increasing attention, and
has a distinctly American worth."

A91. "G in the Klondike." Brooklyn *Daily Eagle*, 25 Jun 1899,
p. 19.
Review of *Goldseekers*. "The poems add nothing to the
interest or charm of the prose story, which is considerable.
Indeed, it is one of the best stories of a wilderness journey that we have ever read."

A92. "The New Books." New Orleans *Daily Picayune*, 2 Jul 1899,
II, 12.
Brief review of *Goldseekers*. Book is "not likely to
broaden" G's reputation. The articles are "undeniably"
clever, "but of a rather hysterical kind of cleverness,

which leaves the reader in doubt as to whether the
author is writing fiction or travel.''

A93. ''Mr. G's Prose and Verse.'' Springfield (Mass.) *Daily Republican*, 10 Jul 1899, p. 4.

Review of *Goldseekers*. ''The echoes of other poets
contained here and there throughout the book would be
of no moment in a writer who has not issued so belligerent a Declaration of Independence as HG's . . . . It is
a quite sufficient piece of originality, however, for a poet
to ride through thousands of miles of wilderness making
poetic records of travel, and it must be allowed that Mr.
G has used his material in an effective and artistic manner.''

A94. Stanley, H. M. ''Late Books on Alaska.'' *Dial*, 27 (1 Aug
1899), 72-73.

Brief mention of *Goldseekers* (72). It is ''a work of
real and vivid power, at once poetic, romantic, realistic.''

A95. ''Three Books on the Klondike.'' *Nation*, 69 (24 Aug 1899),
155-156.

Review of *Goldseekers* (156). The book presents with
''wonderful vividness the hardships and miseries of the
unknown trail.'' Although it is unimpressive as a travel
book, ''as a personal narrative in connection with an
historic movement it will be read with much interest,
even long after the movement itself has ceased.''

A96. ''Books of the Week.'' *Outlook*, 63 (21 Oct 1899), 463-465.

Brief note announcing that a new edition of *MTR*, HG's
best work, has been issued with several new stories
added.

A97. Mendum, E. Bedloe. [Review of *MTR*]. Boston *Courier*,
22 Oct 1899.

A series of short stories all describing ''the penalty''
of civilization and depicting the tedium and duress on
the part of the Westerner supporting the Eastern professional.

A98. ''Books of the Week.'' *Outlook*, 63 (9 Dec 1899), 887-891.

Very brief review of *Boy Life* (887). "No one has better described life on a great farm," and the book "brings very graphically before the reader the movement of a life distinctly American and now fast receding into the past."

A99. "Books for the Young." *Dial*, 27 (16 Dec 1899), 500-503.
Brief mention of *Boy Life* (500). This is "a book in which the author is much more at home than he was in telling what little girls did under somewhat similar circumstances."

A100. "Literature." *Independent*, 52 (4 Jan 1900), 65-73.
Very brief review (73) of new edition of *MTR*.

A101. "Klondyke in American Literature." *Athenaeum*, No. 3767 (6 Jan 1900), 13.
Review of *Goldseekers*. The "best thing of the kind that has been published," *Goldseekers* demonstrates the value of "studied simplicity and clearness." Again, HG's poetry is "poor."

A102. "New Editions." *Book Buyer*, 20 (Feb 1900), 64-67.
Brief mention (65-66) of the first three volumes of the uniform edition of HG.

A103. "American Fiction." *Athenaeum*, No. 3774 (24 Feb 1900), 235.
Review of *Boy Life* and *Folks*. HG has skill as a story teller, but *Boy Life* is not interesting because the boys described are "types rather than individuals" and not quite real. All of HG's attempts at poetry are failures. *Folks* is exactly the same with the characters a bit older.

A104. "New Novels." *Athenaeum*, No. 3811(10 Nov 1900), 611-613.
Brief review of *Eagle's Heart* (613). The novel is full of HG's "characteristic energy." The hero is "uncommonly well portrayed," although one "hardly feels much attracted to the man." But HG's "skill is so great that one follows ... [the hero's] fortunes with excitement,

21

and with that artistic sympathy which every piece of work thoroughly well done must excite." Finally, although HG is a "master... of every sort of American slang, he avoids it in his narration, and writes good straightforward English."

A105. Boyce, Neith. "HG's *Eagle's Heart.*" *Bookman* (NY), 12 (Dec 1900), 351-352.
Review. The main character in the story "is real enough, and his life narrated here has the outline and much of the detail of reality." However, a "crudity of style, as well as a certain conventionality in the manner of looking at life," especially women characters, weakens the work.

A106. "The Season's Books/The Notable Novels." *Outlook*, 66 (1 Dec 1900), 805-812.
Review of *Eagle's Heart* (808-809). Describes the novel in terms of epic quality and poetic sensitivity to the West: "...most elaborate and important presentation which has yet appeared in our fiction."

A107. "Flights of Fiction." *Independent*, 71 (7 Dec 1900), 1265-1266.
Very brief review of *VO's Discipline* (1265). Book "has value only as a collection of seances well narrated" because HG "fails to impress us with the truth of the psychic, perhaps on account of...[his own] personal skepticism."

A108. "Recent Publications." New Orleans *Daily Picayune*, 16 Dec 1900, III, 5.
Review of *Eagle's Heart*. Brief plot summary which concludes by saying that, "The story is not at all like Mr. G's other books, and is all the better for that."

A109. "Mr. HG's New Novel." Brooklyn *Daily Eagle*, 22 Dec 1900, p. 6.
Review of *Eagle's Heart*. This novel "cannot be ranked with Mr. G's best work in fiction. There is too much sketchiness; it lacks intensity. His principal character is not a type, nor is he drawn with sufficiently

winning attributes to make him a favorite . . . . The
background against which he is projected is, however,
fine . . . . On the side of fidelity to nature and pictur-
esqueness of description it is the best novel of the
range and the round-up of its civilizations and its
barbarisms that has yet been published."

A110. Payne, William Morton. "Recent Books of Fiction." *Dial*,
30 (16 Feb 1901), 109-111.
Brief review of *Eagle's Heart* (109). HG's work lacks
art, humor, and finer graces of style. But he is earnest
and forceful in his work. The characterization leaves
much to be desired, and "the people of whom he writes
are not convincing presences."

A111. Flower, B. O. [Review of *Eagle's Heart*]. *Arena*, 25 (Mar
1901), 343.
HG's "picture of a rapidly disappearing phase of life
in the Far West" and his ability "to catch and reflect
with almost photographic accuracy passing phases of
life" are praiseworthy. The novel "is full of human
interest and is one of the strongest and best long
stories . . . from the pen of Mr. G."

A112. "News and Views of Books." N.Y. *World*, 13 Apr 1901, p. 8.
Review of *Mountain Lover*. The story is told in a
breezy manner and a "not too obtrusive realism in
incident."

A113. "The Novel of the Week." Brooklyn *Daily Eagle*, 13 Apr
1901, p. 7.
Review of *Mountain Lover*. "This is a book to do one
good; a real tonic, as fresh and cleansing and stimulating
as the mountain air whence it comes." It has "that
charm whether of novelty or strength or style--which com-
pels one to read on and on without skipping, and makes
even the press of duty a vexatious interruption."

A114. "Books of the Week." *Outlook*, 67 (20 Apr 1901), 920-926.
Review of *Mountain Lover* (922). "The minor characters of the book have little reality, and the plot is
merely a rather poorly constructed vehicle for the ex-

hibition of the one interesting character.''

A115. ''HG's *Mountain Lover.*'' N.Y. *Times Saturday Review of Books and Art,* 20 Apr 1901, p. 270.
Review. *Mountain Lover* misses being ''a very strong book'' because HG cannot handle his love stories without indulging in sentimentality. His presentation of the character of Mary Brien shows his inability and lack of skill ''in psychological portraiture.''

A116. ''A Yankee in England.'' *Canadian Magazine,* 17 (May 1901), 90.
Review of *Mountain Lover* (90). This brief review points to the interest and accuracy of the Western hero's criticisms of the old world, praises the characters and descriptions, but criticizes the ''sentimental windup'' of the novel.

A117. ''New Novels.'' *Athenaeum,* No. 3841 (8 Jun 1901), 721-723.
HG captures the American cowboy hero in this novel. His descriptions of America are interesting, but the real human interest comes in the sections dealing with England.

A118. Payne, William Morton. ''Recent Fiction.'' *Dial,* 31 (1 Jul 1901), 25-30.
Review of *Mountain Lover* (26-27). HG's move from the Middle West to Far West is a move ''for the better.'' ''The finer graces of diction'' are out of HG's domain, ''but he is acquiring a certain rough force and breadth of style that make his work impressive.'' Traces of Bret Harte are visible in the story. The book shows development in the art of HG.

A119. Irwin, Grace Luce. ''Current Books.'' *Overland,* 2d S, 38 (Sep 1901), 233-238.
Review of *Mountain Lover* (235). HG's art is ''strong, '' and he paints ''with a virile, large brush, and spends no time on mere ornamentation.'' ''The charm of the book lies largely in the humor of Matteson's words and actions, and in the description of natural scenery. But nothing in the book is more realistic than the personality of Mary herself.''

A120. "The White Man's Road." *Harper's Weekly*, 46 (5 Apr 1902), 432.

Extended review of *Captain*. In this novel, HG "has fulfilled his early promise." Elsie is "the most successful woman study that Mr. G has drawn," and *Captain* is the best story he has ever written. It is "as frankly idealistic as ... [*Rose*] was frankly realistic." Its "chief merit" is "the power with which Mr. G has interested us in his men and women--they are alive, keenly alive--and the skill with which he has made them develop his plot."

A121. "Books of the Week." *Outlook*, 70 (12 Apr 1901), 926-930.

Brief review of *Captain* (926). "Mr. G tells a clean, entertaining story, with some serious motive relating to the fair treatment of the Indian."

A122. "HG's *Captain*." Philadelphia *Times*, 19 Apr 1902.

Review. *Captain* is closer to the quality of HG's short stories. HG is not an artist, but his character studies are deeper and more complex than previously.

A123. Mabie, Hamilton Wright. "The Fiction of the Season." *Outlook*, 71 (24 May 1902), 208-216.

Brief review of *Captain* (210). "The novel deserves wide reading at this time, not only because it is a vigorous piece of story-writing, but because it brings freshly before the mind those iniquitous spoliations of the Indians which form one of the most disreputable chapters in our history."

A124. Halsey, Francis W. "Some Books To Read This Summer." *Review of Reviews* (American), 25 (Jun 1902), 700-707.

Very brief review of *Captain* (707). "The love story is interesting, and has a happy solution; but this, perhaps, charms not more than the skill with which the author has drawn Indian life and Indian character. Mr. G has done nothing worthy of more attention than his latest volume."

A125. Payne, William Morton. "Recent Fiction." *Dial*, 32 (1 Jun 1902), 385-389.

Review of *Captain* (387). HG "has been apt to let his interest in causes get the better of his artistic judgment, but in this case he has made a book which does not suffer in romantic interest from the obtrusion of the underlying argument." It is "a well-informed and warm-hearted book, that is good to read, and is likely to prove an effective ally in the work of dealing justly and humanely with the Indians."

A126. Flower, B. O. "Books of the Day." *Arena,* 28 (Jul 1902), 98-110.

Review of *Captain* (103-106). Flower reviews HG's career and connection with the *Arena* and states that HG's high moral purpose seemed to be faltering as evidenced by *Rose.* Flower had believed that HG would "become the leader in a virile literary movement, in which the highest ethical and social ideals would be so emphasized as to do much to awaken the sleeping conscience of our nation"; consequently he rejoices that with *Captain* "we meet the G of other days again."

A127. "The Book-Buyer's Guide." *Critic,* NS 41 (Sep 1902), 274-284.

Review of *Captain* (278). The reviewer is confused about HG's real position, for "on the one hand, he takes a very roseate view of the Indian character; on the other, the idea of grouping the Indians in villages is certainly following the line of least resistance, and as certainly their treatment has not been just. It is impossible to judge the book simply as fiction, and equally impossible to pronounce upon its merits as a sociological study."

A128. "New Novels." *Athenaeum,* No. 3913 (25 Oct 1902), 547-549.

Review of *Captain* (547-548). "The author has very happily hit upon a fresh line of fiction which he follows in a style of his own with laudable reserve and parsimony. The heroine is a clever amateur artist, yet Mr. G has been as merciful in restricting the amount of painter's cant as in limiting his output of native dialogue and pow-wow, cowboys' slang, and scenes of

actual peril and violence. The result is an even current of interest, enlivened by occasional rapids and an
impression of reality which are far more satisfactory
and healthy than the feverish illusion momentarily in-
duced by complicated mystery and highly coloured rep-
resentations of superhuman achievement.''

A129. "Novel Notes." *Bookman* (London), 23 (Dec 1902), 109-
112.
Brief review of *Captain* (109). Recounts the plot of
the novel and concludes by saying that: "It is a fine
book; it has its humour, its touches of restrained pathos;
and the characterization is extremely able.''

A130. "Novel Notes." *Bookman* (NY), 18 (Mar 1903), 101.
Review of *Captain*. "The book has the colour and
atmosphere of the place and people it is concerned
with, and the struggle of the old order as it slowly,
inevitably gives place to the new is faithfully ren-
dered throughout.''

A131. [Review of *Hesper*]. Indianapolis *News*, 11 Oct 1903.
Hesper is a distinctively American book with a
tempered restraint that has not marked HG's earlier
novels.

A132. [Review of *Hesper*]. Springfield (Mass.) *News*, 15 Oct 1903.
Life in a mining camp is described in all its primitive
and vigorous energy. It is the strongest story by HG
to date.

A133. "The Heroic Cowboy in G's Novel." Brooklyn *Daily Eagle*,
16 Oct 1903, p. 12.
Review of *Hesper*. The hero of the book is likened to
Wister's and Remington's cowboys, who remain the
American heroes of romance. "G will always be a
Romanticist.''

A134. [Review of *Hesper*]. N.Y. *American*, 17 Oct 1903.
"A work of remarkable realism and dramatic intensity.''

A135. "Fiction of the Day." Springfield (Mass.) *Republican*, 18 Oct 1903, p. 23.
　　　Review of *Hesper*. HG's new style is of less literary significance than that in earlier works, less striking and original.

A136. [Review of *Hesper*]. Brooklyn *Standard Union*, 18 Oct 1903.
　　　Mining life is graphically described in all its primitive and unconventional vigor.

A137. "Realism and Romance." N.Y. *Public Opinion*, 22 Oct 1903.
　　　Review of *Hesper*. The novel is a curious mixture of realism and romance. Character transformation of the heroine is too quick to be credible.

A138. "Among Late Works of Fiction." N.Y. *World*, 24 Oct 1903, p. 9.
　　　Review of *Hesper*. HG is no realist, but an incorrigible romanticist who admires and praises realism.

A139. Peattie, Elia W. [Review of *Hesper*]. Chicago *Daily Tribune*, 24 Oct 1903, II, 17.
　　　HG's literary career is summarized. With *Hesper*, HG has discovered the pathos, calm, and loveliness in literature that he lacked previously.

A140. [Review of *Hesper*]. N.Y. *Mail and Express*, 24 Oct 1903.
　　　HG is successful because he believes deeply in the potent charm of the West and deeply desires to communicate his enthusiasm.

A141. [Review of *Hesper*]. St. Louis *Republic*, 24 Oct 1903.
　　　Atmosphere and local color are the major achievements of the book.

A142. "Some New Books." Nashville *Banner*, 24 Oct 1903, II, 2.
　　　Review of *Hesper*. The characters are well delineated, and the West is remarkably described with all the primitive force of its stormy existence.

A143. "HG's Mining Story." Denver *Republican*, 25 Oct 1903.

Review of *Hesper*. HG has still not caught the skill of giving an "inside" viewpoint in writing of the Far West. *Hesper* has less of reality than HG's earlier novels.

A144. [Review of *Hesper*]. Pittsburgh *Press*, 26 Oct 1903.
Hesper features "vigorous, primitive and unconventional description."

A145. [Review of *Hesper*]. Omaha *Bee*, 28 Oct 1903.
Hesper is a fascinating love story with a thrilling background of mining camp adventure.

A146. Lee, Guy Carleton. [Review of *Hesper*]. Baltimore *Sun*, 29 Oct 1903, p. 8.
Wholesome story with picturesque details of Colorado life.

A147. "Mining Life." Rochester *Herald*, 30 Oct 1903.
Review of *Hesper*. It is a sane and natural novel that is refreshing after all the bizarre sensationalism these days.

A148. "The Courting of Ann." Boston *Daily Advertiser*, 31 Oct 1903, p. 8.
Review of *Hesper*. Here HG reaches literary maturity. Previously he was distressingly argumentative.

A149. "HG's Latest." Detroit *Free Press*, 31 Oct 1903, I, 8.
Review of *Hesper*. Picturesque in description, vivid in incident, graphic in narration.

A150. "New Books." Albany *Evening Journal*, 31 Oct 1903, p. 9.
Review of *Hesper*. HG possesses tremendous skill and accuracy in treating the West, but as he ventures East his powers decline.

A151. "New Books." St. Paul *Daily Pioneer Press*, 31 Oct 1903, p. 8.
Review of *Hesper*. Characters and plot are irresistible in this tale of social intrigue and unconventional romance.

A152. [Review of *Hesper*]. Detroit *Journal*, 31 Oct 1903.
The novel arouses the reader to go West and enjoy
the company of people close to the heart of nature.
Hesper is compared to Wister's *Virginian*.

A153. "Stories of American Life." N.Y. *Churchman*, 31 Oct
1903.
Review of *Hesper*. HG is a prophet of strenuous unconventionality. Exciting incidents and strongly penned characters overcome the improbable love story.

A154. "G's New Novel." Kansas City *Journal*, 1 Nov 1903.
Review of *Hesper*. In this charming, picturesque
novel, HG recaptures his descriptive genius of earlier
novels.

A155. [Review of *Hesper*]. Charleston *Sunday News*, 1 Nov 1903,
III, 21.
HG's work is the soundest and most sincere of all
now being done by American authors. HG is at his
best when he writes about the West.

A156. [Review of *Hesper*]. N.Y. *Newsdealer and Stationer*, 1 Nov
1903.
Hesper is an impressive and knowledgeable handling
of exciting Western events.

A157. "Gentility and the Far West." Chicago *Chronicle*, 2 Nov
1903.
Review of *Hesper*. HG broadens horizons and is
"richer for it." The narrow theories and unconventionality of earlier works lacked attractiveness.

A158. [Review of *Hesper*]. Albany *Law Journal*, 3 Nov 1903.
A dashing story comparable to Owen Wister's
Virginian.

A159. "Books of the Week." *Outlook*, 75 (7 Nov 1903), 607-614.
Brief review of *Hesper* (609). "'Mr. G is at his best
in showing us the miner and the cowboy as they are,
without the glamour of romance, sturdy, rough, and
reckless, with here and there a man of early culture

and strong character." But "how do Mr. G's heroines stand the ponderous, point-blank, stodgy compliments with which his men continually bombard them!"

A160. Lee, Guy Carleton. "Out West." Los Angeles *Times*, 7 Nov 1903, II, 2.
Review of *Hesper*. HG has improved both style and method. The local color contains a realism well-appreciated after the "guide-book" descriptions of most authors.

A161. [Review of *Hesper*]. Buffalo *Express*, 7 Nov 1903, p. 8.
In this "worthy successor to *Captain*," comedy and pathos are well blended.

A162. [Review of *Hesper*]. Denver *Times*, 7 Nov 1903.
This book is a luminous glance into Western working life and the building up of a new country.

A163. [Review of *Hesper*]. Toledo *Blade*, 7 Nov 1903.
Hesper is not a great book, but it is strong and intensely interesting because of its graphic narration.

A164. "Romance of Mining Camp." St. Paul *Dispatch*, 7 Nov 1903.
Review of *Hesper*. HG has turned from the fiery and passionate resentment of earlier novels to discover and celebrate life's sweetness. A calm has come over him and with it artistic advancement.

A165. "With Books and Writers." Atlanta *Constitution*, 8 Nov 1903, p. 11.
Review of *Hesper*. G is without a peer in describing Western life.

A166. [Review of *Hesper*]. Chicago *Interior*, 12 Nov 1903.
In this well-written book, the characters are drawn with HG's usual firm pen.

A167. "Life in a Mountain Mining Camp." Boston *Times*, 14 Nov 1903.
Review of *Hesper*, a "worthy successor to *Captain*."

A168. M., A. B. "HG's New Story." Louisville *Courier Journal*, 14 Nov 1903, p. 5.
  Review of *Hesper*. A primitive and vigorous display of the passions of the Far West.

A169. "Mr. G's New Book." N.Y. *Times Saturday Review of Books and Art*, 14 Nov 1903, p. 810.
  Review of *Hesper*. The novel is "romance of a fascinating sort, but hardly a presentation of cold, hard facts." It "bears about the same relation to the pursuit of the miner that *The Virginian* does to that of the cowboy. In both there is a tremendous amount of the idealizing of the good aspects and suppression of the unpleasant aspects of the situation . . . ."

A170. "Brief Notes on Some New Fiction." Cleveland *Plain Dealer*, 15 Nov 1903, IV, 8.
  Plot summary of *Hesper*.

A171. [Review of *Hesper*]. Philadelphia *Public Ledger*, 15 Nov 1903.
  HG has told a familiar, simple drama in an unfamiliar way. The fresh, virile style lends importance to the work.

A172. [Review of *Hesper*]. Hartford *Times*, 18 Nov 1903, II, 15.
  Hesper is an excellent story of mining life in which the heroine is depicted admirably.

A173. [Review of *Hesper*]. Philadelphia *Record*, 20 Nov 1903.
  HG's tendency for exaggeration in character and plot mars artistic effort. *Hesper* should be a popular success nevertheless.

A174. [Review of *Hesper*]. Boston *Herald*, 21 Nov 1903, p. 11.
  HG's latest and best work stands high in current fiction. *Hesper* has freshness and the enthusiasm of the reality of Western life.

A175. [Review of *Hesper*]. *Zion's Herald* (Boston), 25 Nov 1903.
  Brief summary only.

A176. [Review of *Hesper*]. Chicago *Advance*, 26 Nov 1903.
Hesper, a strongly penned story, is one of the best in the way of description of mining and range life.

A177. [Review of *Hesper*]. *Presbyterian Banner* (Pittsburgh), 26 Nov 1903.
The novel combines a happy style with simple, well-constructed plot.

A178. [Review of *Hesper*]. *Congregationalist* (Boston), 27 Nov 1903.
HG's people are knowledgeably drawn with both insight and power.

A179. MacArthur, James. "Books and Bookmen." *Harper's Weekly*, 47 (28 Nov 1903), 1921-1922.
Review of *Hesper* (1921). "The years [since *MTR*] have brought Mr. G a larger and more generous vision; he has ceased to be parochial in his view of life, and has learned, so to speak, to reckon with the universe." *Hesper* "is a worthy successor" to *Captain*, "and will undoubtedly enjoy a still greater popularity."

A180. "New Novels." *Athenaeum*, No. 3970 (28 Nov 1903), 714-715.
Review of *Hesper* (714). Happily, HG has returned to "the romantic elements of his own imagination" and "to the West." The psychological interest of the book lies in "the passage of this girl's soul to the awakening, its return to the healthier condition of nature."

A181. [Review of *Hesper*]. Indianapolis *Sentinel*, 29 Nov 1903, IV, 14.
Exciting scenes and incidents are acted out by characters of every shade of life.

A182. "A Story of Strenuous West." Des Moines *Register and Leader*, 29 Nov 1903.
Review of *Hesper*. The descriptions of mining camps contain realism, and the sketch of the hero is comparable to Wister's Virginian. HG judges *Hesper* to be his best book.

A183. [Review of *Hesper*]. *Standard* (Mass.), 1 Dec 1903.
Howells contributed to HG's prominence; HG has matured in moving from the darkness and doom of his earlier writing to the larger and more generous vision of the present.

A184. [Review of *Hesper*]. Boston *Watchman*, 3 Dec 1903.
HG exhibits new life and power in writing of that which he knows best--the free and young frontier.

A185. "The Fiction of the Season." *Outlook*, 75 (5 Dec 1903), 843-854.
Very brief mention of *Hesper* (854), "a strenuous and realistic tale of a miners' strike, with a fine background of mountain peaks." [Complete comment.]

A186. "A Story of Western Life." Kansas City *Star*, 5 Dec 1903, p. 5.
Review of *Hesper*. This good story is eminently readable in its vivid appreciation of the unsubdued West.

A187. [Review of *Hesper*]. Seattle *Post Intelligencer*, 6 Dec 1903, p. 31.
Hesper is a refreshing and breezy novel, free from the sociological motifs that marked earlier works.

A188. [Review of *Hesper*]. Indianapolis *Journal*, 7 Dec 1903, p. 7.
Hesper is a welcome relief from the "morbid and neurotic" stories of the day. It is warmer and more human than HG's earlier chillingly realistic efforts.

A189. [Review of *Hesper*]. Worcester (Mass.) *Evening Gazette*, 9 Dec 1903.
Hesper is a thrilling and intense book with credible characters and exciting incidents.

A190. [Review of *Hesper*]. St. Louis *Globe-Democrat*, 12 Dec 1903, p. 6.
Hesper is HG's most ambitious character; however HG succumbs to·convention and leaves the taint of triteness on the tale.

A191. [Review of *Hesper*]. Omaha *World Herald*, 13 Dec 1903.
This book has augmented confidence that HG will write the Great American Novel. It lacks literary finish that makes for a great novel, but simplicity, naturalness, and intensity are certainly there.

A192. [Review of *Hesper*]. Richmond *Dispatch*, 13 Dec 1903.
Hesper is one of the strongest of recent publications. The bold and free spirit of the West contrasts with the petty conventions of the East.

A193. [Review of *Hesper*]. N.Y. *Christian Intelligence*, 16 Dec 1903.
A relevant study of mining strikes which provides a backdrop for a realistic romance.

A194. Collins, Derfla Howes. [Review of *Hesper*]. Utica (N.Y.) *Observer*, 18 Dec 1903.
Under HG's skillful tutelage, the romantic story becomes credible and realistic.

A195. [Review of *Hesper*]. *Lutheran Observer* (Philadelphia), 18 Dec 1903.
Hesper marks an advance for HG over previous novels.. It is a dramatic and realistic rendering.

A196. "The Wild and Wooly G." Providence *Sunday Journal*, 20 Dec 1903, III, 21.
Review of *Hesper*. The book is escapist literature designed for the reader of undiscriminating taste.

A197. [Review of *Hesper*]. Brooklyn *Times*, 23 Dec 1903.
HG demonstrates customary vigor and spirit in a distinctly American novel.

A198. [Review of *Hesper*]. N.Y. *Independent*, 24 Dec 1903.
HG falters when he ventures into a romantic love story, but in a Western this is always subordinate. He excels in describing the moods of the West.

A199. "Lengthy, But Interesting." San Francisco *Argonaut*, 28 Dec 1903.

Review of *Hesper*. In such an unconventional setting, the story, despite its length, gains in the freshness and freedom of atmosphere.

A200. [Review of *Hesper*]. Chicago *Journal*, 29 Dec 1903.
In *Hesper*, the miners' strike incident is overdone and tedious. HG has much room for improvement.

A201. Payne, William Morton. "Recent Fiction." *Dial*, 36 (1 Jan 1904), 18-22.
Review of *Hesper* (19). "*Hesper* represents the best work that Mr. G has done; in it he has sloughed off most of his earlier defects of thought and expression; his asperities have become softened, and his rawness has undergone a transformation into something very like urbanity." It is "a far cry from [*MTR*] to the present volume; it seems almost too far to be accounted for by a mere matter of fifteen years."

A202. [Review of *Hesper*]. *Christian Work* (N.Y.), 3 Jan 1904.
Hesper contains a vivid picture of a Western mining camp with a sympathetic look at the conditions of the miners.

A203. Haynie, Henry. "Love Making While Working on a Gold Mine." Boston *Times*, 9 Jan 1904.
Review of *Hesper*, a fascinating story of dramatic intensity with the effete East pitted against the rugged West.

A204. "In the Far West." N.Y. *Press*, 9 Jan 1904, p. 7.
Review of *Hesper*. It is a conventional novel of He getting She which doesn't make the lengthy reading worthwhile.

A205. "HG and the West." Boston *Evening Transcript*, 13 Jan 1904, p. 16.
Review of *Hesper*. HG now stands in the forefront of American literary artists. "Although a professed realist, G does not follow blindly the dictates of realism." Some parts of *Hesper* are highly romantic.

A206. "To the Hesperian Mountains with HG." N.Y. *Sun*, 16 Jan 1904.

Review of *Hesper*. Facetious description of the novel .

A207. [Review of *Hesper*]. Boston *Evening News Review*, 23 Jan 1904.

Of lesser excellence than *Captain*, *Hesper* is free of the faults of which HG once seemed enamoured.

A208. "My Lady Disdain." Toronto *Globe*, 6 Feb 1904.

Review of *Hesper*. This well-written story is faithfully descriptive of the West.

A209. [Review of *Hesper*]. Chicago *Standard*, 13 Feb 1904.

HG's unconventional style finds worthy expression in this novel, which dignifies the true and real in life.

A210. [Review of *Hesper*]. Boston *Christian Register*, 18 Feb 1904.

Combines early earnestness and poise with dramatic interest and romance. Social and cultural contrasts handled realistically.

A211. "G's New Story." N.Y. *Times Saturday Review of Books*, 4 Jun 1904, p. 384.

Review of *Star*. HG seems "intent rather on the setting forth of a theory than the telling of a mere story. He outlines in the guise of fiction a programme for the upbuilding in New York of a paying taste for wholesome and homely native-grown American plays."

A212. "New Novels." *Athenaeum*, No. 4002 (9 Jul 1904), 42-43.

Review of *Star* (43). HG offers the novel "as a serious study of theatrical life and...temperament. It is, however, about as near to reality as a schoolgirl's dream." The book is romantic and sentimental. HG should return to the West in his fiction.

A213. "Notes on New Novels." *Dial*, 37 (16 Jul 1904), 40-43.

Brief review of *Star* (41). "Remembering Mr. G's earnest protest against literary abuses of one sort and another in his earlier works, it is something of a surprise

to find here no adverse criticisms of the combination
of theatrical managers which has styled our American
drama, and this not withstanding the fact that all the
action of the story depends upon this lamentable condition of affairs. The novel is unusually short, and
not entirely convincing."

A214. *"Star." Reader*, 4 (Sep 1904), 470-471.
The opening chapters of the novel "are perilously
near to artificial melodrama, both in atmosphere and
dialogue." But, "stripped of its propagandist purpose and false theatrical atmosphere, the human story
in *Star* is entirely worthy, and of captivating interest."

A215. [Review of *Hesper*]. Montreal *Herald*, 23 Dec 1904.
HG is likened to Bret Harte in his ability to capture
life in the Far West.

A216. "List of New Books and Reprints." *Times Literary Supplement*, 4 (19 May 1905), 163.
Review of *Tyranny*. HG exhibits some power in
several of his descriptions, but he is "a little vague
about our English institutions."

A217. "Books of the Week." *Outlook*, 80 (27 May 1905), 244-
248.
Very brief review of *Tyranny* (248). It is "a book of
more than ordinary power to hold the reader."

A218. "A Story of Psychic Mystery." N.Y. *Times Saturday Review
of Books*, 27 May 1905, p. 343.
Review of *Tyranny*. "Regarded as fiction simply
Tyranny is too much encumbered with laborious arguments and citations.... The book would be improved
if divested of its fictitious form, and presented as a
contribution to the documents of psychic phenomena."

A219. "Notable Fiction of Spring and Summer." *Review of Reviews* (American), 31 (Jun 1905), 755-764.
Very brief review of *Tyranny* (763). "It is a pity that
Mr. G should have lent the authority of his style and
name to things that at best are unproved and hence

negligible, and at worst the humbug of swindlers or the raving of people whose only place is that of clinical material to a specialist in diseased psy-chology.''

A220. ''New Novels.'' *Athenaeum*, No. 4049 (3 Jun 1905), 684-686.

Review of *Tyranny* (685). ''It is a good and interesting tale; but perhaps it suffers a little from the vehemence of its author's contempt for what is respectfully called psychical research--for all that the man in the street means by the word *spiritualism*.''

A221. Horwill, Herbert W. ''Literature/Recent Fiction.'' *Forum*, 37 (Jul 1905), 99-114.

Review of *Tyranny* (113). ''With all his exposition, Mr. G does not make clear his own view of spiritualism, and, by closing the story where he does, he evades the most difficult of the problems which he raises,'' namely whether Viola's liberation will be permanent. ''His style is disfigured by some painful examples of fine writing.''

A222. ''Occult, Real and Apparent.'' *Public Opinion*, 39 (1 Jul 1905), 26.

Review of *Tyranny*. ''The story is an interesting one; in places it grips you. But, compared to some of Mr. G's earlier writings, it must be said regretfully that the book is a disappointing piece of work. The Mr. G of the prairies and the mountains is greatly preferable to the Mr. G of the darkened room.''

A223. ''Books of the Day.'' *Reader*, 6 (Aug 1905), 357-362.

Review of *Tyranny* (357-358). The book is ''well written'' on a theme which is of great popular interest. Both the plot and treatment of it are ''original.'' HG merely presents his story and lets the reader judge for himself.

A224. ''More Novels.'' *Nation*, 81 (10 Aug 1905), 122-123.

Review of *Tyranny* (122). The novel is ''interesting,'' but ''it ends a chapter too soon.'' We want to know what happened to Viola and her young scientist. The "scientific portions" of the book "are the finest and the most absorbing."

A225. "The Book-Buyer's Guide." *Critic*, NS 47 (Sep 1905), 283-288.
Review of *Tyranny* (284). "It is very delicate and exacting material that Mr. G has chosen for his latest novel, and very crudely has he handled it. If he ever possessed any art or any insight, they deserted him during the composition of this story of a young spiritualistic medium and her scientific lover."

A226. "Novels of the Occult." *Independent*, 59 (7 Sep 1905), 575-576.
Review of *Tyranny* (575). "Nothing" HG does now "has the vividness and life of his early Western stories." "We do wish he would hit the trail once more, or take a ranch in the arid region."

A227. "Recent Fiction." *Nation*, 83 (13 Sep 1906), 227-228.
Review of *Witch's Gold* (228). "The story does not represent Mr. G at his best; it is simply an amiable frontier romance, altogether barren of the grim power of *MTR*, though it was apparently written at about the same time."

A228. "A Guide to the New Books." *Literary Digest*, 33 (22 Sep 1906), 393-394.
Brief review of *Witch's Gold* (394). It is "a simple, healthful love-tale of the West, adapted to beguile an idle hour."

A229. "*Witch's Gold.*" N.Y. *Times Saturday Review of Books*, 22 Sep 1906, p. 581.
Review. "The tale, probably most attractive in a cruder and more elusive form, suffers in the lengthening, or rather, as we are told, in the printing of the hitherto republished original form."

A230. "Comment on Current Books." *Outlook*, 84 (6 Oct 1906), 335-338.

Review of *Witch's Gold* (338). "Whether Mr. G has bettered his original story ["The Spirit of Sweetwater," first published in 1898] in this new version is an open question. The earlier story is more artistic in construction and an adequate development of the same theme."

A231. "Current Fiction." *Nation*, 84 (9 May 1907), 434-435.
Brief review of *Long Trail* (435). *Long Trail* is "a boys' book." Parents "will fully approve its tone of manliness, decency, and respect for law."

A232. "Mr. G's New Story." N.Y. *Times Saturday Review of Books*, 18 May 1907, p. 321.
Review of *Long Trail*. "It is a book of few complications, but with every incident developed in the most absolutely convincing manner."

A233. "Our Library Table." *Athenaeum*, No. 4152 (25 May 1907), 633-635.
Brief review of *Long Trail* (634). "This is an excellent book for a boy's holiday reading, thoroughly wholesome and stimulating, and in no part dull."

A234. "A Guide to the New Books." *Literary Digest*, 34 (15 Jun 1907), 961-962.
Brief review of *Long Trail* (961). "While appealing primarily to youthful readers, with whom it is sure to be a favorite, the story will be enjoyed almost as much by older persons who have not lost taste for outdoor adventure and the alluring life of the gold-camp."

A235. [Review of *Long Trail*]. N.Y. *Press*, 17 Aug 1907, p. 5.
Long Trail holds special fascination for boys with its intimate spirit of the wilderness. HG is one of the rare writers to capture the terror, monotony, and depression of the wilds.

A236. "New Books of the Autumn Season." N.Y. *Times Saturday Review of Books*, 19 Oct 1907, pp. 664-669.
Review of *Money Magic* (664). One-sentence summary of plot and a statement that the book is "an interesting study of the mixed life in a Western city."

A237. "New Novels." *Athenaeum*, No. 4175 (2 Nov 1907), 545-547.

Brief review of *Money Magic* (546). "By some the story may be thought a trifle too long; but it is good, stirring narrative throughout, and the development of character through incident and emotional crises is highly interesting."

A238. "Current Fiction." *Nation*, 85 (14 Nov 1907), 446-447.

Brief review of *Money Magic* (446). Since *MTR*, HG's development has been "entirely towards conventionality, without a corresponding gain in finish of manner or thought."

A239. [Review of *Money Magic*]. *Independent*, 63 (14 Nov 1907), 1177.

In this novel, HG "has achieved a better hero than ever before."

A240. Payne, William Morton. "Recent Fiction." *Dial*, 43 (16 Nov 1907), 317-319.

Review of *Money Magic* (318-319). "There is a certain amount of truth in this narrative, and fairly effective characterization, although the latter must be described as crude rather than subtle. Mr. G has done much better work than this, and will, we trust, do it again."

A241. "Comment on Current Books/Novels and Tales." *Outlook*, 87 (30 Nov 1907), 744-746.

Brief review of *Money Magic* (744). The novel has "little originality."

A242. Van Westrum, A. Schade. "Mr. G's *Money Magic*." *Bookman* (N.Y.), 26 (Dec 1907), 417-418.

Review. It is "far and away the best and most significant novel that Mr. G has written in many years. It has perspective, it is firm of plot, rich in colour, full of movement, unflaggingly interesting, its characters are deftly and understandingly individualized--it has the semblance of life."

A243. "G's Trip to Shadow Land." N.Y. *Times Literary Section*, 23 Oct 1908, p. 586.

Review of *Shadow World*. "Mr G writes with a fine and doubtless sincere attempt at impartiality and open-mindedness.... The whole book is an amusing reminder of the many letters that come to *The Times*, all beginning: 'I am not a Christian Scientist, but--,' and then going on with new 'evidence' that Eddyism must be true. So Mr. G is not a Spiritualist, but--."

A244. "Autumn Fiction." *Independent*, 65 (19 Nov 1908), 1181-1183.

Brief review of *Shadow World* (1183). HG is "quite convinced of the truth of what he has seen," but he "will hardly convince the sceptics."

A245. "Books for Christmas Presents." *Independent*, 65 (26 Nov 1908), 1243-1245.

Brief review of *Shadow World* (1245). It is "a book sure to prove attractive to every crank who is not violently cranked the other way."

A246. "Comment on Current Books." *Outlook*, 90 (28 Nov 1908), 748-752.

Brief review of *Shadow World* (752). HG "shows himself amazingly uncritical in his treatment of the more celebrated 'psychics' of whom he writes." "For the benefit of those inclined to take his book at all seriously it may be added that the 'phase' of mediumship with which it is almost wholly concerned is precisely that which has been most conclusively demonstrated to be permeated through and through with fraud."

A247. "Current Fiction." *Nation*, 87 (24 Dec 1908), 631-633.

Review of *Shadow World* (631-632). The autobiographical nature of the book, which is not quite scientific nor literary, will bring the subject before numerous people.

A248. Dunbar, Olivia Howard. "The Shadow World." *North American Review*, 189 (Mar 1909), 455-458.

Review of *Shadow World*. Dunbar praises HG's attempt to analyze a "taboo" subject. She criticizes the weak narrative of the book but points out that it is "a substantial popular tract" rather than literature. The theories which the book proposes are examined in some detail.

A249. *"Moccasin Ranch."* N.Y. *Times Saturday Review of Books*, 16 Oct 1909, p. 611.

Review. "Mr. G has written longer and more important novels than this, but he has written nothing finer or more powerful in its presentation of human passions or more beautiful in style."

A250. "The New Books/A Few of the **Season**'s Novels." *Review of Reviews* (American), 40 (Nov 1909), 635-636.

Very brief one-sentence mention of *Moccasin Ranch* (636).

A251. "Current Fiction." *Nation*, 89 (4 Nov 1909), 433-434.

Review of *Moccasin Ranch* (433). Although there is "a touch of strain in the speech and conduct" of the four major characters, the "moving thing is that atmosphere of place which Mr. G knows how to make us breathe."

A252. [Review of *Cavanaugh*]. Duluth *News Tribune*, 10 Apr 1910, IV, 5.

Characterization is vivid. The love story overrides the whole of the novel.

A253. Markham, Edwin. "Bookland." San Francisco *Examiner*, 23 Apr 1910, p. 11.

Review of *Cavanaugh*. It is vivid, interesting, and delightful.

A254. Colbron, Grace Isabel. "HG's *Cavanaugh*." *Bookman* (N.Y.), 31 (May 1910), 309-310.

Review. "The theme at the heart of his book so absorbed the writer that he has not made the human story of it as interesting as he might have done." This is true only of the first half of the book, however; for after

that "we get the swing of events of importance far beyond and above any personal interest in either hero or
heroine." Thus, as a novel purely, the story is "weak";
but "as a picture of very important phases of our national life," it is "of great interest and great value."

A255. "Current Fiction." *Nation*, 90 (12 May 1910), 483-485.
Review of *Cavanaugh* (484). Since *MTR*, HG's work
has been "a series of diminishing echoes." The present book is "earnestly and painstakingly written"; but
the characters "are but pale figures," for HG "had a
speech to make, not a story to tell." As fiction, it belongs "to a mediocre sort."

A256. "Literary News and Reviews." N.Y. *Evening Post*, 14 May
1910, Sat. Suppl., p. 7.
Review of *Cavanaugh*. The novel is earnestly and
painstakingly written, but it does not come up to the
standards of *MTR*.

A257. "A Guide to the New Books." *Literary Digest*, 40 (21 May
1910), 1037-1038, 1040-1043.
Mostly descriptive review of *Cavanaugh* (1037-1038).
"It is safe to assume that Mr. G had a purpose in writing the book other than the desire to entertain."

A258. [Review of *Cavanaugh*]. *Independent*, 69 (26 May 1910),
1138.
Cavanaugh is "a travesty on the West . . . unredeemed
by so much as a single page of sincere description."
The characters are "tawdry prigs."

A259. "The New Books/Some of the Season's Fiction." *Review
of Reviews* (American), 41 (Jun 1910), 759-761.
Very brief review of *Cavanaugh* (760). "As an interpretation of the life and ambitions of that fine body of
men who care for the nation's forests in the Far West
the book is well worth while."

A260. [Review of *Cavanaugh*]. Chicago *Interior*, 21 Jul 1910.
Cavanaugh is a delightful romance exposing the
problems confronting the forest service.

A261. "Readable Novels." *Spectator*, 105 (13 Aug 1910), 249.
  Very brief review of *Cavanagh*, "a powerful story of life in the Far West."

A262. "Current Fiction." *Nation*, 91 (27 Oct 1910), 391-392.
  Review of *Other MTR* (391-392). "The privations and squalor of the farmer's life--a life in which the writer himself had played his painful boyish part--had overwhelmingly impressed the young man on his return from the East. Cherished platitudes about the return to nature, the beauty of contact with the soil, had become a mockery in his ears, and these tales express an almost fierce recoil."

A263. "The New Books." *Outlook*, 96 (29 Oct 1910), 515-516.
  Brief review of *Other MTR* (516). "The power that shows in his tales is a penetrating force, and one puts the book down shaken to the center of one's being by the simple story of what the working farmer and his weary wife endured, and even now endure."

A264. Marchand, J. "HG's *Other MTR*." *Bookman* (N.Y.), 32 (Nov 1910), 305-306.
  Review. "In this new collection of earlier stories we find the same strength of portrayal of life in the Middle West, the hard life of the farmer, unvarnished, as it is in actuality--also with something of its underlying realities--as in the *MTR*." "A Day of Grace" and "Lucretia Burns" are singled out for special praise.

A265. "Some Notable Books of the Year." *Independent*, 69 (17 Nov 1910), 1087-1104.
  Brief review of *Other MTR* (1092). "To the reader who has viewed the West as an Eldorado these stories will be disillusioning."

A266. Sherwood, Margaret. "Lying Like Truth." *Atlantic*, 106 (Dec 1910), 806-817.
  Review of *Cavanagh* (809). *Cavanagh* is "an interesting story, with a certain vitality, much realistic detail, and often beauty of line and color. Even if we

find here no new and original nature-sense, no new interpretation of human character, there is a breeze-like quality of enthusiasm in the tale, and there is pleasure in sharing the wide spaces of the range.''

A267. "Our Library Table." *Athenaeum*, No. 4339 (24 Dec 1910), 791-793.

Brief review of *Other MTR* (793) points to the realism of the descriptions and characters, praises "Elder Pill" as one of the best stories (it is touched with a "gentle sense of humour"), and expresses the hope that HG will write a big novel on "the Granger States."

A268. "New Novels." *Athenaeum*, No. 4381 (14 Oct 1911), 452-453.

Review of *VO's Discipline* (452). HG is not "convincing" because "in a tale of commonplace contemporary life [he] introduces into his very machinery a sequence of occurrences beyond the general experience or belief of his public."

A269. "HG's Tract." N.Y. *Times Review of Books*, 15 Oct 1911, p. 617.

Review of *VO's Discipline*. "When an author writes a spiritualistic tract and masquerades it as a novel, what is his point of view? Should his work be treated as fiction or as spiritualistic propagandism?" As "a defense of spiritualism the book is perhaps as successful as most any report of the investigation of a medium by a believer. As fiction it is deplorable."

A270. "The New Books." *Outlook*, 99 (21 Oct 1911), 430-433.

Brief review of *VO's Discipline* (431). "If one has a taste for good English, or for moderately attractive people his patience will desert him early in the reading."

A271. "Notable Autumn Fiction." *Literary Digest*, 43 (4 Nov 1911), 797, 807-808.

Brief review of *VO's Discipline* (808). Despite an "interesting love-story," the book is, "primarily, spiritualistic propaganda and contains little else to hold the interest of the reader."

A272. "Current Fiction." *Nation,* 93 (9 Nov 1911), 444-446.
Review of *VO's Discipline* (445). HG's Victor Olnee
"and the other human figures in the book do not strongly
take hold of the reader's imagination. The 'love interest'
is labored, the plot as a whole is of little importance,
and the whole performance is a bit of commentary rather
than of creation."

A273. "Mr. G's Story of an Outdoor Life." N.Y. *Times Book Review,* 15 Feb 1914, p. 72.
Review of *Forester's Daughter.* "In the world of
humanity Mr. G is not always quite at ease. His dialogue
is often stiff, sometimes forced; many of his characters
resemble figures in a melodrama rather than flesh and
blood people; but once up amid the trees and the crags,
the valleys and wide, solitary spaces, he enters into
his own, and the narrative becomes plastic, swift-moving,
full of life and color."

A274. "HG in Colorado." Boston *Evening Transcript,* 18 Feb 1914,
p. 22.
Review of *Forester's Daughter.* "No one who reads
his story will regret that ... [HG] could not resist the
impulse to turn ... [to] pure romance--pure in every
sense of the word."

A275. "Current Fiction." *Nation,* 98 (26 Feb 1914), 210-211.
Review of *Forester's Daughter* (210-211). One finds
here "no signs of fresh treatment at the hands of the
present writer." HG seems not to be capable of extended narrative. He should return to "the sincere mood
and restrained hand which produced those little classics
of Middle Western literature [found in] *MTR.*"

A276. "The New Books." *Outlook,* 106 (28 Feb 1914), 503-505.
Very brief review of *Forester's Daughter,* a "slight
but graphic romance" (504).

A277. "Literary Notes." *Independent,* 77 (23 Mar 1914), 419-421.

Very brief descriptive review of *Forester's Daughter* (420).

A278. Cooper, Frederick. "The Art of Looking On and Some Recent Novels." *Bookman* (N.Y.), 39 (Apr 1914), 203-210.

Review of *Forester's Daughter* (206). The sentimentality and romance in *Forester's Daughter* make it "hard to believe that this story came from the same hand that once gave us a book of real strength, *Rose*."

A279. Hopkins, Mary Alden. "*Forester's Daughter*." *Publishers' Weekly*, 85 (18 Apr 1914), 1342.

Review, almost entirely descriptive. HG "has undertaken to reverse the assignment of the noble qualities always bestowed upon a pair of lovers, and has succeeded admirably in his novelty."

A280. "Fiction with a Purpose and Stories That Entertain." *Review of Reviews* (American), 49 (May 1914), 625-629.

Very brief review of *Forester's Daughter* (629). "Breezy, vigorous, and wholesome."

A281. "HG's Tales." Springfield (Mass.) *Sunday Republican*, 14 May 1916, p. 15.

Review of *High Trails*. "Mr. G is unique among present-day writers who essay to depict the old West. He seems to write with complete knowledge and familarity of the scenes he pictures--indeed, he is worthy to be compared with Bret Harte." "The Trail Tramp" is "perhaps the most interesting" of the stories.

A282. "Mr. G's Stories." N.Y. *Times Book Review*, 14 May 1916, p. 202.

Review of *High Trails*. HG covers much material that Bret Harte did not deal with. "The Lonesome Man" is "typically American in spirit," and it "reflects the grimness of the literature of Russia. The two characters move toward their fate as inevitably as the people in the sharp, unhappy tales of that tragic country." "Mr. G is to be congratulated on the simple, direct manner in which he has told his tales. They are atmospheric and real, and you feel their sincerity.''

A283. M., D. L. "The High Trails." Boston *Evening Transcript*, 27 May 1916, III, 10.
Review of *High Trails*. HG "has introduced many characters who live in a way out of all comparison with the space he has devoted to them." Review is largely descriptive.

A284. "Novels for Summer Reading." *Review of Reviews* (American), 53 (Jun 1916), 758-760.
Brief review of *High Trails* (760). In these character sketches HG shows knowledge of "his mountain West and its human denizens."

A285. "The American Short Story." *Independent*, 86 (19 Jun 1916), 486.
Brief review of *High Trails*. Although HG "writes of the outdoors understandingly," when "he sets people to influencing people his insight is less true," he "falls back on the accepted formulas of magazine fiction, and the men and women in his stories fail to live up to the possibilities of their setting."

A286. Hale, Edward E. "Recent Fiction." *Dial*, 61 (22 Jun 1916), 26-28.
Review of *High Trails* (27-28). Although HG "has probably not succeeded in doing in this book all that he had in mind to do" and although he hasn't "wholly avoided the conventional probabilities of such books," it is nonetheless "a beautiful piece of work."

A287. "Book Selection Department/Fiction." *Wisconsin Library Bulletin*, 12 (Jul 1916), 322-323.
Brief review of *High Trails* (322). The book pictures "faithfully and vividly" the frontier type.

A288. "Current Fiction." *Nation*, 103 (10 Aug 1916), 132-133.
Favorable review of *High Trails* (132-133). "Mr. G's book sticks in the memory longer as one of the few in which the America of our transitional day has really found voice." Comparatively, Zane Grey's *The Border*

Legion is much too theatrical.

A289. "Tales of City, Town, and Country Life." N.Y. *Times Review of Books*, 18 Mar 1917, p. 1.

Review of new edition of *High Trails*, mostly a summary of Howells' introduction to this edition. Stories are "richly and truthfully expressive of the basic things in national character."

A290. "A Wisconsin Boyhood in the Sixties." N.Y. *Evening Post*, 25 Aug 1917.

Review of *Son*. The discussion of the Civil War, ending at the beginning of the book, should prove a diversion for the reader from the present interminable war. The autobiography ends too early; the reviewer questions if the new dawn of the country that HG saw after the Civil War is valid in 1917. He writes of a personal interview with HG.

A291. Howells, William Dean. "*Son* by HG/An Appreciation." N.Y. *Times Review of Books*, 26 Aug 1917, pp. 309, 315.

Extensive review of *Son* which also includes Howells' memories of HG in Boston. *Son* ranks among great literary autobiographies for its "incomparable novelty as a study of the most characteristic of human conditions in the years that have passed since our race laid hold upon the continent, and began to shape it into the homes of men." Howells criticizes HG for "want of tenderness" in the "characterization of the Father." But *Son* is "the memorial of a generation, of a whole order of American experience"; it is "an epic of such mood and make as has not been imagined before."

A292. E[dgett], E[dwin] F[rancis]. "*Son*." Boston *Evening Transcript*, 29 Aug 1917, p. 6.

Review of *Son*. "It possesses the dual glamour of fact and fiction. Its basis is reality and it is written with the imaginative vigor of a man who by avoiding the dull routine of the matter-of-fact chronicle knows how to make events that happened seem all the more plausible and convincing written in retrospect...." *Son* is "a contribution to American autobiographical literature."

A293. Bashferd, Herbert. *"Son."* San Francisco *Bulletin*, 8 Sep 1917.
>Review. A distinctly American piece of literature.

A294. Cloves, S. T. [Review of *Son*]. Richmond *Journal*, 8 Sep 1917.
>Belle Garland is a tragic figure. *Son* is not only an autobiography but also a chronicle of the times and experiences that thousands of American families went through in taming the West. Crudities of text prevent *Son* from being really great.

A295. "The New Books." *Outlook*, 117 (19 Sep 1917), 100-103.
>Very brief review of *Son* (100). It is "admirable and charming, inspired too with genuine and racy Americanism," a book "well worth reading and re-reading."

A296. [Review of *Son*]. St. Joseph *Gazette*, 21 Sep 1917.
>It is unfortunate that so few authors write autobiography. HG's book, while not great, is truly representative of American life. It is his crowning literary achievement. It encompasses a view larger than himself.

A297. "The Old Middle West/HG's Memoirs." Springfield (Mass.) *Sunday Republican*, 23 Sep 1917, p. 15.
>Review of *Son*. "Mr. G has written a book deserving of a wide reading, and likely to get it by virtue of the style in which it is written. The narrative flows easily-- a little diffusely, in fact--with a great fund of incidents, keen observations and incisive albeit idealized portraits of character." Most of this review is an extremely long summary of the book, often punctuated with quotations.

A298. "The New Books/Biography and Recollections." *Review of Reviews* (American), 56 (Oct 1917), 439-440.
>Brief review of *Son* (439). HG presents the life of the plains with "striking fidelity." *Son* is a graphic portrait of the generation following the war.

A299. B., R. "The American Adventure." *New Republic*, 12 (20 Oct 1917), 333-334.

Extended review of *Son*. The ecstatic review summarizes much of the book but also points out that HG
has found his form in the reminiscence and that he is
the best subject for his work. If there is any defect
in the book, "it is the romantic treatment which at
times almost approaches obstinacy."

A300. Kelly, Florence Finch. "A Group of American Biographies."
Bookman (N.Y.), 46 (Nov 1917), 325-330.
Review of *Son* (327). "Singularly interesting and
characteristically American as the story of one life,
Mr. G's book is of vastly more consequence as the epic
tale of a section and a period." [An enthusiastic review.]

A301. "New Books Reviewed." *North American Review*, 206 (Nov
1917), 793-800.
The book is "not only rewarding as reminiscence, but
also rich in the imaginative and emotional values of the
author's best fiction." "There is something unfeignedly
optimistic in the tone of the whole narrative, despite its
grimness in some particulars; a joy in homely and familiar things and a confidence in the right tendencies that
ultimately control the world."

A302. [Review of *Son*]. *Booklist*, 14 (Nov 1917), 57.
Very brief, almost entirely descriptive review.

A303. [Review of *Son*]. *Open Shelf* (Cleveland), Nov 1917, p. 126.
Very brief and largely descriptive. *Son* is "a notable
memorial of a bygone phase of American life."

A304. "The End of the Trail." *Independent*, 92 (3 Nov 1917), 256,
258-259.
Review of *Son*. Although, because HG was "a bookish
lad whose tastes were cultural and never agricultural,"
experiences "that would have been a matter of course
or even interesting to a 'born farmer' or a biologist"
revolted him, this book is "great and true." It is "a
contribution to our annals of the settlement of our country; as well as a story of unusual interest and even fascination."

A305. [Review of *Son*]. N.Y. *Evening Post*, 3 Nov 1917.

Son arouses interest in the historical and social periods it covers. It has an almost epic quality if HG is thought of as a typical American child observing the conquest of the West. It is refreshing and poetic.

A306. "Vestigia Retrorsum." *Nation*, 105 (27 Dec 1917), 719-720.

Extensive review of *Son*. The book is notable: "As an autobiography, as a literary chronicle, and as the record of an important phase of our national life, it has extraordinary merits." HG's attempt, along with that of Norris and Fuller, to develop "a new and vigorous American realism" failed along the way. In HG's work one finds a tension between city and country; his real love was of the city and literary company. HG is "a writer of sentiment with the touch of a naturalist; an artist, moreover, with an odd grudge against his predestined materials."

A307. "Other Books Worth While." *Literary Digest*, 56 (26 Jan 1918), 36, 38-39.

Brief review of *Son* (36). Largely descriptive comment labels *Son* "simple" and "straightforward." [The same review was printed in *Literary Digest*, 55 (27 Oct 1917), 42.]

A308. Trueblood, C. K. "Background Without Tradition." *Dial*, 64 (28 Feb 1918), 194-195.

Review of *Son*. HG's picture is "a large and broad one, occasionally too sardonic in its fidelity to fact." Trueblood wonders if HG's feeling that social injustice, in the form of the lack of a single tax, is responsible for most of the hardships, has not "partially impaired the artist's perception of the dignity and antiquity of his material .... Has not the determined *actualism* which Mr. G here so sternly reasserts, really been the refuge in adversity of a strongly romantic talent, a talent thwarted by the barrenness of its material?"

A309. [Review of *Son*]. *Educational Foundation* (N.Y.), Apr 1918.
"I have read a great book." The reviewer finds realism and beauty in the description of the Middle Border, a world now becoming part of the tradition of America, and interprets the book as a success story designed to inspire young boys of humble beginnings.

A310. Bowen, E. W. "HG the Middle-West Short-Story Writer." *Sewanee Review*, 27 (Oct 1919), 411-422.
Review of *Son*. HG's return trip West after his first stay in Boston "was important in the procession of HG's struggling fortunes, for it marked the beginning of his career as a writer of fiction." HG's realism did not come suddenly but through Whitman, Howells, and James. *Son* is "a human document of permanent value not only because it contains the entertaining and instructive record of its author's struggle to success, but also because it is an interesting history of the pioneer days on our Western frontier."

A311. Fuller, Henry B. "Three Generations." *Freeman*, 4 (9 Nov 1921), 210-211.
Review of *Daughter*. The work "admirably supplements" *Son*, "or, rather, complements it, being in no sense secondary or subordinate: it is not at all inferior in the interest of its materials, and it is perhaps superior in the manipulation of them, as well as in the matter of general construction."

A312. V[an] D[oren], C[arl]. "The G-McClintock Saga." *Nation*, 113 (23 Nov 1921), 601-602.
Review of *Daughter*. The book "is a precious document on the literary history of Chicago and none the less so because it illuminates the entire profession of literature in America during the Age of Roosevelt." The Garlands and McClintocks, much as HG loves them, "keep their human proportions and frailties. They are the most vivid pioneer families in American literature."

A313. Chamberlin, Joseph Edgar. "*Daughter*." Boston *Evening Transcript*, 10 Dec 1921, IV, 7.

Review of *Daughter*. "It is a strange book ... pure
literary autobiography, sometimes egotistic, frequently
direct and simple to the point of naivete, but interesting
and for the most part really significant in its record of
American intellectual development."

A314. "The New Books." *Outlook*, 130 (11 Jan 1922), 70-71.
Very brief review of *Daughter* (70). The book is
"agreeably written" and "equally readable" and constitutes "a part of the intimate social history of midland America."

A315. Hawthorne, Hildegarde. "A Record of Vanished America."
N.Y. *Times Book Review and Magazine*, 15 Jan 1922,
pp. 14, 19.
Review of *Daughter*. The "better portions" of *Daughter* are those that have to do with Wisconsin. Although
it has little of the "stirring pioneer element" of *Son*,
"it holds you." It is "an American record, and there
is probably no other man in the country who could have
produced such a study of American life, or done it more
simply and effectively."

A316. [Review of *Daughter*]. *Billboard*, 18 Mar 1922.
Interesting as history.

A317. Jones, Richard Foster. "News of New Books and Those
Who Write Them." St. Louis *Post Dispatch*, 29 Mar 1922,
p. 23.
Review of *Daughter*. The book has a spirit of dignity.
HG is a poetic realist.

A318. Shaw, Albert. "Records of Northwestern Pioneering." *Review of Reviews* (American), 65 (Apr 1922), 419-424.
Review of *Son* and *Daughter* (421-423). In *Son*, HG
writes "with a fidelity ... that will ensure for this book
a permanent place in American biography, and give it
standing as a valuable picture of our formative life in
the Northwest." Discussion of *Daughter* is largely
descriptive. *Captain* is also mentioned as a classic
Indian story.

A319. "Briefer Mention." *Dial*, 72 (May 1922), 535-539.
   Brief review of *Daughter* (535). "Mr. G is less happy
   as he gets further away from his boyhood. This book is
   too self-conscious for a saga and too superficial for
   autobiography."

A320. Van Doren, Carl. "The Roving Critic." *Nation*, 114 (24
   May 1922), 622.
   Review of Harper's 12-vol. Border Edition of HG's
   work. HG is "an historian of importance--the most
   important one who has used fiction to present the
   shifting panorama of the upper Middle West and the
   Rocky Mountains." However, as he goes further West
   "something grandiose creeps into his work." He has
   no rivals as far as the Middle Border is concerned.

A321. Gale, Zona. "National Epics of the Border." *Yale Review*,
   NS 11 (Jul 1922), 852-856.
   Review of *Daughter* and *Son* (Border Edition). The
   "unashamed provincialism" of the Middle Border books
   is "their glory." It is "the perfection of the willingly
   provincial--not on the defensive, not in any challenge,
   never by a breath apologetic. But completely articulate."
   Daughter "wins respect and delight" and "fixes HG for
   all time among the beloved figures in American literature."

A322. Hawthorne, Hildegarde. "A Middle West Chronicler." N.Y.
   Times Book Review, 30 Jul 1922, p. 10.
   Review of Border Edition. "We can be thankful to
   Mr. G for these books, all of them. Without them we
   should lose a precious portion of our American story.
   They are not, taken singly, great books. But they are
   a great achievement in their totality."

A323. Nevins, Allan. "G and the Prairies." *Literary Review of
   The N.Y. Evening Post*, 19 Aug 1922, pp. 881-882.
   Extended essay-review on occasion of the publication
   of the Border Edition. The stories of *MTR* "remain
   significant because they deal not with the temporary but
   the permanent seaminess of rural existence; not with the
   accidental but the inevitable difficulties and defeats of
   the frontier." G's decision to abandon the short story

for the novel was "natural" but not altogether satisfactory, for, in his stories, "all the threads are loose,
just as in life"; while, in the novels, G "thought he
had to tie all his threads into a neat and happy conclusion." G's talent is that he is "a master of situation" but "he is a poor handler of plot." His skill
is "reproductive rather than inventive" but *Son* is
"the best description of rural life in the Northwest
ever written."

A324. "*Son.*" *Times Literary Supplement*, 21 (31 Aug 1922), 554.
Review of *Son*. The book "deserves a welcome from
English readers on more grounds than one. It is a picture, by an author who has perfected his method, of an
important phase in the development of American life of
which both the details and the inspiration are little
known to us; it reaches at least its author's highest
previous level of achievement; and it is that unusual
thing--reversing a procedure which has lately been
fashionable--autobiography in the form of fiction."

A325. "The Rainbow's End." London *Times*, 12 Sep 1922, p. 15.
Review of *Son*. The book "will live," because the
personal narrative is "of secondary interest." "The
real theme is the conquest of what the geographies and
maps of seventy years ago called the Great American
Desert."

A326. Lovett, Robert Morss. "The Two Frontiers." *New Republic*, 32 (27 Sep 1922), 14, 16.
Review of Harper's 12-vol. Border Edition of the work
of HG. The collection presents "a considerable variety
and diversity of literary method and value." The stories
begin with the "severe realism of *MTR*, written in the
late eighties," and show "a progressive dilution with
popular romance, culminating in *Captain*." "Mr. G's
realistic method carried him to the edge of his experience; beyond this his imagination failed to penetrate."

A327. Hewlett, Maurice. "Biography and Memoirs." *London Mercury*, 7 (Nov 1922), 106-108.

Enthusiastic review of HG's work. The quality of his fiction is attributed to the fact that his works are autobiographical accounts of life in the Middle West.

A328. "The Middle Border." *Times Literary Supplement*, 21 (23 Nov 1922), 759.

Review of *Daughter*. Although "inevitably" this book "has something less of the epic quality" than *Son*, together they "form a footnote to the social history of modern America, without which something would be lacking, a generation or two hence, to the understanding of the period to which they relate."

A329. Phillip, Peter. "Plain Tales from the Plains." N.Y. *Times Book Review*, 14 Oct 1923, p. 5.

Review of *American Indian*. HG stands between "the romantic evil of Fenimore Cooper ... | and | a utilitarian school [which] has viciously rationalized for popular consumption the vanishing folk tales and customs of the Red Man" in his fictional treatment of the American Indian. HG is like Kipling in his attempt to make the problems of the Indian relevant to the people. He keeps to the facts and researches his material well. The book is a crowning achievement to HG's canon of literature.

A330. [Review of *American Indian*]. *Booklist*, 20 (Dec 1923), 95.

Very brief, entirely descriptive review.

A331. "Two American Artists." *Times Literary Supplement*, 22 (27 Dec 1923), 908.

Review of *American Indian*. Although Remington's drawings are "quite irrelevant" to HG's text, the combination of the two "gives us a readable and attractive volume."

A332. [Review of *American Indian*]. *Literary Review of the N.Y. Evening Post*, 29 Dec 1923, p. 412.

"This is a fitting memorial to the American Indian by two remarkable artists [G and illustrator Frederic Remington] who really knew the race."

A333. Austin, F. Britten. "The Noble Savage." *Bookman* (London),

66 (Sep 1924), 317-318.

Review of *American Indian*. "This book, delightfully
written by Mr. HG and beautifully pictured by the veteran
artist Mr. Frederic Remington, is a splendid memorial"
to the passing of the North American Indian. HG presents the Indian "not in the general terms of the scientific anthropologist, but in fictional typifications of
him, vivid with essential truth," and "never perhaps has
the soul of the American Indian been presented with more
sympathy and insight."

A334. Brooks, William E. "Books and Their Authors." Morgan-
town (W. Va.) *Post*, 13 Oct 1926, pp. 6, 7.
Review of *Trail Makers*. Taken together, the Middle
Border books "have preserved an epoch within their
covers." Reviewer expresses interest in the stress
HG "puts in these books on the influence of song in
the lives of the pioneers."

A335. "HG on Familiar Ground in the Middle Border." St. Louis
Daily Globe-Democrat, 16 Oct 1926, p. 12.
A summary of *Trail Makers*.

A336. **Bussey, Garetta. "The Middle Border Trilogy." N.Y.**
Herald Tribune Books, 24 Oct 1926, p. 25.
Review of *Trail Makers*. "It is a tale of adventure,
and its best moments are those of action"; but "the
men, who are all strong and noble, and the women, who
are all virtuous and fair, move like wooden figures about
the set, making speeches devoid of individuality."

A337. F[arrar], J[ohn]. "The Editor Recommends." *Bookman*
(N.Y.), 64 (Nov 1926), 349-353.
Review of *Trail Makers* (349). HG's work is compared
with Louis Bromfield's *Early Autumn*. "Mr. G is secon-
darily the novelist, and first the historian.... In the
new book, which is far and away better than the others,
he proves himself one of the few realistic chroniclers
of pioneer days who maintain verisimilitude and refrain
from sentimentality."

A338. "A Selected List of Current Books/Fiction." *Wisconsin*

Library Bulletin, 22 (Nov 1926), 297-299.
Brief review of *Trail Makers* (298). Brief summary.

A339. "G Portrays U.S. Grant." *Literary Review of the N.Y. Evening Post*, 6 Nov 1926, p. 3.
Review of *Trail Makers*. "There are times when the reader forgets that it is fiction; wonders whether it is fiction at all. The narrative moves with directness and simplicity. Little use is made of the stock contrivances of fiction. As in real life certain persons appear for a brief moment to play their little parts in the scheme, then to disappear forever, like ships passing in the night."

A340. Nevins, Allan. "HG's Trilogy." *Saturday Review of Literature*, 3 (6 Nov 1926), 270.
Review of *Trail Makers*. The volume "lacks the pulse and color of Mr. G's own autobiography. He has not taken advantage of the license of his romance form to inject purely imaginative materials, and in filling in the outlines of his family chronicle . . . he lacks the vitalizing aid of personal experience." It is "the least vivid and forcible" of the three Middle Border books. But it is still "a valuable addition to our shelf of studies of pioneer life," although it "would be more valuable if Mr. G had treated some parts of it with greater realism and less sentimentality."

A341. "HG Tells a New Tale of the Middle Border." N.Y. *Times Book Review*, 7 Nov 1926, p. 7.
Review of *Trail Makers*. HG's work is quite authentic, and the theme is "well in line with his own tastes and experience." Constance Garland's line drawings in the novel and the physical make-up of the book are well done. "Thus adorned, Mr. G's authentic and moving tale should stand in the vanguard of American historical novels."

A342. Chamberlin, Joseph Edgar. "*Trail Makers*/HG Again Writes of the Middle Border." Boston *Evening Transcript*, 13 Nov 1926, Bk. Sect., p. 3.

Review of *Trail Makers*. It is "fiction, but fiction marvellously true to life, informed with verity, most interesting in its vital details of the period when the workers of New England were throwing down their tools, quitting their farms or their stores and shops, and trekking to the West to make a country and grow up with it."

A343. [Review of *Trail Makers*]. *Open Shelf* (Cleveland), Dec 1926, p. 138.
Very brief and largely descriptive. *Trail Makers* is "a stirring tale."

A344. "Survey of the Past." *Review of Reviews* (American), 74 (Dec 1926), 669-671.
Brief review of *Trail Makers* (670). Graphic in its description and in its treatment of "real pioneers," *Trail Makers* presents an interesting picture of Grant's early days as leader of an army.

A345. "New Books in Brief Review/Fiction." *Independent*, 117 (11 Dec 1926), 681-682.
Brief review of *Trail Makers* (681-682). The book is "every bit as fine as" *Son* and is "a splendid piece of historical writing and a fascinating story in the bargain."

A346. "Novels in Brief." *Nation*, 123 (29 Dec 1926), 696.
Brief review of *Trail Makers*. "It possesses a certain sturdy narrative integrity--sometimes plodding and sometimes poetic--and it earnestly seeks to recapture the flavor of life by honest--rather than melodramatic--devices."

A347. [Review of *Trail Makers*]. *Booklist*, 23 (Jan 1927), 176.
Very brief, entirely descriptive review.

A348. "The Bookman's Guide to Fiction." *Bookman* (N.Y.), 65 (Mar 1927), 76-78.
Very brief mention of *Trail Makers* (77). "Worthy to follow its predecessors."

A349. "HG Completes 'Middle Border' Quadrilogy." Milwaukee
Journal, 17 Nov 1928.
Review of *Back-Trailers*. It is, unlike the other volumes in the series, in no way a novel; but it is fascinating and throws new light on HG, the dean of American
realists.

A350. Chamberlin, Joseph Edgar. "Receders from the Middle Border." Boston *Evening Transcript*, 24 Nov 1928, Bk.
Sect., p. 4.
Review of *Back-Trailers*. The Border series would be
"as good without this fourth volume." "It becomes a
purely reminiscental [sic] book. It is rich in this regard.
But it loses the character of American social history as
reflected in a typical New England migrating family.
The volume strikes fire here and there, especially in
quoted remarks of notable persons." [Review devotes
much space to HG's impression of notable persons like
Conrad and Hardy. The Trail books are "an important
and very interesting addition to American literature."]

A351. "HG's Later Life and Views." Springfield (Mass.) *Sunday
Union and Republican*, 25 Nov 1928, p. 7-E.
Review of *Back-Trailers*. This volume "contains
much that is of interest to those who like to study the
changing environment and racial influences in America,
the conflict of the generations in literary history and
the economic background of the artist's or writer's life
in our land."

A352. Hayes, Marion D. [Review of *Back-Trailers*]. San Jose
Mercury, 2 Dec 1928.
HG is an aristocrat among American writers, and the
book itself is charming.

A353. [Review of *Back-Trailers*]. *Northwestern Christian Advocate*, 6 Dec 1928.
HG reveals more joy in the past and more faith in the
future.

A354. "HG Writes Some of His Experiences." Boston *Morning
Globe*, 8 Dec 1928, p. 6.

Review of *Back-Trailers*, a recital "delightfully reminiscent of Mr. G's later pioneering in the East."

A355. Knowlton, Kent. "The Last of the Middle Border Series." Lowell *Citizen*, 8 Dec 1928.
Review of *Back-Trailers*. The book is well written, but the readers need a familiarity with other books in the series fully to appreciate the point of view.

A356. Nevins, Allan. "Indian Summer." *Saturday Review of Literature*, 5 (8 Dec 1928), 453-454.
Extended review of *Back-Trailers*. "If not as exciting as the record of the crusading years," this book "has a mellow fulness." Its "intimacy" is "always appealing and sometimes touching." The "best parts of this volume are the glimpses of a zestful domestic comradeship"; the "next best part is furnished by the strokes sketching the contemporary elders of Mr. G's literary world."

A357. [Review of *Back-Trailers*]. *Oklahoma News*, 8 Dec 1928.
HG tells tales with charm and geniality.

A358. [Review of *Back-Trailers*]. Savannah *Press*, 8 Dec 1928.
HG's style is graceful and charming, and the story is simple and unaffected. *Back-Trailers* is a pure delight.

A359. Anderson, R. Walter. "Middle Border Book is Fourth." New Bedford *Standard*, 9 Dec 1928.
Review of *Back-Trailers*. HG has a fine style, clear diction, and a wholesome tone.

A360. Sharaf, Lester. "HG Ends His Saga." Brooklyn *Daily Eagle*, 12 Dec 1928, Bk. Sect., p. 4-B.
Review of *Back-Trailers*. A pedestrian book without the high adventure, swing and sweep of the earlier books, it is nevertheless charming.

A361. Senseman, Claire D. "HG Completes Annals of Pioneer Family." Philadelphia *Public Ledger*, 15 Dec 1928, p. 14.

Summarizes *Back-Trailers* and finds it absorbing.

A362. [Review of *Back-Trailers*]. *Watchman Examiner*, 20 Dec 1928.

The book puts the reader under many obligations.

A363. "The Last of the Cycle." Waterbruy (Conn.) *Republican*, 23 Dec 1928.

Review of *Back-Trailers*. The four Middle Border books come as close to an American epic as any attempt in this century.

A364. "Saga of G Family Closes on Victorious Note." *Salt Lake Tribune*, 23 Dec 1928, p. 9.

Summarizes *Back-Trailers* and concludes that the book moves along leisurely and quietly without the element of drama alive in the earlier books.

A365. Titsworth, Mary. "G Re-treks to the East." Knoxville *News*, 23 Dec 1928.

Review of *Back-Trailers*. "This interesting family is pleasantly described."

A366. Maurice, Arthur. "Scanning the New Books." *Mentor*, 16 (Jan 1929), 61-65.

Brief review of *Back-Trailers*. An entirely descriptive review. No critical content.

A367. "Books and Their Writers." Davenport (Iowa?) *Democrat and Leader*, 6 Jan 1929.

Review of *Back-Trailers*. HG is an historian as well as an author, and this book has worth both as history and literature.

A368. Woods, Katherine. "Along the Back Trail from the Middle Border." N.Y. *Times Book Review*, 13 Jan 1929, p. 2.

Review of *Back-Trailers*. "If Mr. G's latest book is representative history in its theme, it is none the less distinctly individual in its personalities and its happenings." *Back-Trailers* constitutes "a collection of exceedingly interesting personal memoirs."

A369. L., H. C. "Book Talk." Des Moines *Sunday Register*, 20
Jan 1929, p. 10-G.
    Review of *Back-Trailers*. The reviewer finds the work
    delightful and readable but resents the fact that the
    author left the Midwest and finds HG's economic reasons
    for doing so insufficient.

A370. Smith, Lewis Worthington. "Of Especial Interest to Iowa."
Des Moines *Sunday Register*, 20 Jan 1929, p. 10-G.
    Brief review of *Back-Trailers*. HG's pronouncements
    on literature are "thoughtful and guarded." The section
    of the book dealing with other authors is especially ef-
    fective.

A371. Mencken, H. L. "The Literary Olio." *Smart Set*, 27 (Feb
1929), 153-159.
    Review of *Shadow World* (153-154). It is "almost as
    entertaining as 'Alice in Wonderland'--which, in more
    than one respect, it resembles." "For all his solemn
    talk of scientific test conditions, G is apparently en-
    tirely unacquainted with the experimental methods of
    true scientists"; and "he seems to be unfamiliar, not
    only with the commonplaces of physical experiment,
    but also with the methods and history of his own occult
    science." The book is, in the end, "superficial and
    amateurish."

A372. "A Saga of the Middle West." *Review of Reviews* (American), 79 (Feb 1929), 84.
    Review of four Middle Border books. "Altogether it
    is a characteristically American story. The European
    mind could hardly be expected to understand or appre-
    ciate it. Possibly the American mind of today will be
    puzzled by its idealism and sentiment, which seem not
    entirely in keeping with the materialistic conception
    of our national growth. Yet we are persuaded that the
    portrayal is fundamentally truthful."

A373. "The Middle Border Books." *Dairyman's League News*,
15 Feb 1929.
    Review of the Middle Border series. The books are
    of compelling interest because they deal with farm

people who belong to the sturdy middle class that led in the conquering of the West.

A374. Jackson, Anne Wakely. "Book News and Reviews." Jacksonville *Daily Journal*, 29 Mar 1929.
Review of *Back-Trailers*. The book is interesting and valuable as social history.

A375. Seitz, Don C. [Review of *Roadside*]. *Bookman* (N.Y.), 72 (Sep 1930), 95.
Entirely descriptive review.

A376. "The World of Books/HG and 19th Century Realists."
Springfield (Mass.) *Daily Republican*, 20 Sep 1930, p. 8.
Review of *Roadside*. The volume is "no attempt at literary history, but an entertaining and frequently significant account of personal acquaintances and encounters."

A377. White, William Allen. "A Bridge into the Past." N.Y. *Herald Tribune Books*, 21 Sep 1930, pp. 1-2.
Review of *Roadside*. The book "is a bridge upon which one may walk into a past that now seems as remote as Ninevah and Tyre, the American life and letters of the seventies, eighties and nineties." No student "of American letters, who wants to know something of how the ancestors of our present writers looked and lived, should ignore it."

A378. Grattan, C. Hartley. "HG/The Metamorphosis of a Literary Radical." N.Y. *Evening Post*, 27 Sep 1930, p. 12.
Review of *Roadside*. It is a "sad" book because it shows that HG "lacked a persistently iconoclastic mind" and had "a confused set of values." But it is also "unflaggingly interesting," "an unusually important literary autobiography," and "superlatively American."

A379. ---. "Ex-Literary Radical." *Nation*, 131 (1 Oct 1930), 351.
Review of *Roadside*. HG "wanted to be truthful in his own stories, but he got himself confused by thinking about 'wholesome' realism. He sensed the immense

brilliance of Stephen Crane, but regretfully concluded
that Crane would never develop like Booth Tarkington
and Owen Wister!'' *Roadside* itself "is a superb literary document, full of information, strewn with brilliant
portraits (brilliant even in their misunderstandings),
and stuffed full of evidence to support Van Wyck
Brooks's most pessimistic generalizations about the
American literary life.''

A380. "The World of Books." *Review of Reviews* (American), 82
(Nov 1930), 10-19.
Review of *Roadside* (12). Mainly descriptive: G has
written about his subject "entertainingly and well."

A381. "New and Special Editions." N.Y. *Times Book Review*, 16
Nov 1930, p. 14.
Review of new edition of *MTR*. The main difference
in this edition is the inclusion of drawings by Constance Garland. The publisher did a poor job in the
physical layout of the book: "The type has no distinction, and no effort has been made at harmonious arrangement of illustrations and text." The book deserves a better treatment because it is one of the landmarks in American literary history. "It is one of the
main stems in the development of fictional realism in
this country."

A382. [Review of *Roadside*]. *Booklist*, 27 (Dec 1930), 155-156.
Very brief, almost entirely descriptive review. The
book is "an important literary biography."

A383. [Review of *Roadside*]. *Open Shelf* (Cleveland), Dec 1930,
p. 152.
Very brief, entirely descriptive review.

A384. Smith, Lewis Worthington. "The Idealism of a Realist."
Christian Century, 47 (3 Dec 1930), 1494-1495.
Review of *Roadside*. This is HG's "most important
contribution to letters so far." For "the intelligent
reader there is a steady glow of interest in the full
pages, and it cannot fail to be useful for reference in
every public library."

A385. Forsythe, Robert S. "Literary Portraits." *Quarterly Journal* (U of North Dakota), 21 (Winter 1931), 169-171.

Review of *Roadside*. Written with HG's "usual honesty, frankness, and Victorianism," it "is not a dull volume, and any reader who is interested in American and English literature of the late nineteenth century will find it valuable in the light it throws upon important persons and personalities of the period." Unfortunately, however, readers of HG's three earlier autobiographical books will find nothing new here, and such a rewriting and rearranging of earlier material "is hardly fair treatment of the reading public."

A386. Paxson, F. L. [Review of *Roadside*]. *Mississippi Valley Historical Review*, 17 (Mar 1931), 652-653.

HG "differed from many of his elder models and his younger friends in that he used no literary disguise, except as he disguised himself to be more visibly himself. And in this lies the value of this book and the significance of the literary career of G."

A387. Chamberlain, John. "In the Literary Desert of the Early 1900's." N.Y. *Times Book Review*, 27 Sep 1931, pp. 2, 12.

Review of *Companions*. HG's middle period (1903-1914) is a descent, falling between *MTR* and *Son*. The years covered in *Companions* are HG's dining out years, his political and social gathering years when he was involved with the Cliff Dwellers and the Institute of Arts and Letters. This volume is "less valuable" than *Roadside*.

A388. White, William Allen. "Bridging Old and New." N.Y. *Herald Tribune Books*, 27 Sep 1931, p. 1.

Review of *Companions*. HG's autobiographical volumes "taken together make a record of American life from the 80's to today that has never been equaled for its veracity, for its intelligent understanding of the middle class American mind in those days and for a certain incorrigible American optimism which is, after all, in spite of the hoots of the sophisticates, our real distinction in the neighborhood of nations."

A389. "The World of Books/HG Continues His Personal Chronicle."
Springfield (Mass.) *Daily Republican*, 3 Oct 1931, p. 10.
Review, largely descriptive, of *Companions*. This
volume is "a pleasant backward ramble."

A390. Hayes, Marion D. "*Companions.*" San Jose *Mercury Herald*,
4 Oct 1931.
Review. *Companions* has enjoyable spontaneity.

A391. Loveman, Amy. "A Goodly Company." *Saturday Review of
Literature*, 8 (10 Oct 1931), 187.
Review of *Companions*. The work suffers from "the
defects of its virtues, for the very multiplicity of personalities it introduces gives to its narrative an episodic
and fragmentary character. It is, indeed, almost a collection of brevities. But they are interesting brevities."

A392. "HG's Literary Life and Views." Columbus (Ohio) *Sunday
Dispatch*, 18 Oct 1931.
Review of *Companion*. The insight into famous men
is interesting.

A393. Hicks, Granville. "G of the Academy." *Nation*, 133 (21
Oct 1931), 435-436.
Review of *Companions*. The book is the "dullest"
of HG's six autobiographical volumes, "partly because
it introduces--without variation to warrant the repeti-
tion--material already presented in earlier volumes, but
chiefly because many of the incidents it describes are
trivial and are narrated with merciless prolixity." Unlike HG's early work, which was "direct, comprehensive,
moving, and savagely honest," this later work is that
of HG, member of the American Academy, "self-satis-
fied, fastidious, undemocratic, out of sympathy with
every vital movement in contemporary life."

A394. [Review of *Companions*]. *Booklist*, 28 (Nov 1931), 101.
Very brief, entirely descriptive review.

A395. "Travel Books." *Survey*, 67 (1 Nov 1931), 168-169.
Very brief review of *Companions* (169). Entirely
descriptive.

A396. Shuster, George N. "Days of Long Ago." *Commonweal,*
15 (4 Nov 1931), 22.
Review of *Companions*. The sketches of famous
figures are interesting, but "undoubtedly the best
part of the book from this point of view is devoted
to the 'trail'--to the vanishing Indian, the changing
West, the whole, huge primitive universe of America."

A397. "Book Notes/Biography and Memoirs." *New Republic,* 68
(11 Nov 1931), 359.
Review of *Companions*. The book is "a sort of
'Pilgrim's Progress' with culture as its objective
instead of salvation"; but "one is moved to wonder
whether Mr. G has not mistaken Vanity Fair for the
Celestial City."

A398. Brooks, Walter R. "Behind the Blurbs." *Outlook and
Independent,* 159 (25 Nov 1931), 411.
Brief review of *Companions*. This is "probably the
most interesting" chapter of "the record of American
life begun in" *Trail Makers*.

A399. [Review of *Companions*]. *Open Shelf* (Cleveland), Dec
1931, pp. 150-151.
One-sentence description.

A400. Stoyle, Lewis E. "An Author's Companions on the Trail."
Boston *Evening Transcript,* 12 Dec 1931, Bk. Sect.,
p. 2.
Review of *Companions*. "It matters little whether
you may agree with the author's theories and opinions
or not. It is sufficient to say that he has gathered together a most interesting collection of sidelights and
observations on the masters of the seven arts of thirty
years ago."

A401. "Check List of New Books/Biography." *American Mercury,*
25 (Jan 1932), iv-ix.
Brief review of *Companions* (vi-vii). HG says nothing
"very illuminating" about his friends, and his literary
judgment is often "somewhat naive."

A402. Hubbell, Jay B. [Review of *Companions*]. *American Literature*, 3 (Jan 1932), 498.

A sequel to *Roadside*, *Companions* is less well organized and somewhat less readable than its predecessor. HG reports having met Emily Dickinson in 1902 when she had already died in 1886. ''Just whom did G meet at Stedman's?''

A403. Chamberlain, John. ''HG's Backward Glancing.'' N.Y. *Times Book Review*, 13 Nov 1932, pp. 5, 14.

Review of *Contemporaries*. The book ''is an example of a mind drawing in upon itself,'' which withdrawal did produce ''two highly estimable chronicles,'' *Son* and *Daughter*; but *Contemporaries* ''is a not very valuable by-product--a sparse record'' which leaves out much that was interesting in the years it records.

A404. MacDonald, William. ''When HG Migrated to New York.'' N.Y. *Herald Tribune Books*, 13 Nov 1932, p. 7.

Review of *Contemporaries*. Almost entirely a summary of the book; no critical comment.

A405. H., G. W. ''HG Proceeds With His Self-Document.'' Providence *Sunday Journal*, 27 Nov 1932, Sec. E, p. 6.

Review of *Contemporaries*. G is ''a stout champion of one hundred percent Americanism--not in so many words, but obviously none the less--something of a bigot in his judgments, a prude. So many times the episodes from his notebooks boil down to a mere listing of goings and comings.'' But G ''has caught much priceless Americana in his books.''

A406. ''A Selected List of Current Books/Biography.'' *Wisconsin Library Bulletin*, 28 (Dec 1932), 334-336.

Brief descriptive review of *Contemporaries* (335).

A407. Stoyle, Lewis E. ''HG.'' Boston *Evening Transcript*, 10 Dec 1932, Bk. Sect., p. 3.

Review of *Contemporaries*. Although through the book ''runs a note of sadness and of baffled effort, a confession that the old order changeth, and that the generation of authors supreme in ... [HG's] day is on the wane,'' it is "unceasingly interesting from cover to cover" and is "an unusually fascinating literary autobiography."

A408. "The World of Books/HG's 'Literary Log.'" Springfield (Mass.) *Daily Republican*, 10 Dec 1932, p. 8.
   Review of *Contemporaries*. "This record of an American author's experiences and impressions is that of a strong, clear and sincere mind. Not all the personal contacts seem important, and some of the judgments, alike of enthusiasm and reprobation, will doubtless provoke varying measures of dissent. But Mr. G's habit of seeing with his own eyes and setting down impressions with his own pen gives the volume pungency and a considerable degree of interpretative significance."

A409. "Mr. G Recalls." *Christian Science Monitor*, 17 Dec 1932, p. 6.
   Review of *Contemporaries*. "Pervading this work is the plaintive note of one who finds himself less and less able to sympathize with a younger generation of 'realistic' writers." The most interesting characterizations in the book are those of HG's English trip in 1932: "These English sketches are less fragmentary and approach more nearly the breadth of treatment that makes *Roadside* the best of the three [autobiographical] volumes."

A410. "Shorter Notices." *Nation*, 135 (21 Dec 1932), 623-624.
   Review of *Contemporaries* (623-624). The book should have been called "A Literary Lag." As HG "proceeds down the years he has less and less to say about literature as it is understood by the present generation and more and more to say about the 'official' writers who are so entirely passé that many youngsters do not even recognize their names. The result is an incredible, weird, hair-raising, sad, silly, irritating, nonsensical, ignorant, and completely fascinating book." *Contemporaries* is "a gorgeous example of the 'official' mind in decay."

A411. Phelps, William Lyon. "Mr. G's Log." *Saturday Review of Literature*, 9 (31 Dec 1932), 355.

   Review of *Contemporaries*. Although Phelps admires *Rose* ("no historian of American literature can afford to neglect this novel") and *Son* ("a permanent contribution to American literature") most among HG's works, he finds *Contemporaries* "mellow and mild" and "interesting." He objects only to "the atmosphere of decay," for "of all false sentiments, none is so false as the apologetic attitude of many old men."

A412. Brickell, Herschel. "Mrs. Woolf as a Critic." *North American Review*, 235 (Jan 1933), 95-96.

   Very brief review of *Contemporaries* (95). No critical comment.

A413. Cournos, John. "Literary Sign-Posts." *Scribner's*, 93 (Jan 1933), 5-7.

   Review of *Contemporaries* (5-6). The third volume of G's "literary log" is pervaded by a sense of death, the death and weariness of the people G has met.

A414. [Review of *Contemporaries*]. *Booklist*, 29 (Jan 1933), 141.

   Very brief, entirely descriptive review.

A415. Clark, Edwin. "Literary Memories." *Commonweal*, 17 (15 Feb 1933), 445.

   Review of *Contemporaries*. The memoirs in this book "contain the swan song of an ex-revoltee .... Having turned his back on the vigor of his youth, G assumed the attitude of the academic sage and from this vantage viewed the arts with lamentation."

A416. Tracy, Henry. "Autobiography, Discursive and Analytical." *Yale Review*, NS 22 (Mar 1933), 619-622.

   Brief review of *Contemporaries* (620). The work is "a serene evocation, as from a secure eminence," which lacks "the epic flow and vigor" of *Son*.

A417. "The World of Books/HG's Impressions." Springfield (Mass.) *Daily Republican*, 10 Nov 1934, p. 10.

Review of *Neighbors*. "The reader will find this
chronicle not free from small beer, but he will also
find much challenge in Mr. G's thoughts about this
day and generation and about himself."

A418. MacDonald, William. "Friends and HG." N.Y. *Herald
Tribune Books*, 18 Nov 1934, p. 10.
Review of *Neighbors*. Largely a summary of highlights of the book. Its "only discordant note" is the
"note of disappointment and bitterness" which runs
through it.

A419. Moffett, Anita. "Celebrities Sketched by HG." N.Y. *Times
Book Review*, 25 Nov 1934, p. 10.
Review of *Neighbors*. Almost entirely a descriptive
summary of the book.

A420. [Review of *Neighbors*]. *Booklist*, 31 (Dec 1934), 127.
Brief descriptive review.

A421. [Review of *Neighbors*]. *Book-of-the-Month Club News*,
Dec 1934, unpaginated.
HG was always in touch with the writers of his time
as well as with public figures. His presentation of
famous literary figures is highly interesting.

A422. Stoyle, Lewis E. "HG with Some of His Afternoon Neighbors." Boston *Evening Transcript*, 1 Dec 1934, Bk.
Sect., pp. 1, 3.
Review of *Neighbors*. HG "has been fortunate in his
friends and . . . he has written about them lucidly and
invigoratingly." *Neighbors* "contains a rich mine of
biographical material that appeals to anyone who has
followed the course of literature during the past half
century."

A423. "Colorful Reminiscences of Three Literary Men." Hartford
Daily Courant, 2 Dec 1934, Sec. D, p. 6.
Review of *Neighbors* which briefly describes the scope
of the book, commenting on G's "hearty, spontaneous
enjoyment of life" which permeates his reminiscences.
It is "a book in which readers of every type should find
something of interest."

A424. "Books in Brief." *Christian Century*, 51 (5 Dec 1934), 1563-1564.

Brief, almost entirely descriptive, review of *Neighbors* (1564).

A425. "Afternoon with Mr. G." *Christian Science Monitor*, 12 Dec 1934, Weekly Mag. Sect., p. 12.

Review of *Neighbors*. HG, "as always, writes competently and his style readily lends itself to reading aloud. What detracts from one's enjoyment is his pessimism and his constant looking to the past as the vanished source of all that's worthwhile."

A426. "Mr. HG." London *Times*, 11 Jan 1935, p. 6.

Review of *Neighbors*, "an entertaining and sage volume."

A427. "The American Scene." *Times Literary Supplement*, 34 (31 Jan 1935), 60.

Review of *Neighbors*. The volume reveals HG as "a personality of great vitality and undiminishing sympathy, alert for new experiences and experiments." The pages on Hardy "are extremely good"; there are "many beautiful portraits of distinguished Americans"; HG "is particularly engaging when he recalls the past and compares himself and his passing generation with the writers of the present moment"; "his mind remains exceedingly fresh and receptive and he accepts with tolerance and inquiry much that he cannot like."

A428. B., M. E. "HG's Book Is Catalog of Literary Names." Cleveland *Plain Dealer*, 3 Mar 1935, Women's Magazine and Amusement Sect., p. 15.

Review of *Neighbors*. "This is a record of an era of American life by a critic who found most of its manifestations distasteful."

A429. Robinson, Ted. "Probes 'Psychic Phenomena.'" Cleveland *Plain Dealer*, 19 Apr 1936, Women's Magazine and Amusement Sect., p. 15.

Review of *Forty Years*. "The book is worthy the attention of the scientist, the spiritist, the skeptic and the religious as well."

A430. Towne, Charles H. "HG's Study of the Occult." Los
Angeles *Examiner*, 21 Apr 1936.
Review of *Forty Years*. Rewritten from copious
diaries that HG kept, the book describes sessions
with psychics. It is scientifically accurate.

A431. "Ghosts and Skeptical Mr. G." N.Y. *Times Book Review*,
26 Apr 1936, p. 9.
Review, largely a summary, of *Forty Years*. "Some
of the results obtained are extraordinarily interesting
and most of them, especially the more recent ones,
make a strong appeal to the intelligence."

A432. "He Keeps an Open Mind." Los Angeles *Times*, 26 Apr
1936, III, 8.
Review of *Forty Years*. The reviewer emphasizes the
authenticity of the phenomena presented by HG and
describes the chapter claiming communications from
William James, William D. Howells, and Walt Whitman.

A433. "Aged Agnostic." *Time*, 27 (27 Apr 1936), 85-86.
Review of *Forty Years*. Book's "sober findings" will
be "respected" by both agnostics and faithful "but will
give little aid and comfort to either." For "those familiar with the popular literature of spiritualism, what re-
searcher G has to tell will be nothing new."

A434. [Review of *Forty Years*]. *Booklist*, 32 (May 1936), 248.
Very brief, entirely descriptive review.

A435. "A Selected List of Current Books/Philosophy." *Wisconsin
Library Bulletin*, 32 (May 1936), 61-62.
Brief review of *Forty Years* (61). The book, an "un-
emotional account" of psychic phenomena, makes no
judgments.

A436. Eberle, Merab. "Spirit World Is Merely New Field of Bio-
logical Research." Dayton *Journal*, 2 May 1936, p. 5.
Review of *Forty Years*. "Here is a book for the many
who wish a clear, dispassionate survey of a research
carried on by brilliant minds in what they believe to be
a vast, uncharted portion of the realm of biology."

A437. J., G. [Review of *Forty Years*]. Providence *Sunday Journal*, 17 May 1936, VI, 8.

> In *Forty Years*, G "asks no one's belief in the supernatural; he simply states the results of his forty years of observations which have convinced him that there is a fourth dimensional power."

A438. "Books in Brief." *Christian Century*, 53 (20 May 1936), 739.

> Brief review of *Forty Years*. "It is Mr. G's story and he sticks to it. But it is not the reader's story, and most readers will neither deny nor believe it."

A439. "Searching for Truth in Realm of Psychic." Springfield (Mass.) *Sunday Union and Republican*, 14 Jun 1936, p. 7-E.

> Review of *Forty Years*. "There is no doubting Mr. G's sincerity. His book, and he probably did not intend it so, is more valuable as a study of his own wanderings than it is in its recital of spirit adventures." "It is a human, moving document."

A440. Crowley, Paul. "Some Recent Biographies." *Commonweal*, 24 (19 Jun 1936), 219-220.

> Review of *Forty Years* (219). Although the work is "valuable Americana" in terms of intellectual history, HG seems "gullible" and "half persuaded he has met with strange goings on."

A441. J., J. [Review of *Forty Years*]. *Saturday Review of Literature*, 14 (18 Jul 1936), 22.

> "The book has the value of illustrating what may happen to a man of abundant talent in one direction, when he ventures into a field requiring an altogether different logical equipment or training . . . ." As "a case-history, the volume is instructive; as a contribution it is hardly to be taken seriously."

A442. Kazin, Alfred. "Thought Forms." N.Y. *Herald Tribune Books*, 19 Jul 1936, p. 16.

> Review of *Forty Years*. The book is "the only type of literature on psychic phenomena that deserves attention and criticism; it is a laboratory notebook that re-

cords definite, planned experiments in a field where
only some of the basic conditions of scientific research can be met." It "should be prized for its lack
of pretense and false encouragement."

A443. " 'A Plain Narrative of Fact.' " *Times Literary Supplement*,
35 (15 Aug 1936), 658.
Review of *Forty Years*. Although HG "is not always
a quite accurate reporter of what he has read" and although "it is annoying that the mediums responsible
for some of the most remarkable phenomena here recorded cannot be identified," the book "is certainly
interesting." The value of HG's testimony is increased
by the fact that "he draws no positive inference regard-
ing the causation of the phenomena."

A444. Thompson, Ralph. "Books of the Times." N.Y. *Times*, 17
May 1939, p. 27.
Review, mainly descriptive, of *Buried Crosses*. "California is a wonderful state, and it is certainly a long
way from the Middle Border."

A445. "Spirited." *Time*, 33 (22 May 1939), 95.
Review of *Buried Crosses*. The "pace and intentional
humor recall the old G." The "unintentional humor"
"fetches many a chuckle."

A446. Drew, Harold D. "Mystic Borderlands." Pasadena *Star
News*, 27 May 1939.
Review of *Buried Crosses*. HG is not dogmatic; he
merely offers testimony. His intellectual integrity is
not to be doubted. *Buried Crosses* is a fascinating
record of a journey into the occult, which presents
evidence and leaves judgment up to the reader.

A447. "HG Writes Again of Experiences with 'Ghosts.' " Honolulu *Star Bulletin*, 3 Jun 1939, Society Sect., p. 14.
Review of *Buried Crosses*. This amusing article
not only discusses the book but also HG's literary
history.

A448. Davenport, Basil. ''Psychic Experiments.'' *Saturday Review of Literature*, 20 (10 Jun 1939), 18.
Review of *Buried Crosses*. HG ''tells his story with evident sincerity, but ramblingly.'' Like ''too many amateur psychicists, he draws no clear distinction between clairvoyance and telepathy, and between these powers and indications of the survival of the personality after death.'' Nonetheless, the reader who feels the fascination of this subject will be interested in the book.

A449. Wiggin, Marian. ''The Rogues' Gallery.'' Boston *Evening Transcript*, 10 Jun 1939, IV, 2.
Review of *Buried Crosses*. ''While we were reading, the whole story seemed most convincing, but the minute we closed the book, it all rolled off like so much water from the proverbial duck.''

A450. Sugrue, Thomas. ''Dreams, Mystery or Facts.'' N.Y. *Herald Tribune Books*, 6 Aug 1939, p. 9.
Review of *Buried Crosses*. The book ''makes a yarn as racy and as exciting as a mystery thriller, despite Mr. G's efforts to slow it down and give it the tone of a doctor's thesis. It just isn't that kind of story, unfortunately for Mr. G's purpose.''

A451. Kuhig, Verna K. [Review of *Buried Crosses*]. *National Spiritualist*, 1 Oct 1939.
The factual evidence displayed in book is described as ''interesting and with overwhelming evidence of the continuity of life.''

A452. Mann, Charles W., Jr. [Review of *CI*]. *Library Journal*, 85 (1 Apr 1960), 1449.
''This book deserved reprinting as a statement of the climate of its time, and as an early defense of an exclusively American literature.''

A453. Tucker, Martin. ''Vintage from the Campus Presses.'' *Saturday Review*, 43 (21 May 1960), 23-24.
Review of new edition of *CI* (24). HG's theory of veritism puts aside use of secondary sources and calls

for direct, "personal observation." The book has
qualities of "ideality and literary independence"
which were or are popular in the late 1950's and
early 1960's.

A454. Marx, Leo. "The Radicalism of HG." *Commentary*, 30
(Sep 1960), 268-271.
Review of Jane Johnson's edition of *CI*. The book
is not the great volume that the publishers of this new
edition claim it to be. It is "shallow" and makes plain
the fact that HG "was no thinker." But "the book's
lack of intrinsic merit does not impair its usefulness
as a historical document." HG, who in *MTR* gave the
appearance of being a literary radical, was really fraud-
ulently avant-garde. In reality, he "tried to use the
surface texture of realism to disguise the premises of
romance."

A455. Butler, Joseph T. [Review of *CI*]. *New England Quarterly*,
34 (Jun 1961), 274-275.
"While *CI* is not in its overall concept a profound
group of essays, it essentially presents a forward
glimpse into the aesthetics of the twentieth century.
Certainly the discussion of impressionism is one of
the most interesting to be found in American literature
of the day."

A456. Hansen, Chadwick. [Review of *Boy Life*]. *College English*, 23 (Mar 1962), 514.
"In spite of its faults, the book is well worth repub-
lishing. HG's boyhood Middle West retains some of
the natural beauty, freedom, and violence of Mark
Twain's, while it anticipates the boredom and inco-
herent longings of Sherwood Anderson's and Sinclair
Lewis's."

A457. Allred, B. W., J. C. Dykes, and F. G. Renner. "A Roundup
of Western Reading." *Arizona and the West*, 4 (Summer
1962), 191-196.
Very brief review of U of Nebraska Press ed. of *Boy
Life* (192). It is "one of G's best books--perhaps his
best."

A458. Anderson, Harry H. [Review of *Boy Life*]. *North Dakota History*, 29 (Jul 1962), 273.

Review of Bison Books (U of Nebraska Press) reprint. "This is a volume that supplies insights into avenues of pioneer experiences that too often are missing from formal studies of homesteading on the frontier."

B. PERIODICAL ARTICLES ABOUT HAMLIN GARLAND

B1. [Chamberlin, Joseph E.] "The Listener." Boston *Evening Transcript*, 28 Nov 1887, p. 4.

Detailed account and critique of speech HG gave to Anti-Poverty Society meeting. HG "failed to prove that the land system was responsible for the present disintegration and overcrowding, and he failed to show just how the change he proposed would work an amelioration." The audience got "the poetry" of the Anti-Poverty movement from HG rather than "the logic of it." HG is described as "a man remarkable in appearance, with thick hair brushed back from his forehead and cut straight off all around; a fine, handsome face, well-chiselled and spirituel [sic]; a full curling beard, that in no sense diminished the aspect of delicacy that his countenance wore; and keen and earnest eyes."

B2. *Standard*, 29 Jan 1890, p. 11.

Announcement that HG and Herne will speak in New York on 2 Feb.

B3. ---, 12 Feb 1890, p. 12.

On 6 Feb, Herne and HG spoke to three hundred citizens of Lynn, Mass., who were "much pleased with the plainness with which the 'cat' was shown." Part of the discussion dealt with the rise of land values.

B4. ---, 16 Apr 1890, p. 11.

HG "addressed the pupils of the school of oratory at Boston yesterday on 'Henry George and the Single Tax.' The address was made by request."

B5.   ---, 23 Apr 1890, p. 13.

    HG addressed a meeting of single-tax people in Boston. He was followed by Herne, who spoke about the single tax for forty-five minutes and then read HG's "Under the Lion's Paw," after which HG answered questions satisfactorily. The 500-seat hall was overflowing; half the audience was ladies.

B6.   "Notes and Announcements." *Arena*, 2 (Jul 1890), i-v.

    Two notes on "Wheel" (iii-iv), which looks forward "to a world built on liberty, justice and fraternity." The plotless realistic play has a plan like life itself and emphasizes character drawing.

B7.   *Standard*, 27 Aug 1890, p. 6.

    Notice that HG will issue "Wheel" in a paper cover very soon at moderate prices, "for the author desires it rather to be widely read than to be a paying production." He has other plays, with reform tendencies, in preparation.

B8.   ---, 3 Sep 1890, pp. 8-9.

    HG is mentioned as one of many welcoming Henry George back to Manhattan. At a Cooper Union conference, HG followed Judge Maguire with a short speech and the reading of a poem by Mrs. Milne of San Luis Obispo, Calif., entitled "January-September, 1890."

B9.   ---, 10 Sep 1890, p. 13.

    Report of conference which took place on 3 Sep at which HG read Mrs. Milne's poem.

B10. "Notes and Announcements." *Arena*, 2 (Nov 1890), xviii-xxi.

    HG's "Return of a Private" will appear in the Dec 1890 issue (xx). It is one of the "strongest and most touchingly beautiful stories we have ever read," and HG is the "most promising young author of the day." He is a "true artist" who understands art as well as reform and duty.

B11. [Chamberlin, Joseph E.] "The Listener." Boston *Evening Transcript*, 1 Nov 1890, p. 6.

Brief account of HG's reading of "Member" at Chickering Hall. "The applause and attention seemed to indicate that the play took hold of the interest and admiration of the audience, especially in the last two acts, which were fuller of passion and emotion than the subject of the buying of a legislature would seem naturally to yield." The play "certainly deserves the test of being acted, to say the least for it."

B12. *Standard*, 19 Nov 1890, p. 11.

Prof. HG will make another trip to the West as far as Minneapolis in December. His headquarters for several weeks will be at Onalaska, Wisconsin. He will speak as often as possible and will read "Wheel" and "Under the Lion's Paw" whenever desired.

B13. "Notes and Announcements." *Arena*, 3 (Dec 1890), xxii-xxvi.

HG's "The Return of a Private," which appears in the Dec 1890 *Arena*, "is one of the finest pieces of realism that has recently appeared" (xxii). HG's scholarly paper "A New Declaration of Rights"--"an important contribution to the social and industrial literature of the day"--will appear in the Jan 1891 *Arena* (xxiii).

B14. *Standard*, 3 Dec 1890, p. 12.

At a meeting of the single-tax state central committee of Massachusetts on 3 Nov. HG was chosen as vice-president. The name of the organization was changed to Massachusetts Single Tax League.

B15. ---, 10 Dec 1890, p. 13.

The Tenth District Single Tax League of Worcester, Mass., expects to have HG and other interesting speakers address them in the near future.

B16. "Notes and Announcements." *Arena*, 3 (Jan 1891), xix-xxi.

HG's "A New Declaration of Rights" in this same issue gives "a strong, clear, and exceedingly entertaining presentation of the single-tax theory."

B17. "Personal." Minneapolis *Tribune*, 6 Jan 1891, p. 5.
    Brief sentence to effect that "Prof. HG read his play 'Wheel' to an audience of the Single Tax League last evening."

B18. *Standard*, 7 Jan 1891, p. 18.
    On Sunday, 28 Dec 1890, the Boston Single Tax League elected HG one of five vice-presidents.

B19. Schindler, Rabbi Solomon. "Nationalism Versus Individualism." *Arena*, 3 (Apr 1891), 601-607.
    HG's "A New Declaration of Rights" is "brilliantly written." But Schindler totally disagrees with HG's position that the single tax will remedy all social ills. He also disagrees with HG's ideas on individualism and socialism.

B20. Wingate, Charles E. L. "Boston Letter." *Critic,* NS 15 (30 May 1891), 289.
    Discussion of the independent theater venture in Boston backed by Herne and "Mr. HG, the warmest admirer of the radical drama . . . ."

B21. "The Latest Western Novelist." Boston *Evening Transcript*, 15 Jun 1891, p. 6.
    Biographical sketch of HG which includes listing of his lecture topics and appreciation of his independence of mind: "It would be impossible for any conventional critic to kill Mr. G with scholarly criticism; he has a buoyancy of indifference to obstacles as free as a cyclone from one of his own Iowa praries."

B22. "Book Chat." *Arena*, 4 (Jul 1891), xxiv.
    This notice that *MTR* will be reviewed in August predicts the book will create a great stir because "it is one of those works which menace the old order of things by making people think."

B23. "An Epoch-Marking Drama." *Arena*, 4 (Jul 1891), 247-249.
    Herne's *Margaret Fleming* was first preformed in Boston's Chickering Hall, 4 May 1891, and HG was in the audience (247).

B24. "Notes and Announcements." *Arena*, 4 (Jul 1891), xvii-xxi.
"A Prairie Heroine," which appeared in the June *Arena*,
is a thoroughly realistic story and is much like photography in art (xviii).

B25. Wingate, Charles E. L. "Boston Letter." *Critic*, NS 16
(18 Jul 1891), 32.
HG is the "leading spirit" of the attempt to establish
an independent theater. "Since Mr. G's new book *MTR*
appeared, a few weeks ago, his friends have been desig-
nating him as the Kipling of the West, and it is certain
his Mississippi Valley stories are bold and strong in
their devotion to realism."
Biographical sketch notes that HG was "devoted to
certain theories--one, of course, being the promulgation
of realism, in every branch of literature, and another
being the rightfulness of individualism, or single tax ...
[;] Mr. G would travel to the North Pole to lecture upon
his pet ideas and not ask a cent of remuneration. It is
a pleasure occasionally to find a man so thoroughly in
love with his self-appointed work."

B26. "Notes and Announcements." *Arena*, 4 (Aug 1891), xxvi-
xxxi.
Quotes a number of reviews of *MTR*, which is causing
great stir (xxx-xxxi). Praises HG's work and mentions
that a London publisher wants to publish *MTR*.

B27. [Crane, Stephen]. "Howells Discussed at Avon-by-the-Sea."
N.Y. *Daily Tribune*, 18 Aug 1891, p. 5.
HG quoted from at length on Howells in lecture HG gave
at the Seaside Assembly.

B28. "Notes and Announcements." *Arena*, 4 (Sep 1891), xxvii-
xxix.
An HG article on the Hernes will appear in the next
issue of *Arena* (xxviii). The HG articles in the September *Arena* show his great and "rare versatility."

B29. Chamberlin, J. E. "HG's Career." *Writer*, 5 (Oct 1891),
208-210.

Extended summary of HG's life to date, with considerable praise for his literary achievements.

B30. Hurd, Charles E. ''HG's Work.'' *Writer*, 5 (Oct 1891), 207-208.
Brief review and appreciation of HG's career.

B31. ''Literary Notes.'' *Arena*, 4 (Oct 1891), xxiv-xxxv.
Brief note (xxxv). ''A Branch Road'' ''is creating considerable controversy through the press.''

B32. ''Notes and Announcements.'' *Arena*, 4 (Oct 1891), xxxvi-xl.
HG's October article on Herne is an excellent and truthful job of reporting (xxxvii).

B33. Wingate, Charles E. L. ''Boston Letter.'' *Critic*, NS 16 (10 Oct 1891), 184-185.
This discussion of Herne's *Margaret Fleming* taunts HG for having backed it and ridicules the advertising campaign he and Herne conducted.

B34. ''The Campaign of '92.'' *Iowa Tribune* (Des Moines), 4 Nov 1891, p. 1.
HG spoke on courthouse steps and is praised editorially as ''a very pleasing, earnest and effective speaker as well as writer.''

B35. ''HG.'' *Iowa Tribune* (Des Moines), 11 Nov 1891, p. 1.
Appreciation of HG, who has been in Des Moines for week participating in People's Party activities. Emphasis on his realism, his fifteen-year residence in Iowa, and his interest in single-tax reform.

B36. *Standard*, 18 Nov 1891, p. 9.
''HG has delivered several single-tax addresses in Iowa within the past few weeks, from which good results are already reported.''

B37. ''The Night Meeting.'' Indianapolis *Sentinel*, 20 Nov 1891, p. 2.
Very brief mention of fact that HG spoke at session of F.M.B.A. and ''dismissed the assembly.''

B38. ''Notes and Announcements.'' *Arena*, 5 (Dec 1891), xlv-xlix.
Arena serialization of *Spoil* will begin in January. It ''will be the first great American novel to deal with

life and conditions as found in the great rural West''
(xlvi).

"Uncle Ripley's Speculations," published in the December *Arena*, contains "rare touches of humor and pathos" and is "vivid and absolutely true to life" (xlvii).

B39. ---. *Arena*, 5 (Jan 1892), xlvii-lii.

Spoil will prove to be "the strongest, brightest, and best American novel of the year, and will place Mr. G in the very front ranks as a novelist" (xlviii).

Jason Edwards, published by the Arena Publishing Co., is "a powerful novel of American life." The novel is summarized (l-li).

B40. ---. *Arena*, 5 (Feb 1892), xlii-xlvi.

Jason Edwards "is a splendid story, strong, healthy, and true to life" (xliii).

Serialization of *Spoil* continues in the *Arena*: "It is a wonderful creation--one of the most noteworthy works of our generation," and it will make HG "the novelist of the West" (xlv).

B41. *Standard*, 3 Feb 1892, pp. 7-8.

For the past week HG has been in Chicago taking an active part in the conference of various political reform groups. He spoke to the club on Thursday about the farmers' movement. The audience was large and attentive but "was not carried away with the notion of leaving the Democrats for a third party--at least, just now."

B42. "Notes and Announcements." *Arena*, 5 (Apr 1892), xlviii-liv.

Excerpts from a laudatory review of *Jason Edwards* which appeared in the Boston *Daily Globe* are reprinted here.

B43. *Standard*, 11 May 1892, p. 5.

HG attended the last meeting of the Chicago Single Tax Club. He joined in the discussion after being asked to and defended the Third Party movement.

He left immediately after, avoiding any debate.

B44. "Literary Notes." *Arena*, 6 (Jun 1892), xlvii-xlviii.
The Arena Publishing Co. is preparing *Spoil* for publication as book. It is "one of the most remarkable,
distinctively American novels that has appeared in recent years."

B45. Flower, B. O. "An Idealistic Dreamer Who Sings in a Minor
Key." *Arena*, 6 (Aug 1892), 288-295.
In this article about Mrs. Moulton, HG is mentioned
along with Ibsen, Tolstoy, and Howells in terms of his
"robust realism," which has been accepted by many
readers because of its essentially moral impulse (288).

B46. Wingate, Charles E. L. "Boston Letter." *Critic*, NS 18
(6 Aug 1892), 72.
"Mr. HG, a well-known apostle of realism in literature,
has come forth in strong denunciation of the military
punishment inflicted at Homestead on Private Iams."
The problem was army treatment of Indians, and HG was
the only literary man who spoke out.

B47. "Notes and Announcements." *Arena*, 6 (Sep 1892), lvii-lxiv.
In *Spoil*, now published in book form, "Mr. G as a novelist is seen at his best" (lx). An excerpt from the Boston
Daily Globe, 26 Jul 1892, mentions HG as President of
the American Psychical Society.

B48. ---. *Arena*, 6 (Oct 1892), lvii-lxii.
Spoil has been "carefully revised, strengthened, and
enlarged by Mr. G and is now one of the strongest and
healthiest works of fiction of the present generation"
(lix).

B49. ---. *Arena*, 6 (Nov 1892), lxxv-lxxx.
In HG's "The West in Literature" we see the author as
the leader of the "new school of veritists or impression-
ists now becoming a real power in literature" (lxxix).
Spoil is "proving immensely popular among thoughtful
American readers who appreciate pictures of real life."
[Two reviews of the novel are reprinted.]

B50. "He Criticizes His Own Books/HG Talks About His Literary Work." Los Angeles *Herald*, 27 Nov 1892, p. 3.
HG discusses political ideas in his works (especially *Jason Edwards*), his objectives in writing, the style of *MTR*, and his plans to use West Coast visit for material for a new book.

B51. "Notes and Announcements." *Arena*, 7 (Dec 1892), xvii-xxii.
HG is on West Coast lecturing on "social reform subjects and . . . 'The West in Literature,' and will give readings from his prose and verse." In literature "no one better represents the Ibsen school of veritists or realists " (xxi).

B52. "Western Literature in 1892." Chicago *Tribune*, 7 Jan 1893, p. 13.
General review of Western literature. "In the department of prose fiction Mr. HG is easily first." *Jason Edwards*, *Member*, *Spoil*, and *Norsk* are all "animated by an earnest purpose, and are characterized by a truthful, vigorous, and sympathetic art."

B53. "Sixth Meeting of the American Psychical Society." *Psychical Review*, 1 (Feb 1893), 290-291.
HG's presidential address summarized briefly.

B54. "Notes and Announcements." *Arena*, 7 (Mar 1893), xxiii-xxxi.
HG's "The West in Literature" stirred up all conventional critics. HG "represents the new school of thinkers who live in the present" (xxiii).

B55. ---. *Arena*, 7 (Apr 1893), xxiv-xxviii.
HG is "in the very front rank of the realistic novelists of America" after only two short years. His "The Future of Fiction" (in current issue of *Arena*) deals with "true realism or veritism of which Ibsen. Count Tolstoi, Mr. Howells, and Mr. G are fair representatives" (xxiv).

B56. "HG." Memphis *Appeal-Avalanche*, 2 Apr 1893, p. 4.
Editorial appreciation of HG in anticipation of his visit to Memphis on 19 April. Emphasis on HG as realist and

as supporter of the single tax.

B57. "New York Notes." *Literary World*, 24 (8 Apr 1893), 112.
HG reported as having left NYC for tour of Southern
States and then on to Chicago. Also included is brief
interview with HG, who comments on regional literature
in the United States and on the moral value of literature.

B58. [Editorial]. Memphis *Appeal-Avalanche*, 16 Apr 1893, p. 4.
Announcement of HG's appearance in Memphis on 19
April for benefit of a new kindergarten, urges readers to
attend.

B59. "Work of the Branches." *Psychical Review*, 1 (May 1893),
385.
Very brief note to effect that HG has started branch of
American Psychical Society in Denver.

B60. "Books of the Day/Notes." *Arena*, 8 (Jun 1893), i-xxi.
Notes the financial failure in Chicago of F. J. Schulte,
HG's publisher. HG had approved of his lending Horace
O'Donohue (his printer) security, a loan which was the
sole cause of the disaster. "For the present" the
Arena Publishing Co. will publish *Folks, Member, Spoil,*
and *Jason Edwards*.

B61. Reid, Mary J. "Western Authors/II. HG." *Literary Northwest*, 3 (Jul 1893), 291-300.
Survey of HG's career to date, punctuated by frequent
quotations from his works and by HG's opinions on
various subjects, either quoted or paraphrased. Among
the things HG comments on are Howells, Zola, the contemporary American theater, Henry James, Mary E. Wilkins Freeman, and American art.

B62. "Octave Thanet on the Short Story/Last Meeting of Authors'
Congress Hears Papers on Modern Fiction." Chicago
Tribune, 15 Jul 1893, p. 8.
HG delivered paper on "Local Color in Fiction." Brief
excerpt from his paper is quoted.

B63. Monroe, Lucy. "Chicago Letter." *Critic*, NS 20 (22 Jul 1893), 60-61.

HG presented "Ebb-Tide in Realism" at a literary congress in Chicago. "Mr. G is the victim of a theory that every novelist should draw his inspiration from the soil, should write of nothing but the country he was bred in and the people most familiar to him"--a theory with which Mrs. Catherwood disagreed. HG was scheduled to present a paper at the Art Institute the following week.

B64. Flower, B. O. "Mask or Mirror--The Vital Difference Between Artificiality and Veritism on the Stage." *Arena*, 8 (Aug 1893), 304-313.

HG is mentioned (305) along with Ibsen, Tolstoy, and Howells as veritists or realists who have not gone as far as they could, but are still "doing magnificent work, and work which is vital because it is true." Also, in an asterisked paragraph at foot of page (305), is a letter to Flower commenting on the power of HG's "Prairie Heroine" to make real the plight of Westerners.

B65. "Leading Articles of the Month/Some Popular Present-Day Authors." *Review of Reviews* (American), 8 (Aug 1893), 211-213.

Summary of Mary J. Reid's interview and article on HG which appeared in *Literary Northwest* (see above).

B66. Zed, X. Y. "Realism with a Vengeance." *Critic*, NS 20 (2 Sep 1893), 158.

Discusses HG's treatment of Eugene Field in the August number of *McClure's*. "Realism is the god that this young writer worships; and, from the persistent manner in which he tells us so, one would think it was a god of his own creating and he its only follower."

B67. "The Literary West." *Saturday Review* (London), 76 (28 Oct 1893), 487-488.

Summary of and adverse comment on HG's "The Literary Emancipation of the West" in *Forum*, Oct 1893. "The West really must have something to show before she can join in the competition with Boston and New York.... The absence of a comb does not necessarily mean genius;

and defective grammar, or lumbering prose, or slang
about 'pooling issues,' is only a mark of bad taste or
defective education.''

B68. ''Books of the Day/Poems by HG.'' *Arena*, 8 (Nov 1893),
i-xxvii.
Stone & Kimball will publish *Songs*. HG is the ''first
realistic novelist who has taken his whole inspiration
from the West.'' The verses in *Songs* are striking because of ''their peculiarly strong combination of realism
and poetry'' (xxiii).

B69. ''Notes and Announcements.'' *Arena*, 8 (Nov 1893), xlv-liv.
In a note concerning the growing interest in the lecture
platform (xlvii), HG is mentioned as a lecturer ''on American literature, on the land question, and various economic problems.''

B70. Mabie, Hamilton W. ''The Most Popular Novels in America.''
Forum, 16 (Dec 1893), 508-516.
HG is mentioned (516) among the ''best names in recent
native fiction'' who are inexplicably left off list compiled
from 100 United States libraries by J. Selwin Tait and
Sons, publishers, of NY.

B71. Fitch, George Hamlin. ''Is the West in Literary Bondage?''
Californian Illustrated Magazine, 5 (Jan 1894), 235-244.
Discusses HG as the new leader of Western writers
crying out against the Eastern establishment, especially
HG's article ''The Literary Emancipation of the West,''
which appeared in the *Forum* (Oct 1893). Praises HG for
a concrete program for the future of American literature
and compares his ''Sim Burns's Wife'' with Turgenev's
''Living Images.'' HG's story is typical of the ''new
Western realism which, however, is as impotent in all the
best spirit of true literature as the evil French system on
which it is patterned.'' Disagrees with HG's claim that
Eastern editors refuse Western authors for magazine publication; many Western writers have neglected form in
their work.

B72. Monroe, Lucy. "Chicago Letter." *Critic*, NS 21 (17 Feb 1894), 115.

The position taken by HG in his lecture on impressionism "is consistent, after all, with his own theories in literature, for he, too, has striven to give truthful impressions of the things he found about him, to paint these Western scenes in the primary colors, which the imagination of his readers may combine." HG's defense of impressionism, however, is weak.

B73. Harte, Walter Blackburn. "HG/A Virile New Force in Our Literature." Chicago *Sunday Inter Ocean*, 18 Feb 1894, p. 31.

Extended interview with HG, who "occupies quite a unique place in American literature, not only because his work has struck an essentially new note in literature, but because he is the forerunner of a great movement that, whatever the excellence or defect of his individual literary work, lends to all he does an added dignity and importance . . . ." Among the subjects discussed are Chicago as a literary center, Shakespeare, G's working habits, his depiction of the working man, and his future plans.

B74. "HG/The Prophet Is Not Without Honor at Home." La Crosse (Wis.) *Evening Chronicle*, 20 Feb 1894, p. 1.

Account of HG's lecture and reading at Universalist Church includes some criticism of HG's theories and practice of realism: "It has been often proven that naked truth may lead her devotees a little astray, since this is a world wherein certain illusions are more true to the average comprehension than the rough realities. Or to state it in another way, Mr. G's literalness portrays, not nature's type, but nature's freak."

B75. "HG and Western Literature." Memphis *Commercial*, 1 Mar 1894, p. 4.

Editorial defending HG's fight for Western literature and putting forward the newspaper as the most democratic arena for literary expression: "The newspaper goes everywhere, from the palace to the cottage, and appeals to every variety of sentiment and intellect."

Urges young writers to submit their work to newspapers rather than magazines.

B76. "HG in Town." Memphis *Commercial*, 2 Mar 1894, p. 2.
  HG, interviewed by reporter, comments on Chicago as a literary center, literature in the South, veritism, and Eastern magazines.

B77. "Modern Novel Analyzed/HG Tells the Difference Between Old and New." Memphis *Commercial*, 3 Mar 1894, p. 5.
  In lecture HG traced development of novel to present and explained and commended the concept of veritism.

B78. "Realism and Romanticism/Discussion Before the Nineteenth Century Club and Its Guests." N.Y. *Times*, 14 Mar 1894, p. 4.
  HG is quoted as participant, with George Washington Cable and Hamilton Mabie, in discussion of "The Realistic and Romantic Schools in Literature." HG spoke on behalf of the realists, Cable for romanticists, Mabie for both.

B79. "Realism and Romanticism in Literature." *Conservator*, 5 (Apr 1894), 30.
  Three-way discussion between HG, George W. Cable, and Hamilton Mabie. HG speaks for realism, Cable for romanticism, and Mabie for synthesis or evolutionary process involving both realism and romanticism, moving from science and fact to eternal verities.

B80. "HG's Literary Methods." *Current Literature*, 15 (Jun 1894), 493.
  This is a reprint of an interview with G by Walter Blackburn Harte which appeared in the Pittsburgh *Dispatch* and other newspapers (see above). It is a brief but revealing discussion by G of his literary methods; especially interesting is his earnestness about literature.

B81. "Notes and Announcements." *Arena*, 10 (Jun 1894), xl-xlvi.
  Brief review of an "interesting and valuable" article by HG on the single-tax in New Zealand (xli). HG is now making his headquarters in Chicago, where he has

become President of the Central Art Association. His lecture topics and his relation with influential artists in all areas are mentioned (xliii).

B82. ----. *Arena*, 10 (Jul 1894), xxxix-xlv.
HG's *CI*, which is "causing much vexation of spirit among parrots and the imitative class, who worship the past and have no faith in anything which is not musty with age or which has not been approved by Europe," will be reviewed at a later date (xlii).

B83. ----. *Arena*, 10 (Nov 1894), lvii-lxii.
HG's 1895 lecture course on "The Development of American Literature" is announced. HG prefers "The Modern Novel," "The Drift of the Drama," "Impressionism in Art," and "Living Authors." Brief explanation of the contents of each lecture.

B84. Monroe, H[arriet]. "Chicago Letter." *Critic*, NS 22 (29 Dec 1894), 449-450.
Mention of HG as President of Chicago's Central Art Association. Although HG "is an extremist in art, as in everything else," "his practice is less exclusive than his theory." "No better man could have been found to execute the purposes of the Association, for he has all the indomitable energy of a pioneer, with a faith in the present and future of American art which will move any mountains that may venture to get in his way."

B85. Inkersly, Arthur. "The Gospel According to HG." *Education*, 15 (Jun 1895), 608-614.
Enumerates, analyzes, and criticizes HG's literary theories. HG is too radical and sets up dichotomies that need not exist. He has gone "too far" in his ideas on impressionism, local color, and the past versus the present.

B86. Monroe, Lucy. "Chicago Letter." *Critic*, NS 23 (29 Jun 1895), 482-483.
"Of all the scattered Chicago writers, Mr. HG is doing perhaps the most serious work." Short discussion of *Rose*.

B87. "New Figures in Literature and Art." *Atlantic*, 76 (Dec 1895), 840-844.
     CI is mere "literary Jingoism"; but HG's theories are truthful although far removed from idol-breaking. The book "reveals a man who, if deficient in critical power and in culture, has certain admirable qualities" which are "moral rather than literary" and "may mean much to the future of his art."
     MTR is marred by stylistic faults and by "brutal realism," which stems from HG's bitterness. The proof of merit of *MTR* is that "it convinces the reader, willy-nilly, of its general fidelity to fact, and lifts him off his critical feet by its sheer brutal force."
     Spoil is a failure because HG "is too young, too immature in his art, too limited in his knowledge of life, to treat well so all embracing a topic."

B88. [Chamberlin, Joseph E.] Boston *Evening Transcript*, 29 Jan 1896, p. 4.
     Defense of HG and *Rose* against reviewer in Springfield (Mass.) *Republican* who disliked novel. *Rose* is worth reading because, "in the picture of the up-growing of a woman in such places and under such circumstances as Mr. G has chosen for his heroine, we get a strong, true, revealing light thrown on the ideas and actions of some millions of people whom it is to our advantage to know well, at the same time that our thoughts are stimulated to action on their own account by Rose's dreams and problems."

B89. "World Biographies/HG." *Literary World*, 27 (22 Feb 1896), 56.
     Brief biographical sketch, followed by list of HG's works to date.

B90. "HG/The Noted Chicago Writer Returns From Mexico." New Orleans *Times-Democrat*, 14 Apr 1896, p. 9.
     HG, in interview, reminisces about his trip to Mexico, particularly about the architecture and people.

B91. "HG's Literary Beginning." *Literary Digest*, 15 (28 Aug 1897), 518-519.

Summary of HG's interview with Frank G. Carpenter from *Home Journal*.

B92. Fuller, Henry B. "The Upward Movement in Chicago." *Atlantic*, 80 (Oct 1897), 534-547.
Very brief mention (546) of HG as founder with his brother-in-law, Lorado Taft, of the Central Art Association of Chicago.

B93. James, Henry. "American Letter." *Literature*, 2 (9 Apr 1898), 422-423.
Brief but significant mention of HG: "I find myself rejoicing...in Mr. HG, a case of saturation so precious as to have almost the value of genius." James sees HG as "the soaked sponge of Wisconsin," adding that "saturation and talent are, of course, compatible."

B94. "HG's Peril/The Novelist Reaches Pine Creek After Running the Gantlet of Starvation and Danger." Brooklyn *Daily Eagle*, 19 Sep 1898, p. 1.
Brief news dispatch on HG's arrival at newest gold-mining camp in Alaska after perilous thousand-mile journey.

B95. "Hardships of HG." N.Y. *Daily Tribune*, 20 Sep 1898, p. 8.
News dispatch on HG's Klondike expedition.

B96. Monroe, Lucy. "HG." *Book News*, 17 (Nov 1898), 113.
Account of HG's life and career to date.

B97. Curtis, W. A. "In HG's Country/Where the Wisconsin Flows." Springfield (Mass.) *Sunday Republican*, 22 Jan 1899, p. 9.
Account of a visit to West Blue Mound, Iowa County, Wisconsin, and description of the locale. Very little explicitly on HG.

B98. "Literary Notes." *Dial*, 26 (16 May 1899), 347.
Brief mention. *Rose* has been published in a "tasteful new edition" by Macmillan.

B99. Bentzon, Th. "Un Radical de la Prairie." *Revue Des Deux Mondes*, 157 (Jan 1900), 139-180.

Extended interview with HG and essay on his work to date.

B100. "HG as Interpreted in Paris." *Literary Digest*, 20 (17 Feb 1900), 209.

Summary of Bentzon's article on HG from *Revue Des Deux Mondes* (1 Jan 1900). See above. Several passages from the essay are here translated.

B101. Howell, Eleanor K. "Against Mr. G's Pictures of Western Farm Life." N.Y. *Times Saturday Review of Books*, 17 Feb 1900, p. 107.

Letter to the editor from "a Western farmer's wife" protesting HG's portrayal of Western farm life. "His stories may be true to his point of view, but they are not representative of life on a Western farm--even a Western farm with a mortgage on it." "I live in what is probably the most cosmopolitan of States [Kansas], and I have seen farmers and farmers' wives from every Western State, and in not one case have I seen the unhappiness depicted by Mr. G...."

B102. "Entertainments." Minneapolis *Tribune*, 22 Feb 1900, p. 6.

Account and appreciation of HG's lecture "Tales of the Trail," given at the Lyceum Theater on 21 February. "As an original recital, his discourse, with the spirit of freedom and unconventionality it involved, was of a very pleasing character, and his audience found great enjoyment in following him." HG followed the lecture with readings from his works.

B103. "Books and Authors." N.Y. *Daily Tribune*, 27 Oct 1900, p. 10.

Reprints a letter to HG from a Texas cattleman praising his fidelity to fact in *Eagle's Heart*.

B104. Barry, John D. "A Note on Stephen Crane." *Bookman* (N.Y.), 13 (Apr 1901), 148.

HG admired *Maggie* and introduced Crane to Howells.

B105. Enneking, J. J. "Mr. Herne as I Knew Him." *Arena*, 26 (Sep 1901), 284-286.

HG introduced Herne to Enneking because all three were interested in the establishment of a *théatre libre* (285).

B106. Routh, James E., Jr. "Insanity in Criticism." *Critic*, NS 43 (Aug 1903), 146-147.
Review of HG's article "Sanity in Fiction," which appeared in the *North American Review*. On HG's criticism of those who don't follow Howells: "The sin to which this other half is shackled, and from which the elect are supposedly free, is an unreasonable preference for passing over the commonplaces of life and picking out the critical moments. These commonplaces, according to Mr. G, should not be passed over, since they constitute the true essence of life, and hence the essence of all that is best in literature." Routh suggests that HG was simply reacting to the non-realistic novels of the day.

B107. Flower, B. O. "Books of the Day." *Arena*, 30 (Oct 1903), 437-443.
In a review of Meredith Nicholson's *The Main Chance* (441-443), HG is mentioned briefly as a writer much like Nicholson in his romances (442).

B108. "HG." Meriden (Conn.) *Record*, 13 Jan 1905.
Praise of HG's lecture "The Indian of Today." HG gives examples of how the Indian has been misunderstood and mistreated. We should help him within his own culture.

B109. "Mystery in the Trail/HG Sees Poetry of Life in Western Wilds." Baltimore *Sun*, 1 Apr 1905, p. 7.
HG enchanted audience at Friends' Meeting House as he told of man's imagination and hardships in dealing with nature.

B110. "G in Ghostland." *Arena*, 34 (Aug 1905), 206-216.
A Study of *Tyranny* in dialogue form. HG's *MTR* marked him "as one of the strongest and most compelling romancers of the veritist or realist schools in the New World," but some of the new book borders "dan-

gerously on the realm of romantic fashion,'' which
realists like HG ''hold in such unfeigned contempt.''
Nevertheless, for the most part, HG ''has adhered
closely to the canons of veritism.''

B111. Lovett, Robert Morss. ''The Beginning of the Short Story
in America.'' *Reader Magazine*, 6 (Aug 1905), 347-
352.
HG mentioned briefly as a local-color writer partly
influenced by Hawthorne (351).

B112. ''HG Here/The Eminent Novelist to Enter the Heart of the
Rockies.'' Pinedale (Wyo.) *Roundup*, 28 Aug 1907.
HG welcomed to Pinedale on his way to explore the
vicinity of Fremont Peak.

B113. ''On the Trail With HG.'' Pinedale (Wyo.) *Roundup*, 11
Sep 1907, p. 1.
Editor tells of his trip into the hills with HG, including a sketch of HG's accomplishments and the
enjoyment of his company.

B114. ''On the Trail With HG.'' *Harper's Weekly*, 51 (5 Oct 1907),
1465.
Account of trip with HG into the mountainous Wind
River region of Wyoming as recorded by the editor of
the Pinedale (Wyo.) *Roundup* (see above).

B115. ''The Cliff Dwellers.'' Chicago *Evening Post*, 25 Jan
1908.
Discussion of HG's residence in Chicago and his
organization of the Cliff Dwellers, a club whose
members represent all the arts.

B116. ''Crowd at Theater.'' *Wisconsin State Journal* (Madison),
29 Jan 1909, p. 8.
Over 100 men and boys appeared at the stage door
of the Fuller Opera House as a result of the advertise-
ment that men were needed for a crowd scene in HG's
''Miller.''

B117. "Drama." *Wisconsin State Journal* (Madison), 29 Jan
1909, p. 4.
Announcement that HG's first play ever to be performed will open at the Fuller Opera House tonight.
That HG chooses Madison for this opening of "Miller"
"is a pretty compliment to us," the citizens of his
native state.

B118. "The Red Man's Point of View." *Daily Cardinal* (U of
Wisconsin, Madison), 29 Jan 1909, p. 1.
In town for the premiere of "Miller," HG speaks to
university students on the mistake of trying to civilize
the Indians.

B119. Robertson, Donald. "Amusements." Appleton (Wis.)
Evening Crescent, 29 Jan 1909, p. [8].
Brief announcement of presentation of "Miller,"
which will play in Appleton. Relates theme of play
to G's work with Henry George.

B120. "Drama." *Wisconsin State Journal* (Madison), 30 Jan 1909,
p. 2.
A review of the first performance of "Miller" focuses
on the actors, concluding that it is unfair to judge the
play on the basis of its first performance.

B121. "G Has Background in Madison." *Wisconsin State Journal*
(Madison), 30 Jan 1909, p. 3.
After speaking of earlier visits to Madison, HG tells
interviewer he has joined with actor-producer Donald
Robertson to produce his "independent" plays in a
small theater in Chicago. The interviewer is surprised
to find HG an ordinary man.

B122. "Drama." *Wisconsin State Journal* (Madison), 1 Feb 1909,
p. 3.
"Miller" was enthusiastically received by the Madison
audience, but it lacked humor and sufficient love interest;
it is thus deficient in poetry.

B123. Mantle, Burns. "News of the Theaters." Chicago *Daily
Tribune*, 4 Feb 1909, p. 8.

Review of "Miller" as performed in Fullerton Hall. HG's "trouble has been in clouding his original intention with too many incidents and in blanketing his theme in an effort to keep all angles of the story in view." HG "also is inclined to make his characters more fanciful than real, and his dialogue bookish rather than natural."

B124. "The Donald Robertson Players/Fullerton Memorial Hall." *Bulletin of the Art Institute of Chicago,* 2 (Apr 1909), 56.

Brief mention of early February Chicago production of "Miller," "one of Mr. G's most serious contributions to the discussion" of "the conflict of Capital and Labor." Notes that "it was found extremely difficult to handle the production on the small stage, and though the audience was one which completely filled the hall, and several hundred people were unable to secure entrance, the play has not been repeated."

B125. "Why HG Finds Wider Fields in the Drama Than in the Writing of Novels." N.Y. *Times,* 11 Apr 1909, V, 4.

Interview. HG plans to concentrate on writing plays because a dramatist can reach more people in a more intimate way, while a novel is printed to sell a number of books without as much thought to the audience. He approves of publishing plays as well as producing them.

B126. "Tributes for Humorist/News of Death Causes Deep Sorrow in Literary Circles." N.Y. *Daily Tribune,* 22 Apr 1910, p. 2.

HG praises Mark Twain as "distinctly American."

B127. Stevens, Ashton. "Give Us Art, But Not Highbrow Art, HG Tells Ashton Stevens." Chicago *Examiner,* 4 Jun 1911, p. 3.

HG explains that the Chicago Theatre Society wants to reach the public with plays that will build up the theater and become increasingly American.

B128. Bennett, James O'Donnell. "News of the Stage." Chicago *Record-Herald,* 11 Jul 1911, p. 8.

Discussion of conflict between Messrs. Shubert of
the New York firm backing the Chicago Theatre Society and HG and others' desire to produce modern
American plays.

B129. Hatton, Frederic. [Discussion of the Repertory of the
Chicago Theatre Society]. Chicago *Evening Post*, 22
Jul 1911.
Secretary of the Chicago Theatre Society praises HG
for using the society to encourage the development of
excellent American drama.

B130. "No Players Signed Yet." Chicago *Examiner*, 22 Jul 1911.
HG announces a tentative schedule of plays. A previously published announcement of players and members
of the Chicago Theatre Society is considered unoffical.

B131. "Music and Drama/Chicago Theatre Society's Repertory
Announced." Chicago *Daily Tribune*, 18 Aug 1911, p. 8.
HG, president of the Chicago Theatre Society, discusses the society's search for appropriate plays for their
repertory.

B132. "No Proofs of Existence of Spirits/HG." N.Y. *Times*, 19
Nov 1911, V, 3.
HG concludes after 20 years of investigation that although he has had experiences with spirit phenomena,
all spiritualism can be explained by physical laws.
He explains that man has psychic powers not yet understood that could explain all.

B133. Hackett, Karleton. "Have We Progressed? Hear HG."
Chicago *Evening Post*, 29 Dec 1911.
HG gives credit to the initiative of the people of
Chicago for the success of the Chicago Drama Players.

B134. Woods, Mary Katherine. "HG Attacks 'The American
Drama'/Thinks Dramatic Quality Sacrificed to Greed."
N.Y. *Morning Telegraph*, 7 Jan 1912, II, [2].
HG gives unsparing arraignment of American drama,
claiming both manager and playwright are only after
money.

B135. Hammond, Percy. "News of the Theaters/*The Maternal Instinct* Worthy and Interesting." Chicago *Daily Tribune*, 23 Feb 1912, p. 9.

HG commended for winning approval to produce modern American drama; and *The Maternal Instinct*, currently being produced by the Chicago Theatre Society, is given a generally favorable review.

B136. Flower, B. O. "Leaders I Have Known: HG, Will Allen Dromgoole, W. D. McCracken, Bolton Hall, Ernest Howard Crosby." *Twentieth Century Magazine*, 6 (Aug 1912), 357-361.

Discussion of HG's social and economic philosophy as evidenced in *Prairie Heroine*.

B137. Howells, William D. "Mr. G's Books." *North American Review*, 196 (Oct 1912), 523-528.

Recounts briefly HG's coming to Boston, his realistic tendencies, his ideas on veritism, and his connection with Henry George. Comments on all of HG's books. *Money Magic* is "possibly the most masterly of the author's books. More than any other since the stories of *MTR*, it expresses constancy to his old young ideal of veritism." Howells laments that in HG's stories, especially *Rose*, *Hesper*, and *Money Magic*, he refuses to recognize "the beast in the man's desire of the woman" and regrets that HG's "Under the Lion's Paw" never got on stage.

B138. "Mr. Howells' Tribute to HG." *Current Literature*, 53 (Nov 1912), 589-590.

Summary of Howells' tribute to HG in *North American Review* (Oct 1912). See above.

B139. "G at Goodwyn." Memphis *Commercial Appeal*, 6 Nov 1913, p. 5.

Announcement that HG will present lecture "With the Forest Ranger" at Goodwyn Institute: "his lecture is non-partisan and presents a comprehensive picture of the whole development of the west."

B140. "Praise for Forests by HG/Large Audience Hears Eminent Author at Goodwyn Institute." Memphis *Commercial Appeal*, 7 Nov 1913, p. 7.
HG pleads for forest reserves and praises the efforts of Gifford Pinchot and Theodore Roosevelt to conserve Western Forests.

B141. Little, Richard Henry. "G Explains Dell's Attack." Chicago *Examiner*, 5 Dec 1913, p. 4.
HG, commenting on Floyd Dell's criticism of Chicago, agrees with him on many points but says it is time Chicago writers quit dealing with the city as though it were on trial.

B142. "G Talks to Students at Drake/Author Sees Highly Beneficial Change in Schools Toward Literature." Des Moines (Iowa) *Register and Leader*, 7 Oct 1914, p. 4.
Account of HG's talk with extensive quotation. HG urged students to recognize great writers as they appear rather than letting them go unappreciated for years as had happened to many members of his generation.

B143. "Talk to the Boosters/HG and Hough Address Chamber of Commerce." Des Moines (Iowa) *Register and Leader*, 7 Oct 1914, p. 5.
In address HG lauds Iowa and claims the basis of his literary development was the environment in which he was reared.

B144. "Banquet Is Finale of Literary Meet." Des Moines (Iowa) *Register and Leader*, 8 Oct 1914, pp. 1, 5.
HG was an after-dinner speaker at the Iowa Press and Author's Club. He paid tribute to Des Moines and to the significance of this banquet.

B145. "G Indorses Capitol Extension/Iowa's Noted Author Speaks at Luncheon in Favor of Beautifying Capitol." Des Moines (Iowa) *Register and Leader*, 8 Oct 1914, p. 3.
HG, during luncheon speech, praises plans to beautify Des Moines.

B146. Weaver, James B. "Back to the Old Home Farm/Some
Memories of the Recent Home-Coming." Des Moines
Capital, 2 Dec 1914, p. 1.
    Includes memories of HG participating in threshing
and being "everywhere in the way and nowhere if
wanted," learning to know the land and people he
later wrote about.

B147. Kilmer, Joyce. "Says New York Makes Writers Tradesmen
HG Laments Metropolitan Influences Which Turn Younger
Literary Generation from Art to Commercial Success."
N.Y. *Times Magazine*, 28 May 1916, pp. 13-14.
    Interview. HG comments at length on the decadent
state of American fiction, the rise of the popular magazine and the consequent materialism of young writers,
the "pernicious" influence on fiction and the drama of
the New York clubs, the state of American poetry, and
the role of the press in America.

B148. "The Joint Committee on Literary Arts." Houston *Daily
Post*, 21 Jan 1917, p. [25].
    HG explains, for the joint committee on literary arts
of which he is chairman, plans for "an informal union
of all the literary forces in the city of New York."

B149. "Fund for Authors' Relief/Incorporation at Albany to Pro-
vide for Extending the Work." N.Y. *Times*, 18 Mar 1917,
II, 3.
    HG quoted as one of incorporators of new fund to help
needy members of writing profession. Very brief news
item.

B150. "A Realist Judges a Realist." N.Y. *Times*, 24 Aug 1917,
p. 6.
    Editorial comment on Howells' review of *Son*, which
is to appear in the next Sunday *Book Review*: "It is
the reaction of one realist to the realism of another
realist of his own school--not, by the way, the school
of the literary photographer, scornful of selection and
under the delusion that anything true is worth telling."

B151. "A Lesson Needed by Critics." N.Y. *Times*, 29 Aug 1917, p. 8.

> Editorial praising Howells for valuing his "opportunity to give deserved praise" in his *Times* review of *Son* rather than "emphasizing excuses for finding fault."

B152. "Mr. Howells's Tribute to the Autobiography of HG." *Current Opinion*, 63 (Dec 1917), 412.

> Summary of Howells' review of *Son* in N.Y. *Times*, 26 Aug 1922.

B153. "Elected to Academy/Brand Whitlock and HG in Arts and Letters." N.Y. *Times*, 12 Jan 1918, p. 11.

> Brief news article on HG's election to American Academy of Arts and Letters.

B154. "Tribute to Lowell Begins This Week." N.Y. *Times*, 16 Feb 1919, II, 1.

> HG quoted on James Russell Lowell centenary celebration being planned by American Academy of Arts and Letters.

B155. "Eminent Men in All Walks Praise Roosevelt." N.Y. *Times*, 26 Oct 1919, X, 1.

> HG quoted in praise of Theodore Roosevelt: " 'He was great not because he knew many definite things, but because he could recall these facts and use them at will.' "

B156. "One Side of Roosevelt." N.Y. *Times*, 18 Apr 1920, VI, 5.

> HG quoted on plan to restore Theodore Roosevelt's New York City birthplace. HG refers to his friendship with Roosevelt: " 'We were staunch friends with common literary interests.' "

B157. Clare, D. G. "G Once Had Job on King Street." (Madison, Wis.) *Capital Times*, 21 Oct 1920 [although the page is is headed 20 Oct, it is clearly part of the edition of 21 Oct], p. 7.

> Visiting Madison for a day, HG remembers when he was a clerk in a Madison Machine Shop for three days in the

early spring of 1882.

B158. "In Honor of Howells." N.Y. *Times*, 27 Feb 1921, VI,
6.
HG quoted at length on background of American Academy of Arts and Letters and on Howells' role in that
organization on the occasion of a memorial meeting
being planned by Academy for Howells.

B159. "A Reviewer's Notebook." *Freeman*, 3 (13 Apr 1921), 118-
119.
Analysis of HG's career to date, as reflected in *Son.*
HG shifted from local colorist to reformer. He lost
"his detachment": "at the very moment when Dakota
had ceased to focus his emotions as a writer, it began
to focus his emotions as a sociologist and a man.
Dakota was no longer a subject that he could leave behind; it had become a problem as well; and Mr. G's
real energy began to flow into the channel of social
reform."

B160. Van Doren, Carl. "Contemporary American Novelists/XI.
HG." *Nation*, 113 (23 Nov 1921), 596-597.
Notes HG's new realistic treatment of the frontier.
HG "had been kindled by Howells in Boston to a pas-
sion for realism which carried him beyond the suave
accuracy of his master to the somber veracity of *MTR*,
Folks, and *Rose*." Both HG and Sinclair Lewis chal-
lenged "the myth of rural beauties and rural virtues . . . ."

B161. "The Evolution of a Literary Radical." *Current Opinion*,
72 (Mar 1922), 389-391.
Summary of Carl Van Doren's article on HG in *Nation*
(23 Nov 1921). See above.

B162. "'Unknown Soldier' Theme Wins Prizes." N.Y. *Times*,
May 22, 1922, p. 4.
News story about 1921 Pulitzer Prizes which mentions
that HG has received biography award for *Daughter.*

B163. "Columbia University Honors Booth Tarkington and Others."
Current Opinion, 73 (Jul 1922), 69-71.

Account of HG's being awarded Pulitzer Prize for *Daughter* as "best American biography."

B164. Coate, D. O. "HG Will Visit City It Is Announced." La Crosse (Wis.) *Tribune and Leader-Press*, 12 Nov 1922, p. 6.

Appreciation of HG's work in anticipation of his forthcoming lecture in La Crosse. HG "has the ability to see the beauty, the poetry, in the common things of life"; he is "a born story-teller"; he "has done that rare and difficult thing of seizing and preserving in attractive artistic form the life and spirit of his own time and his particular place."

B165. "HG Lectures About Middle Border/Daughter Assists in Second Number of Civic Course Presented Here." Dayton (Ohio) *Journal*, 17 Nov 1922.

Report of HG's lecture about Middle Border and the experiences of his own family.

B166. "Middle Border Poet Talks of His Own Life/HG Tells of His Own Boyhood, Travels and Family Life." Dayton (Ohio) *Evening Herald*, 17 Nov 1922.

Report of entrancing lecture by HG and daughter, including memories of Middle Border.

B167. Coate, D. O. "HG Is Genius With Pen/Comes Next Week." La Crosse (Wis.) *Tribune and Leader-Press*, 18 Nov 1922, p. 4.

Announcement of HG's forthcoming lecture. Article is mainly concerned with the intangible touch which separates the hack from the successful and inspired writer.

B168. Borresen, Lily M. E. "HG's Books Deal With Great Outdoors Including Many Novels." La Crosse (Wis.) *Tribune and Leader-Press*, 19 Nov 1922, p. 12.

On occasion of HG's forthcoming talk, local librarian briefly describes each of HG's books to date and quotes from opinions of his work and from his own remarks on his books.

B169. Gunther, John. "The Views of Mr. HG and Mr. Ludwig
Lewisohn/[HG]." Chicago *Daily News,* 22 Nov 1922,
p. 13.
  In interview, HG criticizes contemporary American
writers, with the exception of Willa Cather, as without
technique. He also criticizes most critics.

B170. "No Successors to Howells, Burroughs Says Mr. G." La
Crosse (Wis.) *Tribune and Leader-Press,* 23 Nov 1922,
p. 6.
  Account of HG's lecture at the Normal School. He
reminisced about his last trip to La Crosse seven years
before, his Wisconsin boyhood, and his friendships with
Howells, James Whitcomb Riley, and John Burroughs.

B171. "Society/'Ye' Olden Time Dinner Function Enjoyed by
Eighty." La Crosse (Wis.) *Tribune and Leader-Press,*
23 Nov 1922, p. 5.
  Account of a dinner party at which HG's daughter,
Mary Isabelle, made a surprise appearance to read
from her father's works.

B172. "G Pronounces Self Old-Fashioned/Deplores Writers of
Cheap Ideas." Peoria (Ill.) *Transcript,* 28 Nov 1922.
  In lecture, HG gives personal reaction to contemporary
English and American writers and pleads for "decency
in decorum" and a stronger English allegiance.

B173. "Early Days of West Recalled by G/Noted Writer Gives Experiences to Historians." Indianapolis *News,* 9 Dec
1922, p. 24.
  HG was principal speaker at the fourth annual conference on Indiana history. He discussed the Middle
Border pioneer.

B174. "The Nomad." Boston *Evening Transcript,* 3 Jan 1923,
II, 2.
  Announcement of a lecture by HG and comment on
his travels.

B175. Hill, E. B. "American First Editions/A Series of Biblio-
graphic Check-Lists/Edited by Merle Johnson and

112

Frederick M. Hopkins/Number 30. HG, 1860.'' *Publishers' Weekly*, 103 (21 Apr 1923), 1270.
List of first editions of HG's books and of books containing HG contributions.

B176. ''Here's a Real Treat Coming to Albert Lea.'' Albert Lea (Minn.) *Evening Tribune*, 15 Nov 1923.
Announcement of HG's forthcoming lecture on ''Memories of the Middle Border'' which is being sponsored by the Teachers' League of the Albert Lea Public Schools, the Parent-Teachers' Association, and other civic groups.

B177. ''HG to Speak at High School Tonight.'' Albert Lea (Minn.) *Evening Tribune*, 19 Nov 1923.
Brief mention of HG's lecture in high school assembly.

B178. ''Beyer Sees Klan Following Fascisti/Hamline Professor Attempts to Define Various Phases of Liberalism.'' St. Paul (Minn.) *Pioneer Press*, 20 Nov 1923, p. 5.
Professor Beyer is reported as having criticized HG--who had spoken recently at Hamline--as ''a traditionalist.'

B179. ''HG/Assembly Room at Central School Nearly Filled With Those Who Came to Hear Him.'' Albert Lea (Minn.) *Evening Tribune*, 20 Nov 1923, p. 4.
Account and critique of HG's lecture-reading. HG's works as read seemed ''extra fine,'' but ''his delivery and lecture'' were nothing ''to get excited over.'' All in all, HG did not compare favorably ''with the usual high class talent coming to Albert Lea these days.''

B180. ''Present Tendencies in American Literature Assailed.'' *Current Opinion*, 76 (Feb 1924), 165-167.
Quotes HG (165-166) from a piece he wrote for the *Times* on the present state of literature. ''Mr. G thinks that a great part of the vulgarity and immorality of our present literary output may be traced to increasing European influence.''

B181. Pattee, Fred Lewis. ''Those Fiery Radicals of Yesteryear/ A Letter to HG on Generations and Literary Manners.''

N.Y. *Times Book Review*, 24 Feb 1924, pp. 2, 23, 26.
Reply to HG's "Current Fiction Heroes" (N.Y. *Times Book Review*, 23 Dec 1923). Pattee basically defends the younger generation of American writers against HG's attacks and says that they are a direct result of the literary radicalism of HG's own generation: "Your disciples have pushed on as far beyond you as you and Crane pushed on beyond Howells and James. We are but reaping the inevitable results of realism, that realism that has made so sterile of great literature the past thirty years."

B182. Lake, Ivan Clyde. "HG's Early Life Recalled by Pioneer Resident of Green's Coulee." La Crosse (Wis.) *Tribune and Leader-Press*, 1 Jun 1924, p. 4.
In an interview, Ira "Ed" Green remembers the young HG as bookish; he was not a very effective worker on the farm.

B183. "HGs Dined." N.Y. *Times*, 19 Nov 1924, p. 2.
Brief news item on celebration of HG's 25th wedding anniversary complete with guest list.

B184. "Wish Denied by Roosevelt/Told G He Wasn't Recluse Enough to Write Life as President." N.Y. *Times*, 20 Nov 1924, p. 8.
News item on HG's lecture "Theodore Roosevelt as an Author" in which HG told how he urged Theodore Roosevelt to write about his life as President. Roosevelt replied that he was too active for such a project.

B185. Hughes, Hatcher. "O'Neill's Art Is Defended." N.Y. *Times*, 10 Mar 1925, p. 20.
Letter to the editor which objects to the *Times* and to HG's assertion that O'Neill's "Desire Under the Elms" was not drawn from American life but rather from a pessimistic philosophy of Europe. The writer insists that the dramatist does not have to deal with what is "typical and representative." He also charges HG with moral naivete for his critical comments which described O'Neill's work as "decadent," "depraved," and "poisonous."

B186. Chatfield-Taylor, H. C. "When the World Came to Chicago."
        Century, 110 (Oct 1925), 679-688.
        Brief mention (688) of HG as founder of Cliff Dwellers
        and the " 'rescuing angel' " of Stephen Crane.

B187. "The Gossip Shop." *Bookman* (N.Y.), 62 (Oct 1925), 231-
        240.
        HG, "having returned from abroad, has taken the Carroll
        Beckwith House at Onteora" (233).

B188. "The Gossip Shop." *Bookman* (N.Y.), 62 (Dec 1925), 517-528.
        HG, "white haired and dignified," was encountered
        strolling on Fifth Avenue (522).

B189. Nixon, Herman C. "The Populist Movement in Iowa." *Iowa
        Journal of History and Politics*, 24 (Jan 1926), 3-107.
        HG is mentioned briefly (59) as having been in Iowa
        with Mary Lease in 1891 speaking about the Populist
        movement. He deserted literary labors in Boston to
        speak for the Populists in Iowa (64).

B190. "Honors Given by University." (Madison, Wis.) *Capital
        Times*, 22 Jun 1926, p. 1.
        HG one of six to receive University of Wisconsin
        honorary degrees.

B191. "Six Given Honorary Degrees." *Wisconsin State Journal*
        (Madison), 22 Jun 1926, p. 1.
        Doctor of Letters conferred on HG by U of Wisconsin.

B192. "The Theatre Discussed." N.Y. *Times*, 15 Nov 1926, p. 23.
        Brief news story on dinner meeting of American Theatre
        Association at which HG called New York "a foreign
        city" and said that "much of the filth in its theatre was
        due to its position as port of entry for all the world."

B193. "HG's 'Middle Border' Pioneers." *Literary Digest*, 91 (27
        Nov 1926), 26-27.
        Quotations from various reviews of *Trail Makers* and
        summary of the narrative.

B194. "The Literary Garlands of HG." *National Magazine*, 55
      (Jun 1927), 425, 442.
      Biographical sketch.

B195. Lapham, J. A. "From the News Columns/Thirty Years Ago."
      Osage (Iowa) *News*, 22 Sep 1927, p. 2.
      Report of article in the Chicago *Pioneer Herald* re-
      lating HG's impressions of his work on his family's
      farm near Osage.

B196. "G Extols Hardy." N.Y. *Times*, 23 Jan 1928, p. 17.
      Brief news story on HG's talk on "Personal Remi-
      niscences of Hardy, Barrie and Shaw" at the West Side
      Unitarian Forum.

B197. "No Supernatural, Says G/Spooks Only Unexplored Biology."
      Sante Fe *New Mexican*, 28 Feb 1928, p. 3.
      Includes report of HG relating to dinner guests many
      incredible personal experiences with the media, but
      claiming they happen in accord with natural laws we
      do not understand and are afraid to study. Also includes
      a report of honorary degree of Doctor of Letters confer-
      red on HG by U of Wisconsin, a brief biographical sketch,
      and a brief review of some of his work.

B198. Raw, Ruth M. "HG, The Romanticist." *Sewanee Review*,
      36 (Apr 1928), 202-210.
      Consideration of major works of three periods of HG's
      career to date as demonstration that he has always been
      essentially a romanticist, "a social and political reform-
      er, an adventurer." In first period (1887-1895), he was
      a romanticist "in two ways: first as an adventurer in a
      new literary form; and secondly, as a social and politi-
      cal reformer." Brief discussions of *MTR* and *Rose*--
      "a transition between his earlier works and his western
      romance"--and *Boy Life*--"idyllic," it "shows the poten-
      tial romanticism of the author."
      During the middle period (1900-1916) of Western romance,
      "all of his pent up adventurous desires of the years were
      released in the travel out of which these romances arose."
      Brief analyses of *Captain*, *Hesper*, *Cavanaugh*, and *Long
      Trail:* "If these books are not so brilliant as those in

his first cycle of stories, it was due not to their more romantic and adventurous quality but rather to the fact that he turned to exposures of legislative corruptions and reforms about which he neither knew nor cared so much as he did about the farmers."

The books of his third period (1917-   ) are "his greatest works." "The events in these books have mellowed through years of experience and time. Although he pictured a hard and oppressed life in the West, still he wants everyone to appreciate the bigness and the out-of-door heavenly glories of the West." Some analysis here of *Son, Daughter* and *Trail Makers.*

In the end, HG *is* a realist "in his point of view" and "in the technique of his books of the first and third periods"; but "in his attitude towards life" he was a romanticist who always had "the hope that somehow, somewhere, and some time, things would be made better, and life would be made happier and more worth the living."

B199. "Skinner Gets Prize for Stage Diction." N.Y. *Times,* 27 Apr 1928, p. 25.

News story on meeting of American Academy of Arts and Letters at which HG advocated awarding of a medal "to the radio announcer who best preserved the traditions of good diction."

B200. "Author to Address Students at Final Convocation Today/ HG to Talk on Westward March of Pioneers." *Minnesota Daily* (U of Minnesota), 24 May 1928, p. 1.

News item on HG's up-coming appearance, which "should be of great interest to Minnesotans, as much of his wealth of information concerns Minnesota."

B201. "Society." Minneapolis *Morning Tribune,* 24 May 1928, p. 18.

Brief note that HG will be guest at luncheon given by Dean and Mrs. Melvin E. Haggerty.

B202. S., D. H. "Garlands?" *Minnesota Daily* (U of Minnesota), 25 May 1928, p. 2.

Editorial chastising students for disrupting HG's lecture by noisily leaving early: "Not one minute of the speech existed which was not attended by the noise of a hurried and careless leaving."

B203. "Society." Minneapolis *Morning Tribune*, 25 May 1928, p. 10.
Brief paragraph on HG's attendance at U of Minnesota College of Education banquet, where he was featured speaker, and at social functions before and after that event.

B204. "The 'Back Trailers.'" N.Y. *Times*, 25 Nov 1928, III, 4.
Editorial comment on HG's notion of the "Back Trailers," a movement paralleled in other writers and in the business field.

B205. Edgett, Edwin Francis. "About Books and Authors." Boston *Evening Transcript*, 15 Dec 1928, Bk. Sect., p. 8.
Appreciation of HG's work on occasion of publication of *Back-Trailers*. The Middle Border books "are a work of high literary and historical quality that amplifies Mr. G's fiction, and that gives to it a visual background."

B206. Blair, Emily Newell. "If You Read to Learn." *Good Housekeeping*, 88 (Jan 1929), 43, 180, 183-184.
HG is mentioned (180) as having prepared the American Library Association course on "The Westward March of American Settlement." He spent his younger days with these Western people and wrote "more than twenty books about the men and women who settled the West."

B207. "HG." *Wilson Bulletin*, 3 (Feb 1929), 466.
Biographical sketch.

B208. "Academy to Pick Star Announcer." N.Y. *Times*, 21 Apr 1929, IX, 16.
HG is quoted as chairman of committee of judges.

B209. "Voice Personality Wins Radio Medal." N.Y. *Times*, 28 Apr 1929, X, 17.

News story on awarding of medal by American Academy of Arts and Letters for radio announcing to Milton
Cross includes brief quote from HG, chairman of the
"radio diction committee."

B210. "Plans Second Award for Radio Announcers/American Academy Will Give Medal for Good Diction at April Meeting."
N.Y. *Times*, 4 Aug 1929, II, 5.
   HG is quoted as chairman of award committee: " 'Our
aim, of course, is not merely to improve the diction of
the announcer but to aid in raising the standard of
spoken English throughout the entire country.' " HG
planned to travel throughout the country listening to an-
nouncers recommended by committee members.

B211. "Chronicle and Comment." *Bookman* (N.Y.), 70 (Oct 1929),
176-192.
   Summary (183-184) of HG's career and accomplishments
on occasion of beginning of serial publication of *Roadside* in *Bookman*.

B212. Hoeltje, Hubert H. "Iowa Literary Magazines." *Palimpsest*,
11 (Jan 1930), 87-94.
   HG mentioned briefly (89) as contributor to the *Midland Monthly*.

B213. "Young Authors." N.Y. *Times*, 23 Jan 1930, p. 22.
   Editorial on older established authors helping young
struggling writers mentions HG's assisting Crane.

B214. Mott, Frank Luther. "Exponents of the Pioneers." *Palimpsest*, 11 (Feb 1930), 61-66.
   HG and Herbert Quick are the two men of letters who
have done the most "distinctive literary service to the
Iowa pioneer." *Son* "is likely to stand as Mr. G's best
piece of work" because HG "has won to a true perspective of the pioneer period" and "as a result he has produced a work kindlier, mellower, deeper than" *MTR*.

B215. Taylor, Walter Fuller. "On the Origin of Howells' Interest
in Economic Reform." *American Literature*, 2 (Mar
1930), 3-14.

HG persuaded Howells to support the single tax (9-10).

B216. Boynton, Percy H. "Some Expounders of the Middle Border."
English Journal, 19 (Jun 1930), 431-440.
HG was a Middle Border writer whose nostalgic return
to the Middle Border in *Son* was greeted with respect
but little enthusiasm by the American public engrossed
in World War I (431-432).

B217. "Enjoys Visit/HG, Novelist and Dramatist, Is Pleased with
College." Beloit (Wis.) *Daily News*, 16 Jun 1930, p. 3.
Very brief interview with HG, in town to receive honorary degree from Beloit College. HG expresses preference for small colleges like Beloit, " 'more like the
ones that I knew as a boy.' "

B218. "Need $435,000 for Coed Dorms, Maurer Asserts/Eighty-
Three Seniors Get Diplomas at College's 83rd Commencement." Beloit (Wis.) *Daily News*, 16 Jun 1930, pp. 1, 2.
Account of Beloit College Commencement at which HG
received the honorary degree of Doctor of Letters. Very
brief mention only of HG.

B219. Calverton, V. F. "The Decade of Convictions." *Bookman*
(N.Y.), 71 (Aug 1930), 486-490.
Brief mention (486) of HG as "one of the first to point
out the real tragedy of defeat that underlay" the struggle
between the farmer and the financier.

B220. "HG is Honored at 70." N.Y. *Times*, 16 Sep 1930, p. 31.
News story on luncheon given by Frank Seaman of
Napanoch, N.Y., in honor of HG's 70th birthday. Guests
listed.

B221. White, William Allen. "A Reader in the Eighties and Nineties." *Bookman* (N.Y.), 72 (Nov 1930), 229-234.
Brief mention (229-230) of HG, who was a "protesting
voice against the smugness of the pastoral writers who
told of the delights of the rural scene" and who submit-
ted his work to Gilder of the *Century*, who feared it
would "corrupt the youth of his subscribers."

B222. Cline, William Hamilton. "World Museum Envisioned/Era-by-Era Representation Feature." Los Angeles *Times*, 21 Dec 1930, p. 9.
HG and brother-in-law Lorado Taft hope to establish, in Los Angeles, world's greatest museum of architecture and sculpture.

B223. [Chamberlin, Joseph E.] "The Listener." Boston *Evening Transcript*, 27 Dec 1930, III, 2.
The Listener reminisces on acquaintance with the young and the old HG, commenting on his changing idealism and on some of his works.

B224. "Roosevelt Medals Awarded to Three." N.Y. *Times*, 24 Jun 1931, p. 7.
HG received a medal for "Distinguished Service." Citation praises him for his writings which are " 'history transposed by the understanding of a poet and lover of mankind.' "

B225. *Spur*, 48 (1 Aug 1931), 25.
HG awarded Roosevelt Medal for Distinguished Service in recognition of his significance as a "social historian."

B226. "G Deplores Modern Book Trend." N.Y. *Times*, 15 Sep 1931, p. 28.
Announcement of publication of *Companions*, with extensive quotations from the book of HG's views on contemporary writers and writing.

B227. Gibbs, Mary Pelham. "Thanks to Mr. G." N.Y. *Times*, 21 Sep 1931, p. 16.
Letter to the editor praising HG for his recent *Times* article condemning present-day American writing. "A distinct vote of thanks should be awarded Mr. G in assuming a real and substantial public of culture which is beside and beyond that mass for whom publishers welcome the questionable."

B228. Edwards, Herbert. "Howells and the Controversy over Realism in American Fiction." *American Literature*, 3 (Nov 1931), 237-248.

HG was defended quite strongly by Howells (245), especially in Howells' review of *MTR*. HG introduced Crane to Howells (247).

B229. "G Sees Here Power and Glory." N.Y. *Times*, 7 Nov 1931, p. 17.
Account of talk by HG at Literary Vespers Institute in which he looked back over his forty-six years as a writer and commented on new writers and on New York as a literary center.

B230. Engle, William. "Setting New Goals at Seventy/Illustrious Dead Live Again as HG Dips Pen Into Past." N.Y. *World-Telegram*, 2 Nov 1931, p. 1.
In interview HG explains how he began writing, affirms his love for writing and his belief in veritism, and expresses appreciation for all his family. Engle tells of HG's vitality at seventy-one and of his influence as a reformer and writer.

B231. Austin, Mary. "Regionalism in American Fiction." *English Journal*, 21 (Feb 1932), 97-107.
Very brief mention (100) of HG's *MTR* as example of regional fiction of Middle Border.

B232. Hill, Eldon C. "HG/A 'Contemporary Immortal.'" *High School Teacher*, 8 (Feb 1932), 44-45, 76.
Hill says that, "Of all contemporary authors few can equal and none can surpass his work for 'simple beauty' and purity of diction, for wholesomeness of content, and for soundness of artistic craftsmanship." Essay traces G's early life in the West, his adventures in Boston with the literary giants and the resultant early books. But balance of the article deals with "the most significant part of the author's significant career--the biographical and autobiographical phase." Hill praises highly the Middle Border books and concludes with a brief review of the later autobiographical volumes, *Roadside* and *Contemporaries*. Hill sees G as the forerunner of many American novelists, such as Sinclair Lewis, Willa Cather, Emerson Hough, Knut Hamsen, and Martha Ostenso.

B233. Badger, Retta. "HG Recalls Famous Friends." Los
Angeles *Times*, 14 Feb 1932, pp. 5, 16.
In interview HG comments on famous friends, his
work for the Indians, his studies of spiritualism, the
importance of good broadcasting, and the need to re-
name the Carlsbad Caverns. He pays his greatest
tribute to Howells.

B234. Suckow, Ruth. "Middle Western Literature." *English
Journal*, 21 (Mar 1932), 175-182.
Brief mention (177), in general study, of *MTR*,
"with its dusty, hard-beaten, vigorous prose--from
which, alas, its author has so far retreated."

B235. "HG Here to Lecture on Life and Work." *Ke Leo O Hawaii*,
1 Dec 1932, p. 1.
HG's welcome to Hawaii and his response to Hawaii
are enthusiastic. He is described as the "embodiment
...of that same prairie life of which he has written so
well and so truthfully."

B236. "Mr. G the Guest." Honolulu *Star-Bulletin*, 13 Dec 1932,
p. 6.
HG has become known on the islands and delivered
a series of very successful lectures at the U of Hawaii.

B237. Shippey, Lee. "The Lee Side O' L.A." Los Angeles *Times*,
11 Sep 1933, p. 4.
HG is the author who "put the Middle West on the
literary map" and who has inspired ten thousand
authors. He will be honored at a dinner celebrating
his birthday.

B238. "HG to Be Honored." Los Angeles *Times*, 14 Sep 1933,
p. 5.
Dinner to be given at the University Club honoring
HG on his seventy-third birthday.

B239. "G Honored at Dinner." Los Angeles *Times*, 15 Sep 1933,
p. 2.
HG guest of civic and educational leaders at University
Club.

B240. "To HG." *Book Shop Talk* (Dawson's Book Shop), 1 (30 Apr 1934), 1-2.
      A poem by L. D. B. paying tribute to HG on his 73rd birthday, and a brief biographical sketch.

B241. "Strawberry Shortcake as HG, Famous Writer of 'Middle Border' Stories, Likes It." *Better Homes and Gardens,* 12 (Jun 1934), 69.
      HG's recipe for his favorite shortcake is given as No. 5 in a series of "Famous Foods of Famous People."

B242. Shippey, Lee. "The Lee Side O' L.A." Los Angeles *Times,* 12 Apr 1935, p. 4.
      HG's real name is Hannibal Hamlin Garland. Quips that HG is to give the Mark Twain Centenary address in Hannibal, Mo. HG could indeed pass for Mark Twain. Conveys HG's plea for a California literature.

B243. Millard, Bailey. "G at Milepost/Noted Writer in Anniversary. Los Angeles *Times,* 14 Sep 1935, p. 1.
      At 75, HG says, "Yes, I am a regular Californian now." In the interview he reviews his early life in South Dakota and his rise as a writer and comments on contemporary fiction.

B244. Shippey, Lee. "The Lee Side O' L.A." Los Angeles *Times,* 14 Sep 1935, p. 4.
      Birthday greeting to HG, America's first great realist, who made his place in American literature "because the books he wrote altered the American point of view."

B245. "HG is 75/Writer, on Birthday, Looks to His New Book on the Psychic." N.Y. *Times,* 15 Sep 1935, II, 5.
      Brief interview. HG gives his views on psychic phenomena and on the movies, which have "cheapened literature by drawing off young men to write hasty scripts when they might have been doing something which would endure."

B246. "Son of the Middle Border." N.Y. *Times,* 16 Sep 1935, p. 18.

Editorial appreciation of HG on occasion of his 75th birthday. "HG exchanged his husking-peg for a pen that has put the Middle Borders into the geography of literature of his day and not only endeared him to his fellow 'Borderers' and 'Back Trailers,' but also given him devoted 'Afternoon Neighbors' around the world."

B247. "Four Given S. C. Honors." Los Angeles *Times*, 24 Nov 1935, II, 1.

HG is one of four to receive honorary doctoral degrees from U of Southern California.

B248. "A Weekly Meditation/'Made Beautiful by Human Sympathy.'" Sioux Falls (S. Dak.) *Daily Argus-Leader*, 24 Nov 1935, p. 6.

Editorial in praise of HG on occasion of his 75th birthday summarizes "A Day's Pleasure" from *MTR* as example of Christian sympathy a propos Thanksgiving season.

B249. "Psychic Research/HG To Tell of Striking Phenomena." Springfield (Mass.) *Sunday Union and Republican*, 12 Apr 1936, p. 7-E.

Announcement of forthcoming publication of *Forty Years*, "a soberly written book."

B250. "Reception Given at S. C. in Honor of G." Los Angeles *Times*, 13 May 1936, II, 1.

Opening of HG exhibit at U of Southern California library described and some highlights noted.

B251. "Arts Alumni Renew Ties/HG Outlines Development of Work in United States." Los Angeles *Times*, 6 Jun 1936, II, 1, 3.

HG tells Otis Arts Institute students their aspirations are beautiful. Tracing art history in America to the arrival of impressionism, he says they are developing themselves as Americans.

B252. Shippey, Lee. "The Lee Side O' L. A./HG, Our Dean of Letters, Is Celebrating." Los Angeles *Times*, 13 Sep 1936, p. 4.

HG, author who "aroused middle western farmers to rebellion against the degrading and drudgery of their lives," today celebrates his seventy-sixth birthday. Still active, he recently published *Forty Years*, and is at work on another book.

B253. Whipple, T. K. "Literature in the Doldrums." *New Republic*, 90 (21 Apr 1937), 311-314.

Brief mention of *MTR* (314). Since HG wrote, "nearly fifty years ago, we have had little incisive treatment of farm life." [Rptd in *Study Out The Land*. Berkeley and Los Angeles: U of California Press, 1943. Pp. 69-75 and 76-84.]

B254. Shippey, Lee. "The Lee Side O' L. A." Los Angeles *Times*, 21 Oct 1937, p. 4.

HG is actor in a charming film of his own life made by a company specializing in educational and biographical films. One sees the honors and tranquility HG has earned.

B255. "Assails 'Shocking' Books/HG Says 'Return to Barnyard Morals' Is Disgusting." N.Y. *Times*, 29 Oct 1937, p. 23.

Brief news story on HG talk before California Writers Guild in which he criticized modern writing as " 'disgusting.' "

B256. S., F. M. "A Picturesque Coulee of La Crosse Valley That Gave Wisconsin a Famous Son." Milwaukee *Journal*, 29 Oct 1937, p. 20.

Stoltenberg's landscape of Green's Coulee is a picture of HG's place, setting for some of his most successful stories and *Son*.

B257. "Where the Responsibility Lies." *Catholic News*, 6 Nov 1937.

HG supports the idea that most current literature is "disgusting" because it is "a return to the morals of the barnyard."

B258. Sherman, Carolina B. "The Development of American Rural Fiction." *Agricultural History*, 12 (Jan 1938), 67-76.
  MTR is "the most significant" of three 19th-century novels (*Hoosier Schoolmaster* and *Story of A Country Town* are the other two) which are "forerunners" of the development of rural fiction in America: "Although ... [HG] did not realize or suggest all that the movement implied in the way of profound social and economic changes, he did catch and transmit a suggestion of it in a realistic rather than a romantic way"; and he "eventually followed through with other books that helped to form the main marching force of this new movement."

B259. "G to Open Exhibit." *Daily Trojan* (U of Southern California), 10 May 1938, p. 1.
  Announcement of HG exhibit at U of Southern California.

B260. "G to Speak at Exhibit/American Author to Place Works in Doheny Library." *Daily Trojan* (U of Southern California), 11 May 1938, p. 1.
  Announcement of exhibit (including correspondence, photographs, and a biographical film) and an address by HG at U of Southern California.

B261. "HG to Speak Today at Doheny." *Daily Trojan* (U of Southern California), 12 May 1938, p. 1.
  Announcement of exhibit, primarily of HG correspondence, and a talk by HG at U of Southern California.

B262. Stegner, Wallace. "The Trail of the Hawkeye/Literature Where the Tall Corn Grows." *Saturday Review of Literature*, 18 (30 Jul 1938), 3-4, 16-17.
  Brief mention (4) of HG as Iowa writer "of the first importance."

B263. Leighton, George R. "Omaha, Nebraska." *Harper's*, 177 (Jul 1938), 113-130; 177 (Aug 1938), 309-328.
  Brief mention (128) of HG's attendance at the Populist Party convention in Omaha in July 1892.

B264. "Writers End Convention/HG Tells of Picture Biography
at Redlands Program." Los Angeles *Times*, 31 Mar
1939, p. 14.
HG closes Redlands Writers' Week with the showing
of a picture biography of himself, calling it "art biography," and crediting Lee Shippey of the Los Angeles
Times with first giving him the idea.

B265. "HG Exhibit of Books, Letters, Manuscripts Shown Here."
Lincoln (Neb.) *Sunday Journal and Star*, 9 Apr 1939,
Sec. D, p. 3.
Description of exhibit at U of Nebraska library, with
specific mentions of particularly interesting items, in-
cluding quotations from some letters to and from HG.

B266. Shippey, Lee. "The Lee Side O' L.A./In Old Chicago."
Los Angeles *Times*, 25 Apr 1939, p. 4.
In lecture, HG recalled organizing the Cliff Dwellers.

B267. ---. "The Lee Side O' L.A./HG." Los Angeles *Times*, 14
Sep 1939, p. 4.
HG celebrates seventy-ninth birthday by being guest
of honor on the "Strange As It Seems" radio program.

B268. "HG's Byway." N.Y. *Times*, 20 Sep 1939, p. 26.
Brief editorial on occasion of HG's 79th birthday and
publication of *Buried Crosses*. "It's a long, long way
from ...*MTR* to *Buried Crosses*--which is as yet only
a human byway."

B269. "G, Author, Ill." Los Angeles *Times*, 4 Mar 1940, III, 1.
HG, recently stating that "when a man gets to be my
age the old engine starts to show signs of wear" but
still robust and vigorous, was stricken with a cerebral
hemorrhage while sleeping.

B270. "HG Ill." N.Y. *Times*, 4 Mar 1940, p. 13.
Brief news story reports that HG has suffered cerebral
hemorrhage.

B271. "Garland Dies After Stroke." Los Angeles *Times*, 5 Mar
1940, pp. 1, 2.

Extended obituary notice.

B272. "HG." Kansas City *Star*, 5 Mar 1940, p. 18.
Editorial occasioned by HG's death. HG's "great contribution was his honest, clear-eyed picture of America. His forthright Americanism changed literary trends and gave him a secure place in the history of letters." Middle Border "trilogy" is "his greatest contribution."

B273. "HG Dies/a Pioneer Writer of West." N.Y. *Herald Tribune*, 5 Mar 1940, p. 22.
Extended obituary notice.

B274. "HG, Novelist, Is Dead." N.Y. *Times*, 5 Mar 1940, p. 24.
Extensive AP obituary notice.

B275. "Author's Final Honor Arranged/Ashes of G to Lie in Wisconsin After Services Here." Los Angeles *Times*, 6 Mar 1940, p. 10.
Funeral announced for HG, acclaimed "dean of American letters," best known for his trilogy of middle-western families.

B276. "He Spoke for America." Long Beach (Calif.) *Press-Telegram*, 6 Mar 1940.
Editorial tribute to HG on occasion of his death. Gratitude expressed to him, prodigious writer and admirable person, for his personal example and support of American democracy.

B277. "HG." Boston *Evening Transcript*, 6 Mar 1940, p. 6.
Editorial occasioned by HG's death. *Son* and *MTR* "were the literary forefathers of *Grapes of Wrath*."
If "his books had spurred the imagination of the people as *Uncle Tom's Cabin* did, we might have had an earlier and more fortunate attack upon our agrarian problems."

B278. "HG." Detroit *News*, 6 Mar 1940, p. 22.
Editorial on occasion of HG's death. "He was, we suppose, the Dean of American Letters, in the sense that the oldest practitioner is dean, but certainly not in the usual connotation of being a survival after his

129

time. His works were modern in the meaning that they deal with verities and enduring values, that they will have a message for generations beyond his and ours." His fiction "was only removed from reality by the flavor of his art."

B279. "HG." Indianapolis *News*, 6 Mar 1940, p. 6.
Editorial on occasion of HG's death. "Beauty and the spirit of youth remained in him to the end." Of "his many great gifts, the greatest was his instinctive devotion to truth."

B280. "HG." Minneapolis *Morning Tribune*, 6 Mar 1940, p. 4.
Editorial occasioned by HG's death. "Because he wrote clearly, objectively and truthfully about a life with which he was thoroughly familiar, HG's works will be read long after many another currently popular novel has been forgotten."

B281. "HG." N.Y. *Herald Tribune*, 6 Mar 1940, p. 24.
Editorial appreciation on occasion of HG's death. HG "was the first American to write successfully about the West and to sell what he had written to the sophisticated publishers and readers of Boston." His style "was as direct and honest and unpolished at times as the country he wrote about." He is "the man who first broke the soil of the literature of the West, who saw in Minnesota and Wisconsin and Iowa the poetry of unplowed places and gave it to his country."

B282. "HG." N.Y. *Times*, 6 Mar 1940, p. 22.
Editorial on occasion of HG's death. *MTR* and *Son*, "in spite of contemporary standards, retain their value and charm as true chronicles of a period and a portion of our social history."

B283. "HG." Washington (D.C.) *Evening Star*, 6 Mar 1940, Sect. A, p. 10.
Extended editorial on occasion of HG's death. HG's "place is secure. His *Rose*, which won him a following in England; all of his 'Middle Border' studies and some of his poems are part of the immortal treasury of Ameri-

can letters, and they cannot die."

B284. "HG." Washington (D.C.) *Post*, 6 Mar 1940, p. 8.
Editorial on occasion of HG's death. Had *Son* been
written early in HG's career instead of late, "it would
have been regarded as a landmark, and the critics perhaps might see in it something of a turning point."
As it was, by the mid-1920's, HG's realism "seemed
pretty tame." But only Willa Cather has "wrought in
the genre of the 'Middle Border' with far greater skill"
than HG.

B285. "HG, Realist." Brooklyn *Daily Eagle*, 6 Mar 1940, p. 14.
Editorial on occasion of HG's death. "The history
of American literature could not be written without expressing its debt to this Son of the Middle Border who
was realism's lone disciple in an age of incurable romanticism."

B286. Millard, Bailey. "HG As I Knew Him." Los Angeles
Times, 6 Mar 1940, II, 4.
Brief biographical sketch.

B287. "Passing of HG, 'A Son of the Middle Border.'" Salt Lake
Tribune, 6 Mar 1940, p. 8.
Long lead editorial on occasion of HG's death. "The
writings he left are voluminous, intensely interesting,
free from sexy or suggestive taints, but wholesome and
sympathetic with the men and women who made our midwest one of the richest regions of the American continent."

B288. "Son of the Middle Border." Cleveland *Plain Dealer*, 6
Mar 1940, p. 8.
Editorial occasioned by HG's death. HG "did much to
put American writing on its feet and to interpret America
to itself." He "has left an indelible imprint on American letters."

B289. "Son of the Middle Border and Ward of New England." Baltimore *Sun*, 6 Mar 1940, p. 10.

Editorial appreciation on occasion of HG's death.
"He remained, of course, a distinguished writer whose
work was indeed that of a pioneer breaking new fields
of subject matter and using, for a time, new implements
of expression. Yet the Middle West did not really find
itself in him, nor did HG really find himself in the Middle West. His fame belongs to it and his influence
probably turned others to it. But his own heart was in
another world and another age than those to which he
had helped give birth."

B290. "A Son of the Middle Border Dies." Philadelphia *Inquirer,*
6 Mar 1940, p. 10.
Editorial. HG's "pictures of Western farm life of a
former day should form a lasting and valuable contribution to American letters."

B291. "G Funeral Today." N.Y. *Times,* 7 Mar 1940, p. 23.
Very brief news item on plans for HG's funeral.

B292. "Mr. HG/Novels of the Middle West." London *Times,* 7
Mar 1940, p. 11.
Obituary which is mainly review of HG's life and
career, also contains some estimate of HG's achievement: "his writings had both a literary and social
significance. They marked and stimulated a revolt
against the idyllic interpretations of rural life which
once dominated American fiction in its pictures of the
Middle West."

B293. "Tribute Paid to G/Academy of Arts and Letters Sends
Message to Late Writer's Widow." Los Angeles *Times,*
7 Mar 1940, II, 3.
Letter from American Academy of Arts and Letters
pays high tribute to HG as a self-made man, recognized writer, and stalwart American.

B294. "Two Pass On." Minneapolis *Star-Journal,* 7 Mar 1940,
p. 14.
Editorial occasioned by deaths of HG and actress
Maxine Elliott. HG "was among the first to bring the
middle-west into literature, and to make us see the

color and drama in 'the settlement of an area considered
poor literary material compared to the 'wild' West.''

B295. ''Solemn Group Pays Tribute to Memory of HG/Worlds of
Arts, Sciences and Letters Represented Among Mourners
at Funeral Services for Noted Author.'' Los Angeles
Times, 8 Mar 1940, p. 18.
At HG's funeral, mourners represented the worlds of
arts, letters, and sciences. Dr. Ernest Holmes, officia-
ating, commented on HG's remarkable intellect. HG's
ashes will be scattered on the hills near his old home
and birthplace at West Salem, Wisconsin.

B296. Uncle Dudley. ''Ancestral Acres.'' Boston *Daily Globe*,
8 Mar 1940, p. 18.
Editorial on the occasion of HG's death discusses
reasons why writers like HG left Boston in the 1890's
and early years of the 20th century rather than remaining to write there.

B297. ''Obituary Notes/HG.'' *Publishers' Weekly*, 137 (9 Mar
1940), 1089.
Biographical sketch. Mentions that HG ''recently''
chose Miami University of Ohio ''as the depository of
the records of his authorship.''

B298. Shippey, Lee. ''The Lee Side O' L.A.'' Los Angeles *Times*,
9 Mar 1940, p. 4.
HG died as he wished to die--active and vigorous until
his stroke. Many groups owe him a debt of gratitude.

B299. ''G, the Son of Wisconsin.'' Milwaukee *Journal*, 10 Mar
1940, Editorial Sect., p. 2.
Editorial occasioned by HG's death. Wisconsin's
gift of HG to the nation ''permanently enriched the
literary lore of America.'' He ''foretold the 'dust bowl'
and its tragedy before John Steinbeck or *The Grapes
of Wrath* were ever thought of.''

B300. ''Died/HG.'' *Newsweek*, 15 (11 Mar 1940), 9.
Brief obituary notice.

B301. "Milestones." *Time*, 35 (11 Mar 1940), 64.
Very brief obituary notice.

B302. L[oveman], A[m]y. [Obituary Editorial]. *Saturday Review of Literature*, 21 (16 Mar 1940), 8.
Brief tribute to HG, who, "though his realism may seem sugar-coated to a generation brought up on Faulkner and Caldwell, was one of the few novelists who in the nineties depicted American life without romantic glamour."

B303. "Obituary/HG." (London) *Times Literary Supplement*, 16 Mar 1940, p. 138.
Brief review of HG's career: although he "was one of the lesser figures of American literature," he was "a figure undoubtedly. The best of his work lives as the first extended expression in genuinely realistic terms of the pioneer life of the rural Middle West."

B304. "HG." *Scholastic*, 36 (18 Mar 1940), 27.
Biographical sketch on occasion of HG's death.

B305. Dresbach, Glenn Ward. "Son of the Middle Border (In Memory of HG)." *Step Ladder*, 27 (Apr 1940), 74-75.
Verse tribute.

B306. "His Last Letters." *Step Ladder*, 27 (Apr 1940), 78-81.
Complete texts of nine HG letters written to Mr. and Mrs. George S. Seymour of The Bookfellows between 10 Jan 1940 and 26 Feb 1940.

B307. "Literary Calendar/April 1940." *Wilson Library Bulletin*, 14 (Apr 1940), 546, 548.
Brief obituary notice.

B308. S[eymour], G[eorge] S[teele]. "Time Marches On." *Step Ladder*, 27 (Apr 1940), 75-77.
Tribute to HG, who was one of The Bookfellows, group which publishes *Step Ladder*. Seymour announces that plans for HG's 80th birthday celebration will be changed to produce a memorial volume to include a bibliography of his published works and a critical sketch of his writings.

B309. ---. "To HG--March 4, 1940." *Step Ladder*, 27 (Apr 1940), 73.
    Brief poetic tribute.

B310. Bacheller, Irving. "HG (A Little Story of a Friendship)." *Step Ladder*, 27 (May 1940), 98-100.
    Memories of a lifelong friendship with HG. [Rptd in *Mark Twain Quarterly*, 4 (Summer 1940), 14, 16.]

B311. "The G Memorial." *Step Ladder*, 27 (May 1940), 100.
    Plans for the HG memorial are proceeding smoothly.

B312. [Seymour, George Steele]. "Books and People." *Step Ladder*, 27 (May 1940), 109-111.
    Includes (109-110) mention of fact that Bookfellow Library has just received copy of HG's *Westward March of American Settlement* (1927). Includes also text of HG letter to Seymour explaining history of this item and Seymour's correction of HG's explanation.

B313. Thomas, Louisa Carroll. "To HG." *Step Ladder*, 27 (May 1940), 101.
    Brief verse tribute.

B314. Blair, Walter. "Roots of American Realism." *University Review* (Kansas City), 6 (Jun 1940), 275-281.
    HG's call in *CI* for a new American literature of "veritism" is used as the introduction to a consideration of how successfully Howells, Eggleston, Kirkland, Norris, Howe, and HG himself answered the call. *MTR* is "an antiromantic work"; many of HG's stories are "freighted with social preachments."

B315. "The G Memorial." *Step Ladder*, 27 (Jun 1940), 143-144.
    Announcement that fund has reached $390. Includes list of Memorial Committee and their states.

B316. Bacheller, Irving. "A Little Story of a Friendship." *Mark Twain Quarterly*, 4 (Summer, 1940), 14, 16.
    [Rptd from *Step Ladder*, 27 (May 1940), 98-100. See above.]

B317. Beard, Dan. "HG, the Poet." *Mark Twain Quarterly*, 4 (Summer 1940), 10.
  Memory of HG having written a poem for Beard one day which latter has used many times since then.

B318. Blearsides, Oliver. "G's Twain Anecdotes." *Mark Twain Quarterly*, 4 (Summer 1940), 13.
  Memories of HG's stories about Twain.

B319. Chamberlin, Joseph E. "G in Boston." *Mark Twain Quarterly*, 4 (Summer 1940), 13.
  Brief memories of HG in Boston in 1880's and 1890's.

B320. Clemens, Cyril. "At Lunch with HG." *Mark Twain Quarterly*, 4 (Summer 1940), 5-8.
  Recollections of HG at lunch in Los Angeles, where he talked of Zane Grey, his own diaries, the writing of his books, Robert Frost, John Drinkwater, influences on his writing, Howells, and Twain.

B321. ---. "HG: 1860-1940." *Mark Twain Quarterly*, 4 (Summer 1940), 1, 20.
  Brief summary of HG's career as introduction to HG Memorial Issue of this journal.

B322. Clemens, J. R. "Good Books: to HG." *Mark Twain Quarterly*, 4 (Summer 1940), 4.
  Brief poetic tribute.

B323. Derleth, August. "Elegy: In March the Wind/For HG." *Mark Twain Quarterly*, 4 (Summer 1940), 2.
  Poetic tribute to HG.

B324. Hamilton, Clayton. [Memorial tribute to HG]. *Mark Twain Quarterly*, 4 (Summer 1940), 4.
  Brief statement: "I admired in particular his steadfast insistence upon the dignity of the profession of letters."

B325. Hill, Eldon C. "HG Collection." *Mark Twain Quarterly*, 4 (Summer 1940), 10.
  Brief account of HG papers at Miami (Ohio) University and tribute to HG.

B326. Meriwether, Lee. "My Friend HG." *Mark Twain Quarterly,* 4 (Summer 1940), 9, 20.
     Memories of HG by a friend who first met him in Boston in the 1880's and last saw him in California in 1939.

B327. Sibley, Carroll. "HG: Delightful Host." *Mark Twain Quarterly,* 4 (Summer 1940), 3-4.
     Memories of HG in California during the last four years of his life.

B328. Stevenson, Lionel. "G's Conversation." *Mark Twain Quarterly,* 4 (Summer 1940), 10.
     Brief tribute to HG for his interest in young writers and for his conversational abilities.

B329. Richards, Grant. "Looking Back." *Monitor* (Boston), 1 Jul 1940, p. 8.
     Reminiscences about times spent with HG in England.

B330. "Plan for the Memorial." *Step Ladder,* 27 (Sep 1940), 162-164.
     Plans include a memorial volume and the erection of an HG guest cottage at the site of the Bookfellows Library. Committee members and their states listed at end.

B331. S[eymour], G[eorge] S[teele]. "Things We Can Do Together." *Step Ladder,* 27 (Sep 1940), 161-162.
     More on the HG Memorial and on the spirit of togetherness indicated by members' willingness to contribute to it.

B332. Simpson, Claude M., Jr. "HG's Decline." *Southwest Review,* 26 (Winter 1941), 223-234.
     Although HG "lived as many years in this century as in the last, he must inevitably be considered as a nineteenth-century author who ceased to grow almost with the first appearance of real success." His decline relates to a dichotomy between a desire for reform and a desire for literary success. *MTR* suggests that HG never went far enough in his realism. He was terribly earnest but not quite truthful in his pictures of the Mid-

West. HG finally gave in to the call of a wider reading public and became engulfed in sentimentalism and gentility as *Spoil* shows. The problem was that he associated realism and reform so that "when he turned his back on the one, he retreated from the other."

B333. "The HG Memorial." *Step Ladder*, 28 (Mar 1941), 71.
Further news on the memorial volume, which has been delayed; so bibliography will include *Fortunate Exiles*, HG's last book.

B334. Flanagan, John T. "HG, Occasional Minnesotan." *Minnesota History*, 22 (Jun 1941), 157-168.
Tracing of HG's associations with Minnesota: biographical details about his early life there and his subsequent return trips to visit friends and to lecture; and mention of Minnesota materials in his works.

B335. "The Beat of Wings." *Step Ladder*, 28 (Oct 1941), 193.
Brief mention of fact that HG family has decided not to publish *Fortunate Exiles*: "We cannot help but think that this decision is an unwise one and is contrary to what he wished and expected."

B336. Dickason, David H. "Benjamin Orange Flower, Patron of the Realists." *American Literature*, 14 (May 1942), 148-156.
Flower assisted HG with generous reviews, praise, monetary aid, and general sponsorship. "Flower and the *Arena* launched G" on his literary career (151-152).

B337. Flanagan, John T. "The Middle Western Farm Novel." *Minnesota History*, 23 (Jun 1942), 113-125.
Brief account (115-116) of HG's farm novels. HG is "the most publicized if not the most gifted of farm chroniclers." "No one before G drew with such bitter truth the hopeless struggles of the coulee dwellers or the efforts of men on the Dakota prairies to raise wheat in the face of wind and drought. His books have influenced every subsequent novelist of the farm." But HG's view, "in one sense," was "distorted," for his "eviscerated farmers had only one objective: to escape from

the farm"; for "only flight promised relief." "It remained for later writers to present a more balanced picture of the farm."

B338. ---. "The Middle Western Historical Novel." *Journal of The Illinois State Historical Society*, 37 (Mar 1944), 7-47.

Brief mention (44) of *CI* as work in which HG prophesied coming of great Middle Western literature, which never materialized.

B339. Hornberger, Theodore. "American First Editions at TxU/I. HG (1860-1940)." *Library Chronicle of The University of Texas*, 1 (Summer 1944), 27-29.

Texas has 39 of HG's 46 books, and 31 are first editions. Lists missing seven and gives brief account of how HG collection at Texas began and grew.

B340. Goldstein, Jesse Sidney. "Two Literary Radicals: G and Markham in Chicago, 1893." *American Literature*, 17 (May 1945), 152-160.

David Lesser Lezinsky introduced Markham to HG by letter; later HG provided Markham with a letter of introduction to Howells.

Markham and HG influenced each other. Markham's poetry shows the influence of HG in both form and content; Markham tried writing a short story ("Old Jerry") according to HG's theory of veritism. HG's essay "New Fields" in *CI* may have been influenced by Markham.

Markham agreed with the position taken by HG in his debate with Catherwood and Warner.

B341. "Letters of a Pioneer Realist." *Newberry Library Bulletin*, No. 3 (Dec 1945), 3-7.

Article deals with Kirkland letters recently given to Newberry Library. G gets some attention (4-6) as one of the critics who praised Kirkland's "Zury, the Meanest Man in Spring County." G mentions in several places his debt to Kirkland and his works and their influence on him. Article concentrates on G's meeting with Kirkland in Chicago early in July 1887 and its subsequent effect on his career, as well as on Kirkland's.

B342. Bucks, Dorothy S., and Arthur H. Nethercot. "Ibsen and Herne's *Margaret Fleming*: A Study of the Early Ibsen Movement in America." *American Literature*, 17 (Jan 1946), 311-333.

HG influenced Herne and the radical drama. He introduced the works of Ibsen to Herne and praised Mrs. Herne for her extraordinary powers and gifts and for her contribution to the writing of *Margaret Fleming*. He struggled for an independent theater in Boston.

Quotations from the *Arena* preserve "several significant passages of the actual dialogue" in *Margaret Fleming*.

B343. Smith, Henry Nash. "The Western Farmer in Imaginative Literature, 1818-1891." *Mississippi Valley Historical Review*, 36 (Dec 1949), 479-490.

HG is discussed at the end (487-490) of this essay. Although HG's work is "seriously deficient as art," he "expresses two things better than anyone else: the evolution which had made it possible to deal with western farmers on their own terms, without reference to their supposedly inferior social status." But he "was not gifted in analysis and could not formulate a theory to account for the plight of his people."

B344. Commager, Henry Steele. "Pioneering on the Farm/Based on *Son*, by HG." *Scholastic*, 56 (22 Mar 1950), 8-9.

Summary and appreciation of *Son* as picture of the West in the 1870's, 1880's, and 1890's.

B345. Culmsee, Carlton. "A Pioneer in Modern Pessimism." *Western Humanities Review*, 4 (Summer 1950), 241-250.

Examines HG's youthful years (referring to *Son*), especially "the collapse of the pioneer's dream" which proved for him a "source of disillusionment." HG's defeat by the hostile forces of nature had the one favorable effect of forcing HG to go to Boston and begin his literary career. His belief in Spencer and evolution did not make him a total optimist because his Dakota years

gave him reason enough to have doubts.
Examines the Middle Border works, pointing out that "running through the entire Border series is sadness at the wretched end of the pioneer's great epic and the change in national spirit." *Back-Trailers* "ends on a strain of weary old age, of disillusionment, of nostalgia."
HG's works are of "permanent value as social history."

B346. Jones, Arthur E., Jr. "Darwinism and Its Relationship to Realism and Naturalism in American Fiction, 1860-1900." *Drew University Studies*, 1 (Dec 1950), 1-21.
HG discussed (15-16) in terms of influence of Darwin on his work, particularly *CI*, and, very briefly, his fiction. In HG's work, emphasis is no longer on what man does to nature, but rather on the effect of environment upon man. "This shift seems almost directly the result of the stress laid upon the function of natural process in the *Origin Of The Species*."

B347. Edwards, Herbert. "Howells and Herne." *American Literature*, 22 (Jan 1951), 432-441.
HG, as a friend of Herne, championed Ibsen (437). Brief reference to the controversy about Howells' reaction to *Margaret Fleming* and whether or not HG quoted him accurately (436n). Other scattered references to HG throughout article.

B348. Bowron, Bernard R., Jr. "Realism in America." *Comparative Literature*, 3 (Summer 1951), 268-285.
Brief mention (278-279) of HG as regionalist who was "less uncompromising" in his treatment of the ugly side of life, especially sex, than some of the other regionalists like Howe and Frederic.

B349. Flanagan, John T., ed. "HG Writes to His Chicago Publisher [text of letters]." *American Literature*, 23 (Jan 1952), 447-457.
Notes HG's importance to the publishing firm of Stone and Kimball and lists works published by them. Although G "had occasion to doubt their business sagacity and their ability to sell books he was enthusiastic

about their artistic ideals.''
MTR was third volume issued by Stone and Kimball;
Songs appeared in 1893; *CI* in 1894; *Rose* and *Folks*
in 1895.

B350. Henson, Clyde E. ''Joseph Kirkland's Influence on HG.''
American Literature, 23 (Jan 1952), 458-463.
Kirkland and HG carried on a correspondence for some
time; and their letters ''reveal the extent to which G
was indebted to...[Kirkland] for the revision of stories
and poems, for advice, and for the sale of some of his
work.'' In *Trail Makers*, HG attempted ''to apply the
objective quality which Kirkland recommended as a
method.'' [Article reprints number of Kirkland's letters
to HG.]

B351. McElderry, Bruce R., Jr. ''HG and Henry James.'' *American Literature*, 23 (Jan 1952), 433-446.
Article centers on the controversy over James's ex-
patriation and HG's statement that James told him he
would be an American if he had another chance. HG
included in *Roadside* an account of a meeting with
James which HG inferred took place in 1899; actually
it occurred in 1906, and the recognition of this fact
gives greater credence to James's statement on his
longing for America.
Quotes all James letters to HG in the Doheny Collection at Southern California.

B352. Carter, Everett. ''The Meaning of, and in, Realism.''
Antioch Review, 12 (Spring 1952), 78-94.
HG and others saw fiction as a kind of history (83).

B353. Dove, John R. ''The Significance of HG's First Visit to
England.'' *Studies in English* (U of Texas), 32 (1953),
96-109.
Examines the conflicting reports of HG's first visit
to England as they appear in *Daughter*, *Roadside Meetings*, and *Mountain Lover*. Suggests that HG always
suffered under a ''profound inner conflict'' concerning
the city and the country. He always felt that his life
in the city was ''a form of betrayal,'' and much of his

early fiction deals with the return of the native from
the city. HG tried to compromise by being a spokesman
for the West while living in the city; but he eventually
rejected the country and accepted the city, and his
trip to England was ''a kind of formal dedication of
it.'' However his literature suffered when he rejected
the West.

B354. Duffey, Bernard I. ''HG's Decline from Realism.'' *American Literature*, 25 (Mar 1953), 69-74.
Examines HG's Boston years (1884-1893), especially
the HG-Gilder correspondence which suggests that HG
was more concerned with literary and financial success
than with reform. HG turned realist for a time because
Flower and the *Arena* offered another chance for literary
success, but HG seems to have always wanted Gilder
at the *Century* to take his work first. Later HG gave up
the *Arena*, though he kept his connection with *Harper's*
and the *Century*. For HG ''reform and realism were never
in themselves primary literary or intellectual pursuits.
They were accessory for a time to his campaign for intellectual and literary success.'' He seemed always
willing to compromise, and his real connection was with
the ''Eastern genteel tradition'' with a few ''lapses in
favor of Flower, Howells, Kirkland . . . .''

B355. Schorer, C. E. ''HG's First Published Story.'' *American
Literature*, 25 (Mar 1953), 89-92.
His first published story, which ''HG hoped that no-
body would look up,'' was ''Ten Years Dead.'' It appeared in *Every Other Saturday* for 28 March, 1885. In
the story ''one finds the influence of Hawthorne in the
characters and in the quality of somberness, mystery,
and fatefulness which G endeavored to impart'' (89).
Much of the detail of the story comes from HG's own
life: ''The historical significance of the details is that
they show G approaching veritism two years before he
met Joseph Kirkland, who is commonly believed to have
started G on his literary way'' (91).

B356. ---. ''HG, of Wisconsin.'' *Wisconsin Magazine of History*,
37 (Spring 1954), 147-150, 182-185.

Summary of HG's "physical connection" with Wisconsin, his early life there, and his return visits--to lecture and to receive honorary degrees--and an analysis of his changing attitude toward the state as reflected in his writing. Schorer sees three phases in this attitude: 1) 1860-1893, the period of his boyhood and early manhood, "appears as a happy time, a time of vital reaction"; 2) 1893-1914, the time of his ownership of a house in West Salem, was "a time of nostalgic residence"; 3) 1914-1940, the period of his removal from Wisconsin and of his "physical and literary decline," was one of "melancholy exile." Essay includes a brief consideration of HG's relationship with Zona Gale. It concludes with mention of HG's books with Wisconsin settings, primarily *MTR*, *Rose*, and the Middle Border works in which HG "glamorized" Wisconsin. In the end, the areas of Wisconsin life which HG has helped us to understand better than any other writer are "the farm life of the coulee country and the university in its early days." He is "Wisconsin's foremost author."

B357. Duffey, Bernard I. **"Mr. Koerner's Reply Considered."** *American Literature*, 26 (Nov 1954), 432-435.

Reply to next article. Duffey responds that he did not say HG was a complete opportunist alone; he was not a monster, but he did rely "upon persons and circumstances which made for literary success rather than upon constant inner convictions." He reiterates arguments which he made in his initial article.

B358. Koerner, James D. "Comment on 'HG's Decline from Realism.'" *American Literature*, 26 (Nov 1954), 427-432.

Protests Duffey's view *(American Literature* [Mar 1953]) that HG was an opportunist and disagrees with Duffey's interpretation of the HG-Gilder correspondence and the genesis of HG's work. HG wrote many of the stories of *MTR* before he met Flower. The Howells-HG relationship shows that HG's integrity and honesty seemed to most people his one vital ingredient, which Duffey denies.

B359. Pizer, Donald. "HG in the *Standard.*" *American Literature*, 26 (Nov 1954), 401-415.

   Examines HG's connection with the *Standard* in an attempt to show his economic point of view and the motives for this view. The single tax "was never merely an economic formula to G, but always, as to George, a means by which the freedom of opportunity which was man's natural right could operate in conjunction with a rich and beneficent nature and the natural law of progress to achieve the millenium."

   In HG's stricter single-tax works ("Under the Lion's Paw" and "Under the Wheel") he stresses the "crushing of individual opportunity by land speculation."

B360. Clark, Harry Hayden. "The Influence of Science on American Literary Criticism, 1860-1910, Including the Vogue of Taine." *Transactions of the Wisconsin Academy of Sciences, Arts and Letters*, 44 (1955), 109-164.

   Mention (114-115) of influence of science, especially Spencer, on HG, as seen specifically in *CI*, and scattered mention (153, 157, 158) of HG's indebtedness to Taine.

B361. Pizer, Donald. "Crane Reports G on Howells." *Modern Language Notes*, 70 (Jan 1955), 37-39.

   Pizer reprints Crane's article which appeared in the N.Y. *Tribune*, 17 Aug 1891 (see above), reporting HG's lecture on Howells. Pizer contends that Crane's literary beliefs were greatly influenced by HG's lecture. "His acceptance of the critical theories of G and Howells which emphasize personal honesty and vision seems to have been his initial step towards this triumphant conclusion," that is, his readjustment of his point of view. Pizer quotes two Crane letters as evidence of his being influenced by HG's presentation of both Howells' ideas and his own.

B362. Ravitz, A. C. "Willa Cather Under Fire: HG Misreads *A Lost Lady.*" *Western Humanities Review*, 9 (Spring 1955), 182-184.

   In a letter to Fred L. Pattee, dated 28 September 1923, HG criticized Willa Cather's heroine, Marian Forrester,

as a "female libertine." Ravitz demonstrates error of
HG's analysis: Marian is "clearly symbolic of the new
spirit of the West," and for HG to be disgusted with
this character was for him "to be disgusted with his
own ethic," his "very own social credo."

B363. Pizer, Donald. "An 1890 Account of *'Margaret Fleming.'"
American Literature, 27 (May 1955), 264-267.
"It was G who was, after their meeting in May, 1889,
the greatest influence on Herne, and who helped turn
him toward the drama of ideas."
HG wrote a review of the play which is an accurate
document for reconstructing the play as it was originally
done. Mrs. Herne rewrote the fourth and fifth acts some
time later.

B364. Stronks, James. "False Dawn in Chicago." *Chicago Review*, 9 (Summer 1955), 107-112.
Review of Bernard Duffey's *The Chicago Renaissance
in American Letters*. Duffey's view of HG as a complete opportunist is only partly right, and Duffey errs
in many of his conclusions about HG's life.

B365. McElderry, Bruce R., Jr. "HG's View of Whitman." *Personalist*, 36 (Oct 1955), 369-378.
Detailed tracing of HG's contacts with Whitman, i.e.,
correspondence between them, accounts of their meetings, summaries of HG's reviews of Whitman's works.
McElderry notes that, late in his life, HG's worship of
Whitman was greatly diminished as his own idealism
and crusading spirit waned.

B366. Ahnebrink, Lars. "G and Dreiser: An Abortive Friendship."
Midwest Journal, 7 (Winter 1955-1956), 285-292.
HG liked *Sister Carrie* but his friendship with Dreiser
never grew "because of differences in temperament and
ideals." During the controversy over Dreiser's *The
Genius* and the attempts by literary people to retain
freedom of expression, HG refused to support Dreiser.
He seemed to be reacting against the Freudians, Dreiser's
pro-German attitude, and the free advertising Dreiser was
receiving. He later became an ardent enemy of Dreiser

and, even though Dreiser later praised him, refused to return the compliment.

B367. Pizer, Donald, ed. " 'The Rise of Boomtown'--An Unpublished Dakota Novel by HG." *South Dakota Historical Collections,* 28 (1956), 345-389.

Pizer contributes an Introduction (345-351) to the edited excerpts from the story, a biographical sketch, and details surrounding the composition of the novel "The Rise of Boomtown," which HG wrote in 1886-1887. "The work is of interest and value, ... both as a contemporary account of a particular phase of Dakota life of the early eighties and as a source work of G's apprenticeship. For from it he derived not only Dakota background, scene, and character for later work but also the experience in depicting social background and genre types which served him so well in all his later middle border fiction."

B368. Ahnebrink, Lars. "Paris in Times of Turmoil: Three Letters of HG to His Parents in 1899." *Études Anglaises,* 9 (Jul-Sep 1956), 246-251.

Introduction by Ahnebrink (246-247) notes how HG went to Paris to see Mme. Blanc (Th. Bentzon) and to see the art of France. During his stay "the Dreyfus Case, the assault on President Loubet and the return of Major Marchand, the African explorer" all took place adding to the excitement of his visit.

Three HG letters to his parents are reprinted (246-251) from the University of Southern California collection.

B369. Edwards, Herbert. "Herne, G, and Henry George." *American Literature,* 28 (Nov 1956), 359-367.

HG was one of the few creative artists who reflected George's economic theories; he was instrumental in converting Herne to the single-tax movement. "Ignoring the basic principle that the temple of the arts may have an altar, but not a pulpit, G tried to introduce the Single Tax into his fiction."

B370. Pizer, Donald. "Herbert Spencer and the Genesis of HG's Critical System." *Tulane Studies in English,* 7 (1957), 153-168.

HG's selective use of Spencer "represents both an important late nineteenth-century intellectual relationship and one of the few attempts to construct a systematic local color aesthetic." He used Spencer to "explain the growing complexity of the novel and to equate this growing complexity with progress." Examines HG's "The Evolution of American Thought" and its reliance on Spencer, Taine, and Posnett.

It is easy to understand HG's admiration for Whitman and the local colorists when one realizes that for HG "American literature must be of the present, and it must deal with the primary characteristic of the present, the common, normal experiences of the people."

B371. ---. "HG: A Bibliography of Newspaper and Periodical Publications (1885-1895)." *Bulletin of Bibliography*, 22 (Jan-Apr 1957), 41-44.

Chronological listing of HG's essays, reviews, and fiction.

B372. Pallette, Drew B. "G and the Prince of Players." *Western Speech*, 21 (Summer 1957), 160-163.

Article examines HG's notebooks dealing with Edwin Booth, whom HG admired greatly. The notes deal with Booth's performances of Shakespeare, especially his interpretation of Hamlet. HG lectured numerous times on Booth when he first began his literary career in Boston. His interest in theater and acting are made clear by his recordings, and "his enthusiasm led him to record many details concerning Booth's methods which are of interest to historians of the American theatre."

B373. Pizer, Donald. "Romantic Individualism in G, Norris and Crane." *American Quarterly*, 10 (Winter 1958), 463-475.

HG, Norris, and Crane belong not only to the naturalistic strain but also to the American romantic individualist strain going back to Jefferson and the transcendentalists. Veron's *Aesthetics* influenced HG's ideas on "impressionistic artistic truth." Veron and HG both felt "the necessity for art to represent change, and it required that this be done through the expression of individual personality, the most important product of evolutionary

progress from homogeneity to heterogeneity."
In *CI* "G stated an aesthetic system in which evolutionary ideas served as the intellectual foundation, impressionism as the artistic method advocated and local color
as the end product in the various arts." Furthermore,
"central to this system--and the emotional center of
reference in all of G's thought--was the right and need
of the individual to be free." [Rptd in *Realism and
Naturalism in Nineteenth-Century American Literature.*]

B374. Duffey, Bernard I. "Progressivism and Personal Revolt."
Centennial Review, 2 (Spring 1958), 125-138.
MTR discussed (129-131) as being concerned not with
economic issues but with "the individual seeking ful-
fillment in a web of circumstance over which he can
triumph only by a heroic degree of individual action."
"Up the Coulé" is used to illustrate Duffey's idea that
the light G "casts by implication on the populist movement is to suggest that its final cause was as much reaction from cultural **barenness, boredom, and ignorance**
or the fear these produced as from specific abuses of
economic or political power. The latter were efficient,
and not ultimate."

B375. Pizer, Donald. "Radical Drama in Boston: 1889-91." *New
England Quarterly*, 31 (Sep 1958), 361-374.
Discusses the rise of the radical drama in Boston under
the impetus of HG and Herne. Through Herne, HG met
many theater people, and his interest in the theater grew
greatly. HG's attacks "on American commercial theater,
and his support of and struggle for an independent theater sprang from his inability to get his own realistic
drama of contemporary social problems produced."
HG's "Jason Edwards" was published by Flower in the
Arena but never produced.
Discusses at some length genesis of HG's "Member"
and also HG's extensive publicity work for the production of Herne's *Margaret Fleming*.

B376. Shuman, R. Baird. "HG on Education." *School and Society*,
86 (25 Oct 1958), 376.

Includes text of HG letter to R. G. Shortlidge of West Chester State Teachers College on subject of teachers. HG considers position of teacher "most honorable and fundamentally important" and feels that "teachers are not paid enough and are not held in as high regard by the community as they deserve."

B377. Pizer, Donald. " 'John Boyle's Conclusion': An Unpublished Middle Border Story" [with text]. *American Literature,* 31 (Mar 1959), 59-75.

This is the first printing of a story written in 1888. The story "is obviously crude and immature in dialogue, credibility ... and style"; but "despite its obvious crudities and slips, it is, on the whole, one of the more compelling revelations of the depth and meaning of G's reaction to Middle Border farm life of the late 1880's."

"In the next few years, he was, through the discipline of revision and the aid of such writers and editors as Joseph Kirkland and R. W. Gilder, to refine his fictional technique and style until they reached the professional qualities revealed in *MTR* and *Folks.*"

B378. McElderry, Bruce R., Jr. *"Boy Life:* HG's Best Reminiscence." *Educational Leader,* 22 (1 Apr 1959), 5-16.

HG's account of boyhood is impressive when compared with other accounts by Aldrich, Clemens, Warner, and Howells. And, aside from *MTR, Boy Life* is "probably the best single book that G ever wrote." Traces orgins of the book and compares it with *Son,* establishing the superiority of *Boy Life.* In *MTR,* HG is "too personally involved"; in *Boy Life* "there is more balance, more restraint." "Despite the apparent discursiveness of the book, unity is achieved by emphasis on the change in the prairie, which parallels and intensifies the boy's growing up." [Rptd as "Introduction" to *Boy Life.* Lincoln: U of Nebraska Press, 1961. Pp. v-xvi.]

B379. Pizer, Donald. "A Summer Campaign in Chicago: HG Defends a Native Art." *Western Humanities Review,* 13 (Autumn 1959), 375-382.

Provides several reasons for HG's move to Chicago and examines his campaign in the summer of 1893 for local-color fiction which is interesting "for both its revelation of the evangelical intensity of G's belief in a native western art and its contribution to the occasionally farcical history of the realism-romanticism conflict of the nineties." Recounts the fact that HG and Mrs. Catherwood got into a "joust" over HG's championing the West and local color and Mrs. Catherwood's defending Eastern romanticism.

Examines HG's article on the "Literary Emancipation of the West" for its important effects on Eastern journalists, writers and magazines, which HG attacked, especially the *Dial*.

B380. Spiller, Robert E. "Man of the Middle Border." N.Y. *Herald Tribune Book Review*, 17 Jul 1960, p. 6.
Review of Jean Holloway's *HG*. HG "was an excellent example of the author whose claim to greatness depends on his response to the vital currents of his times rather than on an ability to rise above his times and reveal universal truths in enduring form."

B381. Simpson, Claude M., Jr. "Wolfe and G." *Southwest Review*, 45 (Autumn 1960), 362-364.
Review of HG studies by Jean Holloway and Donald Pizer, along with two books on Wolfe.

B382. Flanagan, John T. "Literary Chronicler." *Minnesota History*, 37 (Sep 1960), 129-130.
Review of Jean Holloway's HG biography, which slights HG's boyhood and early manhood.

B383. Gullickson, Rachel. "G Marker Dedication Addresses." West Salem (Wis.) *Journal*, 15 Sep 1960, p. 1.
Text of Rachel Gullickson's address at the unveiling of the HG Historical Marker.

B384. "HG Historical Marker Unveiled at Impressive Ceremony." West Salem (Wis.) *Journal*, 15 Sep 1960, p. 1.
A large crowd attended unveiling of HG Historical Marker at Swarthout Lakeside Park on Sunday, 11

September, and a smaller marker at the HG family plot
at Neshonoc Cemetery.

B385. Wulling, Emerson. "G Marker Dedication Addresses."
West Salem (Wis.) *Journal*, 15 Sep 1960, p. 1.
Text of Dr. Wulling's address at the unveiling of the
HG Historical Marker.

B386. Pizer, Donald. "The G-Crane Relationship." *Huntington Library Quarterly*, 24 (Nov 1960), 75-82.
Attempt to clear up the discrepancies in dates of the
G-Crane meetings, caused in part by HG's having
changed certain accounts and telescoped meetings
and dates in his autobiographical writings. [Rptd in
*Realism and Naturalism in Nineteenth-Century Ameri-
can Literature.*]

B387. Harwick, Robert. [Review of *HG/A Biography* by Jean
Holloway.] *College English*, 22 (Dec 1960), 207.
Unfortunately Holloway offers "little that is new"
dealing with HG's movement away from realism. She
accepts Wagenknecht's explanation of the decline
partly in terms of "worldly wisdom" and partly because HG "exhausted his middle-border material."
She should have attempted an explanation of "what is,
after all, the main consideration in G criticism."

B388. Pizer, Donald. "Jean Holloway's *HG.*" *Nineteenth-Century Fiction*, 15 (Dec 1960), 275-277.
Review. As an "outline, it will be extremely useful";
but "on the level of a probing of G's lifelong excessive
need for the patronage of the successful and wealthy, or
of a search for the unifying thread binding together his
often ludicrously diverse reform interests, of a study of
the relationship between fact and fancy in his autobiographical writing--in these and in other such fertile
fields Mrs. Holloway is for the most part silent." HG
was, "in a special sense, a Victorian author--that is,
he was a man of letters as well as an artist, an active
participant in his literary and social worlds rather than
alien from them . . . . "

B389. Whitford, Kathryn. "Patterns of Observation: A Study of HG's Middle Border Landscape." *Tranactions of The Wisconsin Academy of Sciences, Arts, and Letters,* 50 (1961), 331-338.

Detailed examination of HG's use of weather, the seasons, vegetation, plant names, animals, and birds in his Middle Border works as test of accuracy of his observations. Conclusions are that: 1) "he works almost entirely from first hand experience, largely uncorrected by subsequent study or learning"; 2) "his observations are typically those of the farmer, the herdsman and the trailer"; 3) "his eye for panorama is better than that for detail, except in those cases in which there is some practical reason for observing detail"; and 4) "he is accurate in what he observes but...his observations would be of little value to a botanist or zoologist."

B390. Boatright, Mody C. [Review of *HG's Early Work and Career* by Donald Pizer.] *South Atlantic Quarterly,* 60 (Winter 1961), 97-99.

Review of HG's career and achievement in connection with Pizer's study.

B391. Walker, Robert H. "The Poets Interpret the Western Frontier." *Mississippi Valley Historical Review,* 47 (Mar 1961), 619-635.

HG's verse is quoted three times (624, 627, 631) in this survey of verse observations on and reactions to Western life.

B392. Pizer, Donald. "Evolutionary Ideas in Late Nineteenth Century English and American Criticism." *Journal of Aesthetics and Art Criticism,* 19 (Spring 1961), 305-310.

HG is one of several critics who relied on "the historical relativism and environmental determinism implicit in the ideas of evolution..." as well as on Herbert Spencer. His reliance on Spencer is documented by a brief analysis of his unpublished "The Evolution of American Thought."

B393. Browne, Ray B. "'Popular' and Folk Songs: Unifying Force in G's Autobiographical Works." *Southern Folklore Quarterly*, 25 (Sep 1961), 153-166.

Traces in the Middle Border books the recurrence of three individual songs and one group of four songs which form basic themes or sub-themes unifying these four works. Music was central to HG's life, and certain songs represented the most compelling drives and emotions in his life on the Middle Border and his writing about that life.

B394. [Review of *HG: A Biography* by Jean Holloway.] *Virginia Quarterly Review*, 36 (Autumn 1961), cxix-cxx.

"Though he was not a great writer, his activities and writings constitute one of the best means by which the student of American culture between the Civil War and World War I can be introduced to the subject."

B395. Matusow, Allen J. "The Mind of B. O. Flower." *New England Quarterly*, 34 (Dec 1961), 492-509.

HG is quoted on his deep respect for Flower's altruism and concern with social progress. Also includes brief discussion of Flower's championing of realism and his association with HG's work which he accepted for the *Arena*.

B396. Fryckstedt, Olov W. "Crane's Black Riders: A Discussion of Dates." *Studia Neophilologica*, 34 (1962), 282-293.

Deals with the difficulty Crane scholars have had in dating Crane's poem. Part of the difficulty stems from the fact that HG is one of the main sources, and his accounts of his meetings with Crane differ in various places. Fryckstedt analyzes HG's accounts of these meetings.

B397. Pizer, Donald. "Evolutionary Literary Criticism and the Defense of Howellsian Realism." *Journal of English and Germanic Philology*, 61 (Apr 1962), 296-304.

Examines the relation of evolutionary thought to literature, especially as a defense of realism, according to the understanding of HG, T. S. Perry, and George Pellew. Discusses HG's unpublished "The Evolution of

American Thought'' as a basis for his defense of
Howells in ''Mr. Howells's Latest Novels'' (*New England Magazine* [May 1890]).

In their argument HG, Perry, and Pellew used two
central ideas in 19th-century thought: ''the material
advances of science and the individual opportunity
and freedom of democracy.''

B398. Daly, J. P., S. J. *''HG's: Rose.''* *The English Language
and Literature* (English Literary Society of Korea), No.
11 (Jun 1962), 51-65.

Most of this article deals with how the reviews of the
1895 edition of *Rose* influenced G in making revisions
in the novel for the 1899 edition. Aside from the minor
stylistic changes G made in the revision, his major al-
terations, in response to many reviewers' objections,
''softened the harshness of the physical and sexual ex-
pressions, omitted the passage referring to the early
love affair of Carl and Rose, and altered the ending substantially with a two-page romantic addition.'' Thus,
G, under the influence of the reviewers, ''was willing
substantially to alter his most sustained effort at veritistic writing into a much weaker semi-romance.''

B399. Stronks, James B. ''Mark Twain's Boston Stage Debut as
Seen by HG.'' *New England Quarterly*, 36 (Mar 1963),
85-86.

Short note on HG's having seen Twain and Cable in
Boston on their reading tour. HG recorded the performance in a ledger he kept at the time (1884) but later
changed the account in *Roadside* (1930), probably because he forgot about the earlier journal. HG praised
Twain's performance.

B400. Lazenby, Walter. ''Idealistic Realist on the Platform: HG.''
Quarterly Journal of Speech, 49 (Apr 1963), 138-145.

Traces HG's career from his first reading of Henry
George's work and his adoption of the single-tax theory
through his public speaking career both for the single
tax and the Populist movement. Brief biography stresses HG's love of public speaking and oratory and his
early years in Boston, where he became a Delsarte

enthusiast. HG's speeches on the single-tax movement used "the poetry rather than the logic of the movement." HG often read his own works, like "Wheel" and
"Member," and his early work "was really inseparable
from the speaking itself," both in its themes and its
"publication to live audiences." *Spoil* throws some
light on HG himself and on his speaking career.

B401. Higgins, John E. "A Man From the Middle Border: HG's
Diaries." *Wisconsin Magazine of History*, 46 (Summer
1963), 294-302.
Excerpted from the diaries are HG's remarks on a
variety of subjects: his mother, his father, his wife,
his daughters, his interest in the automobile, the radio,
and the movies, his writing habits, his political views,
his friendships, and his response to old age.

B402. Mane, Robert. "Une Rencontre Littéraire: HG et Stephen
Crane." *Études Anglaises*, 7 (Jan-Mar 1964), 30-46.
Detailed examination of relationship, professional
and personal, between HG and Crane.

B403. Stronks, James B. "A Realist Experiments with Impressionism: HG's 'Chicago Studies.'" *American Literature*,
36 (Mar 1964), 38-52.
Examination of "Chicago Studies," which has recently
been published. In the mid-nineties "the erstwhile angry
young practitioner of the New Realism was no longer
very angry, nor very young...nor was realism itself any
longer a very fresh impulse." HG began to move from
objective realism to impressionism, and by 1893 he
"thought of impressionism as a special--more vital and
more wholly truthful--kind of realism" though he didn't
understand it fully because he confused painting and
writing techniques.
HG might have been influenced by Stephen Crane, who
was a natural impressionist in his writings.
HG never repeated his "Chicago Studies" experiments.

B404. Durbin, James H., Jr. "Ayot St. Lawrence and the Middle
Border." *Coranto*, 1 (Spring 1964), 3-13.

HG's relationship with George Bernard Shaw is detailed through excerpts from HG's books and through quotations from the cards Shaw wrote HG.

B405. Reamer, Owen J. "G and the Indians." *New Mexico Quarterly*, 34 (Autumn 1964), 257-280.

HG's work treating the American Indian "reveals the man and also his eventual mastery of a clear, effortless narrative prose style, the style of his better known 'Border' series." HG's concern with the plight of the Indians was prompted by his concern for all downtrodden people. He was sensitive to the dilemma of the Indians torn between custom and tradition and the white man's ways.

HG's best story is "The Silent Eaters," in *American Indian*. "It is a simple, straightforward prose, packed with concrete, realistic details, and it flows along unobtrusively as the style of a good story-teller should." HG knew his material. Reamer disagrees with Gronewald's assertions in "The Social Criticism of HG" (Unpublished dissertation; see under "Books") relating to HG's motives for helping the Indians. He was deeply concerned; he even urged President Roosevelt to come to their aid.

B406. Whitford, Kathryn. "Crusader Without a Cause: An Examination of HG's Middle Border." *Midcontinent American Studies Journal*, 6 (Spring 1965), 61-72.

Focuses on the movement of HG's work from the Middle Border to the Far West. A close examination of the Middle Border works reveals that seeds of HG's later romanticism were contained in the early "naturalistic" fiction and that the "swift change in land economics" in the Middle Border forced HG to move west to new frontiers. *MTR* and *Son* show that HG's Middle Border protests and crusades were cultural: "G thus finds himself combating phantoms much of the time. He can emphasize the hardships of toil, of climate, of poverty, but he cannot bring himself to exaggerate the evil qualities in his characters themselves and make the borderers the victims of their own natures or of man's injustice to his fellow man." Because he was part of that

157

life he didn't allow himself to "make their lives sordid
enough to compete with the developing naturalism of
Stephen Crane and Frank Norris."
HG did not fully understand all the implications of
the single tax. "In a real sense the Middle Border failed G by becoming history while he was still in mid-ca-
reer."

B407. Pitzer, Paul C. "HG and Burton Babcock." *Pacific Northwest Quarterly*, 56 (Apr 1965), 86-88.
Discusses HG's relationship with Babcock, a childhood
friend from Iowa who appears in *Son* and who later went with
HG on his Klondike expedition. Later in their lives,
Babcock asked HG for help in acquiring a piece of land
in Washington. HG's letter to Gifford Pinchot, Chief
Forester, is included. HG's attempt failed and Babcock
died in 1911. He "exemplified G's homesteader, and the
hardships he endured were typical; yet G never used this
incident in his published writings."

B408. Saum, Lewis O. "The Success Theme in Great Plains Realism." *American Quarterly*, 18 (Winter 1966), 579-598.
HG's realism in *MTR* and *Jason Edwards* is not totally
pessimistic (586-592).

B409. Roselle, William C. "A HG Letter to Herbert Stuart Stone."
Books at Iowa, No. 4 (Apr 1966), 9-11.
Examines a letter sent by HG to Stone and Kimball in
an attempt to throw light on the relationship between
HG and his publisher. The letter contains comments by
the publishers written in after receiving the letter from
HG, and Roselle examines these comments.

B410. Williams, John Joseph. "HG's 'Sidney Lanier.'" *English
Language Notes*, 3 (Jun 1966), 282-283.
Brief mention of HG's knowledge of Lanier's work and
of Lanier's influence on HG's poetry, which, according
to HG himself, was not to any "marked degree."
HG's early commemorative poem "Sidney Lanier,"
which was later reconstructed by him from memory and
published in the *Southern Bivouac*, is reprinted.

B411. Leonard, Neil. "Edward MacDowell and the Realists."
   American Quarterly, 18 (Summer 1966), 175-182.
   MacDowell, impressed by *CI*, became friends with HG.
   HG made several suggestions to MacDowell about his
   music, and just before MacDowell died, HG moved in
   with him at his hotel. HG was "especially active in
   perpetuating MacDowell's name after his death."

B412. Miller, Charles T. "HG's Retreat from Realism." *Western
   American Literature*, 1 (Summer 1966), 119-129.
   Examination of differences between HG's early fiction
   and the thirteen books published between 1900 and 1916
   in effort to show how, under the pressure to make money,
   HG turned to romantic fiction. "It seems incredible that
   he did not recognize the laxity and diffuseness of plot,
   the sterotyped situations, the naive motivations, the
   shallow characterizations, and the frequently sloppy literary expression of these works. At best, they reverted to
   the earlier local color movement, with its virtues of authentic scenery, dialect, and mannerisms, and with its
   many faults augmented by a responsible writer who, by
   the year 1900, should have known better."

B413. Kirk, Clara M. [Review of *Realism and Naturalism in Nineteenth-Century American Literature* by Donald Pizer.]
   Criticism, 8 (Fall 1966), 398-401.
   Kirk says that HG was "a confused romantic, too
   easily bowled over by the more potent minds he encoun-
   tered too late in his life"; and "the Chicago Exposition
   of 1893, and an invitation to deliver a series of summer
   lectures there, brought into focus the wealth of ideas
   simmering in G's mind."

B414. Pizer, Donald. "HG's Son: An Appreciation." *South Atlantic Quarterly*, 65 (Autumn 1966), 448-459.
   Examines themes and form of the book. HG's "changing relationship with his parents, from rebellion and
   desertion to guilt and rescue, is the narrative and emotional center of the book." This is same theme of "de-
   sertion-guilt-rescue" which appears in "A Branch Road"
   and "Up the Coulé" in *MTR*.

HG was also torn between the West and its hardships (his father) and the East and culture (his mother), which leads to the theme of HG's discovery of self as an artist and as a Westerner. He both loved and hated the West as other writers hated and loved their homes (Joyce, Wolfe, and O'Casey).

Finally, "Much of the force and richness of *Son* stems from G's ability to combine the intensely personal theme of his family conflict with the objective reality of the setting in which it occurs, to combine the personal with a larger cultural theme which emerges out of the setting and thereby to invest the cultural with some of the intensity of the personal." [Rptd in *Essays in American and English Literature Presented to Bruce Robert McElderry*, eds. Max F. Schulz, William D. Templeman, and Charles R. Metzger.]

B415. Pilkington, John. "Henry Blake Fuller's Satire on HG." *University of Mississippi Studies in English*, 8 (1967), 1-6.

Description and analysis of "The Downfall of Abner Joyce," in Fuller's *Under the Skylights*.

B416. Holsinger, Paul M. "HG's Colorado." *Colorado Magazine*, 44 (Winter 1967), 1-10.

Examines HG's work between 1898 and 1914, most of which dealt with Colorado in some way, and gives a brief description of those works, finding *Money Magic* to be "G's most outstanding Colorado work." Though the novels dealing with Colorado aren't great novels, the descriptions in them are often magnificent.

B417. Wertheim, Stanley. "Crane and G: The Education of an Impressionist." *North Dakota Quarterly*, 35 (Winter 1967), 23-28.

HG distorted the facts about his relationship with Crane because he disapproved of Crane's supposed bohemianism. There is evidence, however, that he functioned as Crane's early literary mentor. He read an early draft of *Maggie*, and his subjective conception of truth in art provided Crane with a theory of the novel that is strongly reflected in *The Red Badge of Courage*.

B418. Meyer, Roy W. "HG and the American Indian." *Western American Literature*, 2 (Summer 1967), 109-125.

Detailed examination of HG's trips to Indian country and of his writings, fictional and nonfictional, about Indians. Specific attention is given to *Captain*, to the stories in *American Indian*, and to HG's essay "The Red Man's Present Needs" in the *North American Review* for April 1902. Conclusion is that he was at his best in the essay where he did not need "to create characters and manipulate a plot" and could "plead his case lucidly, often eloquently." But he did not create one memorable character in the fiction and HG's command of language, while "at times characterized by a tension, an economy, and an aptness," is "too often slovenly or turgid or both."

B419. Whitford, Kathryn. "'Miller': HG's Labor Play." *Midcontinent American Studies Journal*, 8 (Fall 1967), 33-42.

"Miller" is important in the history of American letters since it is the only HG play to be produced and since it stands as the "culmination of his long interest in writing for the theater." An "extensive examination of the labor situation," it extends HG's realism later than most critics admit and suggests that HG's "career as a Single Tax advocate has a stronger basis in the plight of labor than has been generally recognized."

B420. Pizer, Donald. "HG (1860-1940)." *American Literary Realism*, 1 (Fall 1967), 45-51.

Bibliographical essay surveying work done on HG to present and indicating areas where further research is needed.

B421. [Katz, Joseph]. "HG's Copy of *The Red Badge of Courage*." *Stephen Crane Newsletter*, 3 (Winter 1968), 10.

Very brief description.

B422. Wertheim, Stanley. "The Saga of March 23rd: G, Gilder, and Crane." *Stephen Crane Newsletter*, 3 (Winter 1968), 1-3.

More on the dating of HG's letter to Gilder recommend-
ing Crane MS. Author considers it unlikely that MS. was
The Red Badge of Courage, thinks it probably was *Maggie*

B423. Monteiro, George. "A Capsule Assessment of Stephen Crane
by HG." *Stephen Crane Newsletter,* 3 (Fall 1968), 2.
Text of late and very short letter to Philip D. Sherman
which "embodies G's ambivalence toward Crane."

B424. Alsen, Eberhard. "HG's First Novel: *Spoil.*" *Western
American Literature,* 4 (Summer 1969), 91-105.
Account of the novel's composition and revision by
HG and brief summaries of its contemporary reception by
reviewers and its later reception by scholars. Latter
seem to agree that *Spoil* fails for two reasons: "first,
because G was more interested in its political than its
artistic success, and, second, because G's realism becomes unconvincing as soon as he leaves the environment of his successful middle border stories." But
Alsen believes that *Spoil* "is a much better novel than
its critics have been willing to see." Its didacticism
"does not become obvious until the last three chapters";
and, even then, the didacticism "is essentially moral
and humanitarian rather than political." HG's "moral
idealism" accounts for "the weaknesses in the delineation of the characters of" Bradley and Ida, who emerge
as "lifeless statues that represent G's view of what human beings ought to be." Only the minor characters,
e.g., Nettie Russel, Judge Brown, and Cargill, are up to
the standards of realism established in *MTR*; but lack of
realism in *Spoil* is "chiefly a matter of characterization,"
not of HG's unfamiliarity with the locales in the second
half of the book. He knew Des Moines and Washington
quite well, and if they appear more unreal and remote,
it may have been intentional on HG's part to show that
Bradley feels "removed from the business of the state
and national legislatures that are described in the second half" of *Spoil.* But, despite its shortcomings, *Spoil*
deserves attention for its "valuable insights into trends
in the American realistic novel and particularly into G's
development as a novelist." Students of American history will also find it of value for its picture of the farmers

revolt and the third party movement in the last three decades of the 19th century. [Rptd as "Introduction" to *Spoil* (Johnson Reprint, 1969).]

B425. Harrison, Stanley R. "HG and the Double Vision of Naturalism." *Studies in Short Fiction*, 6 (Fall 1969), 548-556.
In an attempt to refine the definition of naturalism, "HG presents the vibrations of hope and despair, naturalism's double vision of life and death, in possibly the most complex fashion of all." Harrison uses *MTR* and *Folks* as a basis for his view that, "In the midst of the destructive economic and natural forces that swirl through his short stories, he provides, not one, but three havens of liberation for his prairie folk and main-travelled roaders: they find respite and transcendent wonder in the physical beauty indigenous to the landscape, spiritual satisfaction in their tragic anger and in their own humanity, and hope in the possibility of eventual escape." Harrison concludes, after examining these three havens of hope, that "Despair is the property of naturalism and death is its end, but the celebration of life is its counterpoint; and G held to this double vision of man's existence throughout his Middle Border years."

B426. Wilson, Edmund. "Books: Two Neglected American Novelists--I--Henry B. Fuller: The Art of Making It Flat." *New Yorker*, 46 (23 May 1970), 112-139.
Article deals extensively with Henry Blake Fuller and G is discussed briefly (120) as the subject of Fuller's "The Downfall of Abner Joyce." G is portrayed as the literary climber who forfeits his best talents for the glamor of popularity and social acceptance. Wilson also points out that G and Fuller remained friends through their lives though G was again satirized in "Addolorata's Intervention." Other brief mentions of G and his relationship with Fuller are scattered throughout the article.

B427. French, Warren. "What Shall We Do About HG?" *American Literary Realism*, 3 (Fall 1970), 283-289.
G's work is not artistically important yet he has generated interest because of his personal activities. Discusses *CI* as an example of G's somewhat confused

thought. All of G's writing was never more than "stylish" journalism. French suggests that G's failure as an artist stems in part from his fear of self-analysis which might have led him to a discovery of homosexual or some other deviant tendancies. This suggestion is based on G's vehement defense of established norms after a brief radical period. "The reason that G remains important is not his individuality, but his typicality. What is needed about him is more theories based on significant contemporary speculation before any more facts can be considered in a meaningful perspective." G needs a good psychological study.

B428. Martinec, Barbara. "HG's Revisions of *MTR*." *American Literary Realism*, 5 (Spring 1972), 167-172.

Detailed collation of the six editions of *MTR* which appeared during G's lifetime in effort to show that, contrary to many critics' claims that G diluted the realism of the original texts in subsequent editions, most of the revisions were stylistic. G was trying "to clarify obscure passages, to eliminate incongruities and needless repetitions, to render dialect more accurately, and to reduce sentimentality."

B429. Irsfeld, John H. "The Use of Military Language in HG's 'The Return of a Private.'" *Western American Literature*, 7 (Summer 1972), 145-147.

Brief examination of the use of military terms in the story in attempt to show that such usage adds "to the effectiveness of the larger metaphor of the story that equates man on the midwestern farm in the late middle nineteenth century with a private in the army of the Union during the Civil War."

C. BOOKS AND PARTS OF BOOKS ABOUT HAMLIN GARLAND

C1. Adams, J. Donald. *The Shape of Books to Come.* N.Y.: Viking, 1944. Pp. 27, 45, 47, and passim as indexed.

HG had in his work "a sporadically bitter portrayal of American farm life"; but he later turned to romance, and hence, Adams says, we had no one in America to compare with the skeptical Hardy, Meredith, and Butler. HG's *MTR* and *Folks* were written without his using Zola; for "they derived directly from HG's own experience, from his memory of the drab and bitter fight for existence which life on the expanding frontier had frequently been."

C2. Adams, Oscar Fay. "G, H," in *A Dictionary of American Authors.* 5th ed. rev. and enl. Boston and N.Y.: Houghton, Mifflin, 1905. P. 143.

Very brief sketch. Lists only seven books.

C3. Abernethy, Julian W. *American Literature.* N.Y.: Maynard, Merrill, 1902. Pp. 458, 464.

HG is "a loyal Western author" who "indulges in a prophecy that is significant, even if over-confident." He is a contributor to new literary types developing out of the West.

C4. Ahnebrink, Lars. *The Beginnings of Naturalism in American Fiction/A Study of the Works of HG, Stephen Crane, and Frank Norris with Special Reference to Some European Influences/ 1891-1903.* N.Y.: Russell & Russell, 1961; originally published by Harvard U Press, 1950.

Several large sections of this book are devoted to HG as follows (there is, in addition, extensive scattered mention):

"HG--1860-1940" (63-89): a biographical résumé with an emphasis on the social and economic forces which shaped HG. Also includes brief descriptions of *MTR, Jason Edwards, Member, Norsk, Spoil, Folks, Rose, Wayside, Grant,* and *Goldseekers.*

"HG and *CI*--1894" (135-150): a detailed examination of *CI,* with consideration of philosophy which underlies it and some analysis of reactions to it.

"Zola and G" (233-249): extended comparison of *Jason Edwards* and Zola's *L'Assomoir* and *La Terre.*

"Turgenev and G" (317-328): influence traced in *MTR,* "Wheel," *Jason Edwards, Norsk, Folks,* and, especially, in *Rose.*

"Ibsen and G" influence traced through *MTR, Jason Edwards, Member* (in great detail), *Spoil,* and *Rose.*

"Books of HG in the University of Southern California Library" (415-434): includes 365 items.

"Other Books of HG" (434-437).

"Books of HG Presented by the Author to the Cliff-Dwellers' Club of Chicago" (437-438).

"Lecture Season of 1885-6" (439-440): "Lecture Circular" (440-441); "The Seaside Assembly" (442-443): reprints various publicity materials which list topics HG is prepared to lecture on and the fee expected.

"Extracts from HG's Lecture on 'The Modern Novel'" (444-447); "Extracts from HG's Lecture on 'The Literature of Democracy'" (447-450).

"HG and the First Independent Theater Association" (451-453): prospectus and declaration of aims of the Association, as laid down by HG.

"HG and *Margaret Fleming*" (453-455): reprinted circular of comment by Flower and HG praising play.

"Reading of 'Member'" (455-458): includes program of reading and some excerpts from opinions of the Boston press.

Aikin, Wilford M. See Rankin, Thomas E., and Wilford M. Aiken.

C5. Alsen, Eberhard. "Introduction," *A Spoil of Office.* N.Y. and London: Johnson Reprint, 1969. Pp. v-xxiii.

[Rptd from *Western American Literature*, 4 (Summer 1969), 91-105. See under "Periodicals."]

C6. *American Authors and Books 1640 to the Present Day*, ed. W. J. Burke and Will D. Howe (rev. and aug. Irving R. Weiss). N.Y.: Crown, 1962. P. 272.
   Listing of HG's works, date and place of birth and death.

C7. *American Literary Manuscripts*, ed. Joseph Jones et al. Austin: U of Texas Press, 1960. Pp. 140-141.
   Listing of libraries holding HG materials.

C8. *American Literary Scholarship--An Annual:* 1963, ed. James Woodress. Durham, N.C.: Duke U Press, 1965. Pp. 56, 112.
   Brief descriptions of HG items written in 1963.

C9. *American Literary Scholarship--An Annual:* 1964, ed. James Woodress. Durham, N.C.: Duke U Press, 1966. P. 116.
   Brief descriptions of three HG items in Louis J. Budd's essay on 1964 scholarship on "Nineteenth-Century Fiction."

C10. *American Literary Scholarship--An Annual:* 1965, ed. James Woodress. Durham, N.C.: Duke U Press, 1967. Pp. 129, 137, 234, 267, 276.
   Various items of HG scholarship and criticism are described and, in some instances, evaluated.

C11. *American Literary Scholarship--An Annual:* 1966, ed. James Woodress. Durham, N.C.: Duke U Press, 1968. Pp. 119-120, 145, 163.
   Brief descriptions and evaluations of scholarship and criticism on HG done in 1966.

C12. *American Literary Scholarship--An Annual:* 1967, ed James Woodress. Durham, N.C.: Duke U Press, 1969. Pp. 141, 167, 299.
   Brief descriptions of HG items written in 1967.

C13. *American Literary Scholarship--An Annual:* 1968, ed. J.
Albert Robbins. Durham, N.C.: Duke U Press, 1970.
Pp. 142, 155.
Brief descriptions and evaluations of G scholarship
and criticism done in 1968.

C14. *American Literary Scholarship--An Annual:* 1969, ed. J.
Albert Robbins. Durham, N.C.: Duke U Press, 1971.
Pp. 178-179, 348.
Brief descriptions and evaluations of work done on G
in 1969.

C15. *American Literary Scholarship--An Annual:* 1970, ed. J.
Albert Robbins. Durham, N.C.: Duke U Press, 1972.
P. 202.
Brief descriptions of G scholarship done in 1970.

C16. Andrews, Kenneth R. *Nook Farm/Mark Twain's Hartford
Circle.* Cambridge, Mass.: Harvard U Press, 1950.
P. 227.
Reference to HG, who worked with Charles Dudley
Warner, Twain's collaborator and friend, in forming the
National Institute of Arts, Sciences, and Letters.

C17. Angoff, Alan. *American Writing Today.* Washington Square:
NYU Press, 1957. Pp. 177, 179, 182.
HG helped place the short story "firmly on the map" in
American writing; and it became "in Stephen Crane, HG,
and Jack London (no doubt influenced by Zola) natural-
istic, reflecting the conditions of American Society."

C18. Arnavon, Cyrille. *Histoire Littéraire Des États-Unis.* Paris:
Hachette, 1953. Pp. 268-270 and passim as indexed.
Biographical summary, with sentence or two on several
of HG's books. Comments on "Return of a Private"
specifically but briefly.

C19. ---. *Les Lettres Américaines Devant La Critique Française*
(1887-1917). Paris: Les Belles Lettres, 1951. P. 118.
Brief mention of HG which includes indication of trans-
lations of his works into French and summary of Bentzon's
essay-interview.

C 20.   Arnavon, Daniel J. "Le roman réaliste et naturaliste aux
          États-Unis (1887-1917)." Unpublished dissertation.
          Uniuersity of Paris, 1950.
          Not seen.

C 21.   Arvidson, Lloyd A. "A Bibliography of the Published
          Writings of HG." Unpublished M.A. thesis. U of South-
          ern California, 1952.
          Not seen. Cf. entry immediately following.

C22.   ---,ed. *HG--Centennial Tributes and A Checklist of The
          HG Papers in The University of Southern California
          Library.* USC Library Bulletin No. 9. Los Angeles:
          U of Southern California, 1962.
          Volume includes a "Foreword" (xi-xii) by Lewis F.
          Steig, USC Librarian, explaining how USC came to
          obtain HG's papers; an "Introduction" (xiii-xvi) by
          Bruce R. McElderry, Jr., which gives a brief review of
          HG's career; "Centennial Tributes" to HG by the fol-
          lowing: John Masefield, Gladys Hasty Carroll, Van
          Wyck Brooks, Isabel Garland Lord, Francis Hackett,
          Kathleen Norris, Constance Garland Doyle, Vilhjalmur
          Stefansson, John Farrar, Harold S. Latham, Hermann
          Hagedorn, M. A. DeWolfe Howe, Josephine Lawrence,
          Homer Croy, Witter Bynner, Lee Shippey, Leland D.
          Case, Donald Culross Peattie, August Derleth, Paul
          Jordan-Smith, Garland Greever, Robert E. Spiller,
          Robert Mane, Donald Pizer, and Robert Lowry; and a
          "Checklist of the HG Papers" compiled by Lloyd A.
          Arvidson.

C23.   Asselineau, Roger. *The Literary Reputation of Mark Twain
          from 1910 to 1950/A Critical Essay and A Bibliography.*
          Paris: Marcel Didier, 1954. Pp. 21-22, 76, 125, 127, 129.
          Text of book includes a very brief excerpt from an HG
          comment on Twain (21-22). The bibliography lists five
          items by HG.

C24.   Atherton, Lewis. *Main Street on The Middle Border.* Bloom-
          ington: Indiana U Press, 1954. Pp. 14-22 and passim.
          Mostly a biographical sketch of HG and his family in
          his early years taken from *Son.* Stresses HG's essential

169

rootlessness because of the innumerable migrations of
his family. Suggests that his early fascination with
the visiting circus led naturally to the use of the circus
performer in *Rose.*

C25. Banks, Rev. Louis Albert. *White Slaves or the Oppression
of the Worthy Poor.* Boston: Lee and Shepard, 1892.
P. 318.
Very brief mention: "If one really wants to see what
is behind the great upheaval in the West, which has its
outward manifestation in the Farmers' Alliance, he only
needs to read Mr. HG's *MTR.*"

C26. Barker, Charles A. *Henry George.* N.Y.: Oxford U Press,
1955. Pp. 541, 559, 591-592, and passim.
Briefly mentions HG's single-tax activities in Boston
initiated by his reading of George's *Progress and Poverty* and his acceptance of its theories. Notes that
"Under the Lion's Paw" and "Wheel" appeared in the
Standard and that Herne predicted the latter would be a
great success. Describes *Jason Edwards* as "a none-
too-successful novel of 1892" which was "in large degree a single-tax tract." Brief mention of HG's attempt
to unite literary people in support of George's attempt
to become mayor of New York.

C27. Becker, George J., ed. *Documents of Modern Literary Realism.* Princeton, N.J.: Princeton U Press, 1963. Pp.
137-138.
In headnote introduction to *CI,* Becker points out that
"It was the disparity between farm life on the frontier
as he knew it and the romantic accounts of the West
appearing in fiction that impelled HG to write his...
MTR (1891), which illustrates the drabness and frustration of the farmer's life." HG's veritism "is a clear
expression of the spontaneous desire for realism in a
new country whose life and experience are falsified
and stunted by existing literary conventions." Laments
that "HG did not long pursue the realistic vein, but
turned to polemical, sentimental, or romantic treatment
of western subjects. Whether this was from economic
necessity or innate preference remains a question."

C28.   Beer, Thomas. *The Mauve Decade*. N.Y.: Knopf, 1926.
       Pp. 66, 70, 92, 200, 202.
          HG mentioned as contributor to *Century*, as Populist
       author whose contributions to the *Arena* were "probably
       not read," and as social commentator.

C29.   ---. *Stephen Crane*. N.Y.: Knopf, 1933, originally published
       in 1927. Pp. 77, 84, 107, 228.
          Mentions the HG-Crane relationship. Emphasis on as-
       sistance HG gave Crane at beginning of latter's career.

C30.   Bennett, George N. *William Dean Howells/The Development
       of a Novelist*. Norman: U of Oklahoma Press, 1959. Pp.
       35, 45, 132.
          Brief mentions of HG, generally in connection with his
       views and memories of Howells, especially in Boston.

C31.   Bernard, Harry. *Le Roman Régionaliste Aux États-Unis
       (1913-1940)*. Montreal: Fides, 1949. Pp. 15, 174, 195,
       201, 209, 212, 248, 266.
          Very brief scattered mention of HG, chiefly as a de-
       picter of various regions of the country.

C32.   Berryman, John. *Stephen Crane*. N.Y.: William Sloane, 1950.
       Passim as indexed.
          Discussion of the HG-Crane relationship.

C33.   Berthoff, Warner. *The Ferment of Realism/American Liter-
       ature, 1884-1919*. N.Y.: Free Press, 1965. Pp. 24, 51,
       134-136, and passim as indexed.
          Points out that *Spoil* has "gone the way, to oblivion,
       of most topical writing and editorializing." HG was
       quite earnest but lacked "discriminating intelligence"
       and a "critical (and self-critical) judgment." But when
       he drew on "childhood recollection, he made a genuine
       contribution to the documentary record of American life."
       MTR, *Folks*, *Boy Life*, and *Son* are "nearly artless but
       grounded in unshakeable personal impressions...."

       Bettman, Otto L. See Brooks, Van Wyck, and Otto L.
       Bettman.

C34. Bidle, Kenneth Eugene. "Impressionism in American Literature to the Year 1900." Unpublished dissertation. Northern Illinois U, 1969. [DA, 30 (1969), 715A-716A.]

"G endorsed impressionism because it allowed him to unite his belief in scientific process with his devotion to aestheticism. His finest pieces of writing, *MTR* and *Rose*, excel because of their impressionistic qualities." HG and Crane are the two "first American literary impressionists."

C35. Blair, Walter, Theodore Hornberger, and Randall Stewart, eds. *The Literature of the United States/An Anthology and a History.* 2 vols. Chicago: Scott, Foresman, 1947. II, 609-610.

HG "lacked the deep-rooted convictions and infinite patience that Howells had; he fought with pitchforks and was easily discouraged." His novels "show an increasing command of structure and are perhaps as good as the better magazine fiction of the period," but "not one of them . . . is truly memorable and some are almost gushingly sentimental." His "greatest weakness as a novelist" is "his thin characterization." His autobiographical works make clear that HG was "never really a rebel": "What seemed like revolt was an intensely personal emotional reaction to a particular situation; the true G was respectful of tradition and of success, wherever he found them." [Anthology includes "Mrs. Ripley's Trip" and excerpt from *CI*.]

C36. Blankenship, Russell. *American Literature as an Expression of the National Mind.* N.Y.: Holt, 1958. Pp. 493-497 and passim as indexed.

HG was the first realist to deal with farm life and was concerned with the "harsh realities of life." He "had none of the optimistic philosophy . . . . The new western writer was grim, pessimistic, almost despairing, when he contemplated the fate of man in the struggle against great odds." HG "embodied the first American appearance of an old world pessimistic realism that was to be of great importance in the development of our literature." Suggests that George's and Flower's influence on HG in terms of luring him to the "field of propaganda and re-

form" was partly the cause of HG's later romantic
tendencies.

C37. Bledsoe, Thomas A. "Introduction." *Main-Travelled Roads/
Six Mississippi Valley Stories.* N.Y.: Rinehart, 1954.
Pp. ix-xl.

Begins with sketch of HG's life and career up to writing
of *MTR*. Power of *MTR* lies in "the quality of indignation"
in the stories; for "only when moved by violent moral indignation could HG discard the romantic cliches his fundamentally conventional cast of mind made natural for him."
Thus, "his talent was for short stories and not for novels,
since novels demand intellectual development as well as
emotional intensity, and, for the same reason, for stories
of situation rather than plot."

Spirit of "guilt" informs stories in *MTR*. HG was very
fond of his mother and felt guilty for leaving or neglecting
her. This appears in stories like "Up the Coulé," "A
Branch Road," and "Return of a Private." Each story
is also animated by the basic paradox of "the conflict between Good--man's better nature, the simple beauties of
the land--and Evil, the injustice of society, the grasping
selfishness that speculation fosters, the bitterness of
the struggle with nature which injustice necessitates."

HG was not a naturalist, for "he never wrote without a
sense of individual responsibility"; and "it is against
the backdrop of the American Dream, of the right and responsibility of every man to be free, to succeed, that
G's tragedies display themselves." For HG, "in spite
of the muck and sweat of the farmyard, the universe was
friendly if only man would make it so." "Among the Corn-
Rows," best among the stories in *MTR*, "most delicately
illustrates the tensions of HG's moral universe."

Contrast between *MTR* and *Son* shows *MTR* superior but
is also fruitful for "the insights these separate outgrowths
of the same period in the author's life can give into the
qualities of his work." Contrary to Mencken and others
who see *MTR* as a tract rather than art, the stories show
HG's "genuine talent for ordering his situations to produce a cumulative result, and for developing each of them

in a thoroughly convincing way." "Return of a Private"
is used as an example of this. His characters show a
balance "between inner theme and external reality."
Finally, *MTR*, as a whole, is a unified book, not simply
a collection of related stories: in it HG develops themes
through a planned sequence, just as in the individual
stories. In later editions of the book, he mutilated it by
diluting "its acrid protest"; but this merely parallels
and documents HG's own "conversion from rebellion to
conformity."

This edition also includes a "Textual Note" (xli-xlii)
and a "Bibliographical Note" (xiii-xiv). The latter is a
very brief listing of primary and secondary sources.

C38. Blotner, Joseph. *The Modern American Political Novel/1900-
1960.* Austin: U of Texas Press, 1966. Pp. 27, 42, 43.
Includes brief discussion of *Spoil*: "Artistically the
book was little better than its immediate predecessors,
replete like them with sentimental clichés and catch
phrases, and containing little exploration in depth of
character and motivation." But it also "made use of
radical political theory including new concepts of
wealth and its production. Beyond this, it . . . advocated
not reform within the old system, but revolution through
class warfare" (27).

C39. ---. *The Political Novel.* Doubleday Short Studies in Political Science. Garden City, N.Y.: Doubleday, 1955. Pp.
36, 65.
Spoil is briefly summarized and commented upon in the
chapter on "The Novelist as Political Historian." Blotner concludes, "A sentimental and somewhat superficial
book which substitutes clichés and catch-phrases for
exploration in depth of causes and effects, *Spoil* is valuable for its recital of the farmer's early role in politics--
if one can bear the surfeit of bucolic virtues and inartic-
ulate devotion to a fair and exalted lady." A second
briefer reference to *Spoil* occurs in the "Labor" sub-sec-
tion of the chapter on "The Novelist as Analyst of Group
Political Behavior."

C40. Boas, Ralph Philip, and Katherine Burton. *Social Back-grounds of American Literature.* Boston: Little, Brown, 1937. Pp. 219, 268.
Mention that *Son* appeared during the war years and received little attention at the time. Notes that "Willa Cather . . . , unlike G, did not weaken her work by prolonged reiteration of material."

Boynton, Henry Walcott. See Higginson, Thomas Wentworth, and Henry Walcott Boynton.

C41. Boynton, Percy H. *American Literature.* Boston: Ginn, 1923. Passim.
Very brief mention of HG as post-war novelist who wrote *MTR* in 1891.

C42. ---. *Literature and American Life.* Boston: Ginn, 1936. Passim as indexed.
HG's *MTR* and *Folks* pictured life on the frontier with a "fidelity that startled and offended both East and West--the West because it was grimly true; the East because it discredited a pleasant myth."

C43. ---. *The Rediscovery of the Frontier.* Chicago: U of Chicago Press, 1931. Pp. 80-85, 155, 158, and passim as indexed.
Brief biographical examination. Says of *Son* that "Through the pathos of distance . . . [HG] captured the glamor of pioneering days, their restlessness, the grim tribute of grinding labor they exacted, the heart-rending sacrifices of the women who had no choice but to follow their men and slave for them, the unrewarded lives of the rank and file in the conquering pioneer hosts, the repugnance to it all that capped a boyhood on the Middle Border." HG's reward for this book came in the form of "election to the American Academy of Arts and Letters, small sales, and a royalty check that bought a new bath and a covered porch for his Adirondack cabin . . . ."

C44. ---. *Some Contemporary Americans/The Personal Equation in Literature.* Chicago: U of Chicago Press, 1924. Pp. 185, 232.

Very briefly mentions HG as one of the American writers who supported idea of a national literature.

C45. Bradley, Sculley, Richmond Croom Beatty, and E. Hudson Long, eds. *The American Tradition in Literature.* Rev. ed. 2 vols. N.Y.: Norton, 1962. II, 799-801.

Biographical sketch. HG "remains in literary memory for the enduring value of the early stories of *MTR*, in which he almost unwittingly contributed to early American naturalism, and for the 'Middle Border' series, in which the history of a family of plain people is given historical and human significance."

C46. Brashear, Minnie M. *Mark Twain/Son of Missouri.* Chapel Hill, N.C.: U of North Carolina Press, 1934. P. 59.

Brief comparison of Twain and HG: "Whatever the former touches that is local becomes generalized, of broad human significance; what the latter writes remains local."

C47. Brashers, Howard C. *An Introduction to American Literature for European Students.* Bonniers: Svenska Bokförlaget, 1964. Pp. 105, 121, 126.

Mention of how Howells helped and encouraged HG and how HG in turn supported Crane. HG was "a little less naturalistic than Crane, but no less realistic."

C48. Bridgman, Richard. *The Colloquial Style in America.* N.Y.: Oxford U Press, 1966. Pp. 62, 236, 237.

Brief mention of HG's dialogue: "Writers like HG and Sarah Orne Jewett wrote of essentially domesticated characters and, as a consequence, their dialogue quieted."

C49. Brigham, Johnson. "HG, Pioneer, Reformer and Teller of Tales," in *A Book of Iowa Authors by Iowa Authors,* ed. Johnson Brigham. Des Moines: Iowa State Teachers Assoc., 1930. Pp. 95-108.

Chapter is mainly appreciative plot summaries of several HG books, specifically *Spoil, Rose, Hesper, Son,* and *Daughter.* Emphasis is on Iowa settings.

C50. Briggs, Austin, Jr. *The Novels of Harold Frederic*. Ithaca, N.Y.: Cornell U Press, 1969. Passim as indexed.
Points out that G's and Howe's realism presents young men and women with hopes and dreams, while Frederic's realism is quite different. Several brief mentions.

C51. Brodbeck, May, James Gray, and Walter Metzger. *American Non-Fiction 1900-1950*. Chicago: Regnery, 1952. Pp. 110-111.
Biographical sketch. Notes HG's move from Chicago to New York where he began his "journalistic studies in autobiography." He "exercised the pioneer's skill in improvising a new technique for handling new materials. He had anticipated the regionalists who were to borrow from him a few decades later. His two important interpretations of American life [*Son* and *Daughter*] were among the few vivid works of a period comparatively barren of such interests."

C52. Brogan, Denis William. *American Themes*. N.Y.: Harper, 1949. P. 193 and passim as indexed.
Brief mention of HG's moving to Boston and of his association with the Populists.

C53. Bronson, Walter C. *A Short History of American Literature*. Boston: Heath, 1900. P. 291.
HG described as "more powerful" than Eggleston. *MTR* "pictures with grim realism the hardships of the Western farmer in his monotonous struggle with poverty; ...[HG's] later works, such as *Eagle's Heart* (1900) and *Moccasin Ranch* (1909), are better as stories but have less reality and force."

C54. Brooks, Van Wyck. *The Confident Years/1885-1915*. N.Y.: Dutton, 1952. Pp. 63-84, 163-184, and passim as indexed.
HG followed the realism of Eggleston and Howells in his early work, "though his touch was rather more drastic than theirs had been; and he liked to describe his own method as 'veritism,' or work that could always be verified in comparison with facts." In his early work, HG prepared "the way for the darker school of realism that

was more and more dominant in time throughout the West"
(63-66). Brief reference to HG's relationship with Fuller
in Chicago. Judges *Rose* "the best of G's novels."

C55. ---. *Howells/His Life and World.* N.Y.: Dutton, 1959. Pp.
116, 166-168, 209, 258, 259, 269.
    Mentions the HG-Howells relationship, with emphasis
on their meeting in Boston when Howells urged HG to
write about what he knew and to return to the West. *MTR*
was the result.

C56. ---. *New England Indian Summer/1865-1915.* N.Y.: Dutton,
1940. Pp. 388-389, 466, and passim as indexed.
    Brief mention of HG's move to Boston, his relation
with Howells, and his feeling, along with Miss Wilkins
and Crane, that a realism more drastic than that of
Howells was needed.

C57. ---. *The Writer in America.* N.Y.: Dutton, 1953. Pp. 40, 58.
    HG is quoted on the longevity of American writers'
popularity and relevance: " 'In America, no man and no
thing endures for more than a generation.' " Also mentions mutual influences of Cather, Rölvaag, Veblen, and
HG on each other.

C58. ---, and Otto L. Bettman. *Our Literary Heritage/A Pictorial
History of the Writer in America.* N.Y.: Dutton, 1956.
Pp. 181-200.
    Critical observations are drawn from *The Confident
Years.*

C59. Brown, Deming. *Soviet Attitudes Toward American Writing.*
Princeton, N.J.: Princeton U Press, 1962. P. 242.
    Mention of HG as one of "first writer-realists who
stepped forth at the end of the last century" and founded
"the general stream of American radical petty bourgeois
literature."

    Burton, Katherine. See Boas, Ralph Philip, and Katherine
Burton.

C60. Cady, Edwin H. *The Realist at War.* Syracuse, N.Y.: Syracuse U Press, 1958. Pp. 142-144 and passim.
Examines HG-Howells relationship and suggests that "There can be little doubt that if G had hewed to that line [Howells' realism] instead of whoring off after *Captain* and, eventually, spiritualism, his would have been a much greater achievement." Points out that "The key to an understanding of G, or at least of his relations with Howells, seems to be the recognition of a tension between G's devotion to Howells and what he stood for and a more natively congenial Midwestern adaptation by G (much like Vachel Lindsay or Carl Sandburg after him) of the gospel according to Walt Whitman."

C61. ---. *The Road to Realism.* Syracuse, N.Y.: Syracuse U Press, 1956. Pp. 12, 87, 230, 232.
HG "found *The Undiscovered Country* in a frontier store in Osage, Iowa, in 1881 and discovered a new mode in literature" (230).

C62. ---. *Stephen Crane.* N.Y.: Twayne, 1962. Pp. 35, 71, 103, and passim as indexed.
Mentions HG as Crane's discoverer and literary mentor.

C63. Cairns, W. B. *A History of American Literature.* N.Y.: Oxford U Press, 1932. Pp. 484, 501, 504-505.
States that "realism was a natural reaction against romanticism, and as practiced by Howells, James, and G was consistent with the older systems of religious and philosophic faith." HG was "the most important local color writer of the Middle West." Suggests that the "reason for the comparative failure of men like Harte, Page, and HG as novelists may be that there is no necessary connection between the quick observant power needed to gather picturesque material and the organizing ability needed to construct a plot on a large scale."

C64. C[allaway], H. L. "G,H." *Cassell's Encyclopaedia of World Literature.* 2 vols. N.Y.: Funk and Wagnalls, 1953. II, 1793.

HG wrote with "mordant realism about the poverty and drabness of prairie life in the period when pioneer hopes were proving false."

C65. Calverton, V. F. *The Liberation of American Literature.* N.Y.: Scribner's, 1932. Pp. 42-48 and passim.
HG was one of the first to reflect a growing pessimism caused in part by the "closing of the frontier and the disappearance of the freedom and autonomy of the West." What HG's work "lacked in structural and aesthetic excellence, it compensated for in social significance."

C66. *The Cambridge History of American Literature*, eds. William Peterfield Trent, John Erskine, Stuart P. Sherman, Carl Van Doren. 3 vols. in one ed. N.Y.: Macmillan, 1943. II, 363, 388, 390; III, 76, 92, 919.
Brief mention of HG in Carl Van Doren's Vol. III essay, "The Later Novel: Howells," and in Fred Lewis Pattee's "The Short Story" in Vol. II. Pattee mentions *MTR* briefly but with praise.

C67. Campbell, Walter S. *The Booklover's Southwest/A Guide to Good Reading.* Norman: U of Oklahoma Press, 1955. Pp. 115, 243, 251.
Annotated checklist that includes HG's *American Indian* and *Captain*. Attacks HG's own "veritism" by accusing him of not caring or knowing very much about Indians, warfare, or adventure.

C68. Canby, Henry Seidel. *Classic Americans.* N.Y.: Harcourt, Brace, 1959. P. 4.
HG's *Son* is a "narrative of settlement" in the tradition of Captain John Smith's *True Relation*.

C69. Cantwell, Robert. *Famous American Men of Letters.* N.Y.: Dodd, Mead, 1956. Pp. 178-179, 187.
Brief biographical sketch and critical note. HG's work "lacked excitement and drama. Indeed, it is only . . . a poignant quality, a suppressed poetic fervor, that lifts HG's work above a drab portrayal of the commonplace."

C70. Cargill, Oscar. *Intellectual America/Ideas on the March.*
N.Y.: Macmillan, 1941. Pp. 82-89, 735.
HG is important for his impressionism, what he called
veritism. Although he approached naturalism, he never
acquiesced to sordidness and animalism. HG, in "The
Return of a Private," is indebted to Hardy's *Return of
the Native.* His novel closest to naturalism is *Rose,*
which is, however, "amateurish and disappointing, perhaps because it promises more than it fulfills."

C71. ---, ed. *The Social Revolt/American Literature from 1888 to
1914.* N.Y.: Macmillan, 1933. Pp. 4, 5, 52, 594.
Reference to HG as contributor to *Arena,* as author of
MTR, "the most provocative volume placed in the hands
of the public up to that time," as the sounder of "the
death-knell of the dream of an agrarian democracy," and
as discoverer of Crane.

C72. Carter, Everett. *Howells and the Age of Realism.* N.Y.:
Lippincott, 1954; rptd Archon Books, 1966. Pp. 18,
120-121, and passim as indexed.
Howells was HG's "master...from whose lips he received the word about realism in literature." HG's
MTR "almost singlehandedly exploded the myth of the
West as the Garden of America.... It was a work...
which expressed the sad spirit of the rural Northwest
from the experiences of one who had been part of what
he saw." Both Howells and HG found the techniques of
the impressionist painters to be like their own in "the
ignoring of photographic representation in favor of
emphasizing those visual aspects which could suggest
the truthful aspect of the complex whole."

C73. Cella, Charles Ronald. "Two Reactions Against the Stero-
type of the Old-Fashioned Girl in American Novels, 1890-
1920." Unpublished dissertation. U of Kentucky, 1968.
[DA, 30 (1969), 1553A-1554A.]
Rose is expressive of HG's implicit rejection of the
"old-fashioned girl" in that the heroine exhibits a conflict "between mind and animal instincts." neither of
which characterized the type. But HG evidently "could

not resolve the conflict in favor of the New Girl without allowing his portrait to incorporate" the old-fashioned girl's "innate purity and sentimental love."

C74. [Center, Stella C.] "HG," in *Prairie Song and Western Story*, ed. Stella C. Center. Boston: Allyn and Bacon, 1928. Pp. 343-346.
This special edition of selections from HG's works, "made in cooperation with the author," for junior high school readers, includes a "Preface" (iii-iv), the above-cited biographical note, "Questions and Topics for Study," a "Word List," and a "Reading List."

C75. Chamberlain, John. *Farewell to Reform/The Rise, Life and Decay of the Progressive Mind in America*. N.Y.: Liveright, 1932. Pp. 95-104, 116-118, and passim.
Traces HG's literary career and refutes his rebel status, suggesting that he was like wax, easily moved by others, and that he was "humorless, idealistic and sentimental," and lacked all power of self-criticism. He was lucky to meet some great minds early in his career, which saved him from "the banality of outlook that gradually usurped his character as he grew older in years." Examines most of HG's works and points out that "For a literary pattern of the Populist revolt" one should look at *MTR*, *Son*, *Rose*, and *Spoil*.

C76. Christman, Henry M. "Introduction," *A Son of the Middle Border*. N.Y.: Macmillan, 1962. Pp. v-xii.
General discussion of social, economic, and political environment surrounding and influencing HG's work. "Just as [Sinclair] Lewis focused a searing light on America's small towns, G stripped away the false aura of romanticism which had pervaded portrayals of rural life."

C77. Chubb, E. W. "HG's Literary Beginnings," in *Stories of Authors*. Freeport, N.Y.: Books for Libraries Press, 1968. Pp. 358-360.
Frank G. Carpenter's interview of HG reveals the influence of Hawthorne and the genesis of HG's first story

"Lost in the Norther." Chubb says, "His vivid descriptions of Western farm-life are not the results of reading and casual observation, supplemented by a vivid imagination; they are the products of actual experiences."

Cleaton, Allen. See Cleaton, Irene and Allen.

C78. Cleaton, Irene and Allen. *Books and Battles/American Literature, 1920-1930.* Boston: Houghton Mifflin, 1937. Pp. 60, 190.

Casual references to HG as a conservative who favored literary censorship and who contributed to the later, restyled "Humanist organ,"*The Bookman.*

C79. Clough, Wilson O. *The Necessary Earth/Nature and Solitude in American Literature.* Austin: U of Texas Press, 1964. Pp. 156, 174, and passim as indexed.

Notes that Howells stirred young men "to look more sharply at their own environment; men like Norris, Stephen Crane, and HG, who exhibited in their output a compound of American idealism, western scenery, and the ironies of man pitted against impersonal, larger-than-human forces."

C80. Coan, Otis W., and Richard G. Lillard. *America in Fiction/ An Annotated List of Novels that Interpret Aspects of Life in the United States.* Stanford, Calif.: Stanford U Press, 1956. Pp. 10, 16, 37, 131, 172.

Various HG novels are listed in different categories, e.g., *Rose* under "Grass," *Cavanaugh* under "Mountain and Desert," *MTR* and *Prairie Folks* under "Farm and Village Life--The Middle West," *Spoil* under "Politics and Public Institutions--The Nineteenth Century," and *Captain* and *American Indian* under "Minority Ethnic Groups--The Indian."

C81. Cole, Cyrenus. *A History of the People of Iowa.* Cedar Rapids, Iowa: Torch Press, 1921. Pp. 443, 499-503.

Quotes from *Son* to show the hardships of Midwest life, where sentiments and feelings were repressed by men and

HG's consequent emotional turmoil which finally led
him to his mother, who was a symbol of culture and the
East.

HG struck the "first great note" in Iowa literature,
and his early writings were "Populism turned into realistic literature." Brief discussion of *MTR* and hint of
annoyance that HG painted a one-sided picture of Iowa,
which was really "a region of natural beauty" containing
"men and women who abounded in generosity."

C82. ---. *Iowa Through the Years.* Iowa City, Iowa: State Historical Society of Iowa, 1940. Pp. 387-388, 475, and
passim as indexed.

Brief biographical sketch of HG and his family stating
that he blamed family troubles "more on the laws of
man than on the laws of nature." He became a radical
realist who insisted on dealing with the grim aspects
of life, and his uncompromising realism was a "taint"
on his writing. Suggests he moved away from his early
ultra-realism in *Son,* which in many parts deals with
Iowa.

C83. ---. *I Remember, I Remember/A Book of Recollections.*
Iowa City, Iowa: State Historical Society of Iowa, 1936.
Pp. 213-214.

Memories of HG's appearance on literary scene with
MTR, which Cole remembers having criticized for what
he then thought was HG's excessively harsh picture of
Iowa farm life.

C84. Commager, Henry Steele. *The American Mind/An Interpretation of American Thought and Character Since the
1880's.* New Haven, Conn.: Yale U Press, 1950. Pp.
60-61.

"Typical of them all [Howe, Kirkland, Frederic, and
Norris], both for what he saw and for what he failed to
see, for the bitterness of his revolt and for its incon-
clusiveness, was HG." Brief comment on *MTR* and
statement that *CI* was "more remarkable for moderation
than for iconoclasm."

C85. *Concise Dictionary of American Literature,* ed. Robert Fulton
     Richards. N.Y.: Philosophical Library, 1955. P. 92.
     Brief sketch of HG's life and career.

C86. Cooke, Delmar Gross. *William Dean Howells/A Critical
     Study.* N.Y.: Dutton, 1922. Pp. 3, 77, 242.
     HG quoted as approving of Howells' desire to abolish
     discipleship and pupilage. Howells quoted on HG's
     handling of erotic themes. HG mentioned for calling
     Bartley Hubbard "the modern substitute for a villain."

C87. Cowie, Alexander. *The Rise of the American Novel.* N.Y.:
     American Book, 1948; 1951. Pp. 537, 552, 699, and
     passim as indexed.
     HG's local-color stories "evoke a strong sense of
     place, but his people are often on the move--generally
     for economic reasons." This questioning of the in-
     justice of the social order is somewhat inimical to the
     local-color story. HG was a follower of Howells, who
     "spread and exemplified the gospel of realism" and
     who aimed his attacks "at human betrayers of mankind,"
     separating himself, therefore, from the pure naturalism
     of the Zola type.

C88. Cowley, Malcolm. "Foreword: The Revolt Against Gentility,"
     in *After the Genteel Tradition/American Writers/1910-
     1930,* ed. Malcolm Cowley. Carbondale: Southern Illinois
     U Press, 1964; originally published by Norton, 1937.
     Pp. 3-20.
     Roger Burlingame of Charles Scribner's rejected an
     early HG novel because of its " 'slang, profanity, vul-
     garity, agnosticism, and radicalism.' " HG founded
     Cliff Dwellers. Sinclair Lewis accused HG of going to
     Boston and becoming " 'cultured and Howellized.' "

C89. ---. "Naturalism in American Literature," in *Evolutionary
     Thought in America,* ed. Stow Persons. New Haven,
     Conn.: Yale U Press, 1950. Pp. 300-333.
     Brief reference to Spencer's influence on HG's thought.

C90. Crawford, Bartholow, Alexander C. Kern, and Morriss H.
     Needleman. *American Literature.* College Outline Series.

3rd. ed. N.Y.: Barnes & Noble, 1953. Pp. 204-207.
Brief account of HG's career, followed by division
of it into three parts: "Early Period: Realism (1887-
1894)"; "Middle Period: Romance (1895-1916)"; and
"Final Period: Autobiography (1917-1940)." Short
summaries of major works of each period are included.

C91. Crouch, Lora, comp. *HG/Dakota Homesteader.* Sioux
Falls, S. Dak.: Dakota Territory Centennial Commis-
sion, 1961.
This 61-page pamphlet reprints HG's "Foreword"
and "HG--A Biographical Sketch" from the text of
the 1939 *Hamlin Garland Memorial* (see below). It
also contains: "Preface" (3-5) by Lora Crouch;
"Drifting Crane," a short story from *Indian* (35-43);
and seven HG poems of life in Dakota. The selections by HG are prefaced by brief "Compiler's Notes."
The pamphlet is illustrated with photographs and
facsimiles of manuscripts; and the editor adds (57-
61) a list of "Major Writings of HG."

C92. Cunliffe, Marcus. *The Literature of the United States.*
Baltimore, Md.: Penguin Books, 1961. Pp. 185, 202-
204, and passim as indexed.
Usual biographical sketch (202-204) suggests that
HG was "perhaps never entirely wholehearted in his
realism" and that he abandoned it later for "spiritualism" (185).

C93. *Current Biography, 1940,* ed. Maxine Block. N.Y.: Wilson,
1940. Pp. 324-326.
Extended summary of HG's life and career.

C94. *Cyclopedia of World Authors,* ed. Frank N. Magill. N.Y.:
Salem Press, 1958. I, 403-405.
A listing of HG's "Principal Works" is followed by
biographical sketch which contains brief estimates of
HG's major works (*MTR* is "one of the most important
books in American literary history"; *Rose* is his "best
novel"), and a short list of "Bibliographical References."

C95.   Deegan, Dorothy Yost. *The Stereotype of the Single Woman in American Novels/A Social Study with Implications for the Education of Women.* N.Y.: Columbia U King's Crown Press, 1951. Pp. 138, 148, 153.
        Brief discussion of Ida Wilbur, reform-minded young woman in *Spoil.* Also mention that *Rose* is one of the first novels to present the woman of talent in America.

C96.   de Mille, Anna George. *Henry George/Citizen of the World,* ed. Don C. Shoemaker. Chapel Hill: U of North Carolina Press, 1950. Passim as indexed.
        Brief mention of HG as follower of George, contributor to the *Standard,* and supporter of George's New York mayoral race.

C97.   Dennis, Charles H. *Eugene Field's Creative Years.* N.Y. and Garden City, N.Y.: Doubleday, Page, 1924. Pp. 130-136 and passim as indexed.
        Focuses on HG's friendship with Fields. Reprints excerpts from Field's Chicago *Daily News* columns that relate the course of a rather minor literary "controversy." Field and Mrs. Mary Hartwell Catherwood are on the side of romance, and HG is on the side of what he called "realism or veritism or sincerity or Americanism (at bottom these words mean practically the same thing)."

C98.   De Voto, Bernard. *Mark Twain's America.* Boston: Little, Brown: Houghton Mifflin, 1951. P. 35.
        Brief mention of HG in connection with the musical quality of Western Americans.

C99.   Dick, Everett. *The Sod-House Frontier/1854-1890/A Social History of the Northern Plains from the Creation of Kansas and Nebraska to the Admission of the Dakotas.* N.Y. and London: Appleton Century, 1937. Pp. 186, 483, 485, and passim as indexed.
        HG's *Son* provides some of the "popular psychology in the eighties" and is used to illustrate the few contacts Mid-westerners had with culture, primarily through the county fairs and travelling vendors.

C100. Dickason, David H. "The Contribution of B. O. Flower and the *Arena* to Critical Thought in America." Unpublished dissertation. Ohio State U, 1940.
Not seen.

C101. Dickinson, A. T., Jr. *American Historical Fiction.* N.Y.: Scarecrow Press, 1958. Pp. 70, 185.
Brief mention of fictionalized meeting of Grant and HG's father in *Trail Makers.*

C102. Dickinson, Thomas H. *The Making of American Literature.* N.Y.: Century, 1932. Pp. 639-641.
"The man who inaugurated the new movement of realism and social revolt in American literature is HG. His later retreat during a portion of his life from the ideals of his youth does not invalidate his title as the first of the realists." Biographical sketch.

C103. Dietrichson, Jan W. *The Image of Money in the American Novel of the Gilded Age.* N.Y.: Humanities Press, 1969. Pp. 301-302, 311.
Mention of Howells' review of *MTR* (301-302) and of HG's unsuccessful efforts to win Howells over to the single tax.

C104. Dodd, Loring Holmes. *Celebrities at our Hearthside.* Boston: Dresser, Chapman & Grimes, 1959. Pp. 126-130.
Reminiscence about HG which says of *MTR*, "The best story in it and one of the most perfect in all American literature is 'Mrs. Ripley's Trip.'"

C105. Dondore, Dorothy Anne. *The Prairie and the Making of Middle America/Four Centuries of Description.* Cedar Rapids, Iowa: Torch Press, 1926. Pp. 316-324 and passim as indexed.
HG gives in his work "not only the fullest presentation but the most satisfying explanation of the ironic paradox that has caused the Middle West, a region celebrated since its discovery in the most hyperbolic terms ... to be the source of our harshest literary realism."

In *CI,* HG "promulgates the code of the realist, proclaiming the local novel as the most promising and sincere of the literary attempts of the day." Long discussion of *Son* as a record of HG's critical theory and his best creative work. *MTR, Other MTR,* and *Folks* "form next to *Son* his most significant work." *Norsk* and *Rose* are flawed in their structure and sentimentality.

C106. Duckett, Margaret. *Mark Twain and Bret Harte.* Norman: U of Oklahoma Press, 1964. Pp. 291-295 and passim as indexed.

HG liked Harte because of his leadership "in the local-color movement, which G considered the most vital development of our literature." Also mentions that HG met Twain, as well as Harte, in London in 1899.

C107. Duffey, Bernard. "HG," in *The Chicago Renaissance in American Letters/A Critical History.* [East Lansing]: Michigan State College Press, 1954. Pp. 75-89 and passim as indexed.

Detailed biographical examination of HG. His life "From the first . . . had in it the elements of conflict and contradiction which were to determine its course throughout." A tension in HG centered on his love for and rejection of the West. Howells' encouragement to use the realistic method "had for him the inestimable advantage of being the only literary technique by which he could hope to use his knowledge of western life" and still retain his connections with the city and culture. Part of HG's problem was his continual desire to be accepted as a writer and to become a literary success on the one hand, and his social reformer tendencies on the other. Duffey sees HG as a "major symbol among the mid-western authors of his time," torn between a utilitarianism which he got from his farm life and a desire to write. He finally gave himself over to the genteel tradition, an act which caused his literary downfall because that tradition was "imaginatively sterile."

Duffey tries to show that HG's final departure from realism was caused by his desire for money, prestige . and a solid identity. He was, in other words, an opportunist.

C108. Duncan, Hugh Dalziel. *The Rise of Chicago as a Literary Center from 1885 to 1920/A Sociological Essay in American Culture.* Totowa, N.J.: Bedminster Press, 1964. Pp. ix-xii, 5, 19, 30-32, 38, 61-63, 69, 78-79, 87, 104-109, 117, 129, 136-138, 141, 147, 172, 179-180.
Considerable scattered mention of HG as one of the leaders in the Chicago Renaissance in the arts. Emphasis is on HG's attempt to make Chicago another Boston, with the latter's genteel and decorous ways.

C109. Dunlop, George Arthur. *The City in the American Novel 1789-1900.* Philadelphia: Privately printed, 1934. Reissued New York: Russell & Russell, 1965. Pp. 64-65.
In *Jason Edwards* (1897), "the impression left upon the reader of the sordidness of poverty in the city and its almost certain federation with crime is a vivid one painted with all the author's powers of Realism." In his novels HG represented poverty "descriptively, rather than through the narrative."

C110. Earley, Jane Frances. "An Edition of HG's 'Miller of Boscobel.'" Unpublished dissertation. Northwestern U, 1969. [DA, 30(1970), 2964A.]
Introduction to text includes history of manuscript and details of 1909 production. Play put into context with "Wheel" and "Member" and "offers proof that HG's realistic period of writing did not end in 1896 . . . but instead extended into the twentieth century." Appendices include fragments of other stages of the play and an actor's script from a 1909 performance.

C111. Edell, Harold. "HG and the *Arena.*" Unpublished M.A. thesis. New York U, 1935.
Not seen.

C112. Edener, Wilfried. *Die Religionskritik in Den Romanen Von
    Sinclair Lewis.* Heidelberg: Carl Winter, 1963. Pp.
    47-52.
    HG is mentioned (47) in section on "Von Hamlin
    Garland bis Henry L. Mencken," in chapter entitled
    "Kapitel: Amerikanische Religionskritik von Sinclair
    Lewis."

C113. Edwards, Herbert Joseph. "The American Controversy
    Over Realism in Fiction (1875-1905)." Unpublished
    dissertation. Ohio State U, 1930.
    Not seen.

C114. ---, and Julie A. Herne. "HG," in *James A. Herne/The
    Rise of Realism in the American Drama.* Orono, Maine:
    U of Maine Press, 1964. Pp. 45-56, 63-69, and passim
    as indexed.
    Biographical sketch of HG's years in Boston; his
    championing of realism under his mentor Howells; his
    economic and political ties with Henry George; and his
    relation with B. O. Flower and the *Arena.* Detailed
    examination of G's interest in the theater in Boston in-
    stigated in part by his contact with the works of Ibsen,
    especially *A Doll's House,* which he saw in 1889. He
    admired Ibsen except in his treatment of women, which
    points up "the gulf that lay between continental realism
    and the American realism of the Post-Civil War period.
    Behind the American novelist or dramatist was a dif-
    ferent tradition--Puritanism . . . and optimism born of
    America's unexampled opportunity and prosperity."
    There were always limits for HG in his realism beyond
    which he would not venture.
    Also a close examination of the HG-Herne relationship.
    HG often read stories from *MTR* to Herne who knew
    "they were masterpieces of realism" but who, of course,
    could not have known that they were "the finest things
    G was ever to do, the most genuine, and the most typical
    of his true talent as a writer. . . ." HG introduced Herne
    to Ibsen's works and to the single-tax theories of George.
    HG is referred to several times as the unofficial press
    agent for Herne's *Margaret Fleming.* He did succeed in

filling the theater for opening night with all of his
literary and intellectual friends in Boston (63-69).

Edwards, Herbert W. See Horton, Rod W., and Herbert W.
Edwards.

C115. Elias, Robert H. *Theodore Dreiser/Apostle of Nature.*
N.Y.: Knopf, 1949. Passim as indexed.
HG commented favorably on *Sister Carrie,* and Dreiser
visited the Cliff Dwellers in Chicago.

C116. Ellis, Milton, Louise Pound, and George Weida Spahn, eds.
A College Book of American Literature. 2 vols. N.Y.:
American Book, 1940. II, 668-670.
Brief biographical sketch with listing of HG's books
and of works about him precedes "Under the Lion's
Paw."

C117. Ernst, Morris L., and William Seagle. *To the Pure/A Study
of Obscenity and the Censor.* N.Y.: Kraus Reprint,
1969; originally published by Viking Press, 1928. Pp.
42, 223.
Brief mention. Although HG's remarks about sex-
obsession in modern literature were often quoted by
the N.Y. Society for the Suppression of Vice, in 1896
there was serious talk of suppressing HG's own *Rose.*

C118. Ewing, Mary Jane, ed. *HG--As West Salem Knew Him.*
West Salem, Wis.: West Salem Journal, 1951.
This brief pamphlet is basically a biographical presentation, with some personal reactions to HG by West
Salem people. The "Preface" (3) reports HG's birth
in West Salem and his later return. Pages 5-27 narrate
the Garland family's move to West Salem (Much of the
material drawn from *Trail Makers*) and HG's life (based
on *Son*). The study attributes parts of *Moccasin Ranch*
and "Old Pap's Flaxen" to West Salem experiences
(1883-1884) and notes that while *MTR* was praised in
the East by Howells and others, it was attacked by
Western reviewers because of its grim pictures of the
West. Chronological record of HG's life and works appears on pages 28-29.

C119. Falk, Robert P. "The Literary Criticism of the Genteel Decades: 1870-1900," in *The Development of American Literary Criticism*, ed. Floyd Stovall. Chapel Hill: U of North Carolina Press, 1955. Pp. 113-157.
In brief scattered comments HG is linked with Howells and H. H. Boyesen as a critic who mixed "idealization of the commonplace" and "a powerful strain of the romantic." Includes a description and analysis of *CI* (139-141) which "dramatized the distinction between the native realism of Howells and the greater objectivity and scientific discipline of Henry James and the French school."

C120. ---. "The Rise of Realism, 1871-1891," in *Transitions in American Literary History*, ed. Harry Hayden Clark. Durham, N.C.: Duke U Press, 1953. Pp. 410, 430, 434, 435, 437, 438, 440.
HG saw the seeds of a vital and original literature in people like Cable, Harris, Eggleston, Jewett, Wilkins, and Harte. He moved to a militant realism; his " 'Veritism' contained the seeds of ardent social reform, and, like Bellamy, [he] combined a realism of subject material with an intensified idealism for greater economic justice."

C121. ---. *The Victorian Mode in American Fiction/1865-1885*. [East Lansing]: Michigan State U Press, 1965. Passim as indexed.
HG "found localism to be the key to the realistic trend" (163) leading to a vital and democratic literature.

C122. Ferguson, Delancey. "Garland, (Hannibal) Hamlin," in *Encyclopedia Americana*. International Edition. N.Y.: Americana, 1969. XII, 294.
Brief review of HG's life and career.

C123. ---. *Mark Twain/Man and Legend*. N.Y.: Russell & Russell, 1965. P. 15.
Twain's Hannibal, Missouri, "cannot be interpreted in terms of that rebellion against village and farm which began with Ed Howe in the 1880's and HG in the 1890's."

C124. Field, Eugene. *Sharps and Flats*. N.Y.: Scribner's, 1900.
I, 47-51.
Reprinting of Field's 27 Jul 1893 newspaper column
attacking HG's realism and the bad influence of
Howells on HG.

C125. Fiske, Horace Spencer. "*MTR* by HG," in *Provincial Types
in American Fiction*. N.Y.: Chautauqua Press, 1903;
Port Washington, N.Y.: Kennikat Press, 1968. Pp.
179-207. See also pp. 150-151.
Chapter on *MTR* consists entirely of long summaries--
with much quoted material--of "A Branch Road," "Return of a Private," and "Mrs. Ripley's Trip." Fiske's
introductory remarks (150-151) note that the volume
"shows a penetration and a knowledge and a sincerity
of sympathy that make . . . [HG's] work vital and effective, even if at times it seems to be too regularly keyed
to misery and hopelessness."

C126. Flanagan, John T., ed. *America is West/An Anthology of
Middle Western Life and Literature*. Minneapolis: U of
Minnesota Press, 1945. P. 265.
"Under the Lion's Paw" and "Color in the Wheat"
are reprinted in this anthology, the former preceded
by a brief, essentially biographical, note: "Although
much of G's work is mediocre, he has an assured place
in the development of American realistic rural fiction."

C127. ---. *James Hall/Literary Pioneer of the Ohio Valley*. Minneapolis: U of Minnesota Press, 1941. Pp. 141, 149.
Hall was less complete than HG, Howe, and Kirkland
in "his delineation." He was a "frustrated realist"
while HG was a "thwarted romantic."

C128. ---. "A Soil for the Seeds of Literature," in *The Heritage
of the Middle West*, ed. John J. Murray. Norman: U of
Oklahoma Press, 1958. Pp. 198-233 and passim as
indexed.
HG discussed on pp. 209, 214, 217, 218. In HG and
others "the realistic movement reached a triumph.
Not only did such writers treat landscape, characters,
and action with fidelity, but they also introduced themes

which had been previously neglected or untouched."
HG and Kirkland "widened the scope of fiction and
gave it a more solid grounding in reality."

C129. Flory, Claude R. *Economic Criticism in American Fiction.*
Philadelphia: U of Pennsylvania Press, 1936. Pp.
119-121, 146-147, 222-223, 247.

HG was the most important writer of economic criticism dealing with the problems of rural America. *Folks*
expresses HG's ideas on economic reform based on
George's single-tax doctrine. Briefly commenting on
MTR, *Spoil*, *Norsk*, and *Rose*, Flory judges *MTR* and
Folks the best of HG's work. *Rose* "lacks the atmosphere of inevitability that contributes greatly to the
strength of his earlier fiction of western farm life."
HG's "pen was not without the knowledge of romance
but when he wrote from the soul he was a consummate
realist, a reformer whose argument was truth."

C130. Flower, B. O. *Progressive Men, Women, and Movements of
the Past Twenty-five Years.* Boston: New Arena, 1914.
Pp. 24, 62, 76, 105, 128, 131, 153-154, 274, 276, 285,
286.

HG told Flower how much George's *Progress and Poverty* meant to him. Flower asserts that HG "gave new
and wonderfully vivid pen-pictures of the hard life of
the prairie farmers" and that he began his literary career with the *Arena*. *Member* reveals HG's belief that
common folks were incapable of solving their own problems. HG's later metaphysical speculations provided
a "paradox in method" for both him and Flower because
of "the intuitionism of the occult versus the empiricism
of secular conceptions of social reform."

C131. Foerster, Norman. *American Criticism.* N.Y.: Houghton
Mifflin, 1928. P. 223.

HG and others ushered in "the realism of the early
twentieth century" which was "hostile to the essentials
of ... [Walt Whitman's] creed."

C132. Folsom, James K. *The American Western Novel.* New Haven, Conn.: College and University Press, 1966.

Pp. 149-160, 180-184, and passim as indexed.

Rather extensive examination of HG's *American Indian*, especially the story "The Silent Eaters." HG felt that the Indians had to accept the white man's ways in order to survive, but he was not insensitive to the difficulties of this acceptance. In "The Story of Howling Wolf" HG puts aside his optimism; "The parable of history in this story resembles that in the Leatherstocking Tales. Change is certain, but it does not represent progress; history records the frustration of hope." Zane Grey echoes HG's "concern over the future of the Indian..." but is often inept in doing so.

Folsom says that HG is "probably the most interesting granger novelist...the bitterness of whose work recalls the pessimism of Howe's view of the rural utopia rather than the often bland critique of Herbert Quick"; but the "bitterly ironic view that the hope for a better life in the West is in its nature self-contradictory is by no means limited, among granger novelists, to G."

C133. Foner, Philip S. *Mark Twain Social Critic*. N.Y.: International Publishers, 1958. P. 262 and passim as indexed.

HG mentioned along with numerous others, including Twain, as one who opposed all "wars for plunder."

C134. Foster, Richard Allen. *The School in American Literature*. Baltimore, Md.: Warwick & York, 1930. P. 132 and passim as indexed.

Suggests that T. B. Aldrich's *The Story of a Bad Boy* (1869) was a forerunner of HG's *Boy Life* and that the work of Horace Bennett anticipated HG's pictures of the humble life.

Franchere, Hoyt C. See O'Donnell, Thomas F., and Hoyt C. Franchere.

C135. French, Warren. *Frank Norris*. N.Y.: Twayne, 1962. Pp. 31, 127.

HG was one of few established writers with whom Norris was intimate and one of very few people who lamented Norris' premature death in print.

C136. Frost, John Eldridge. *Sarah Orne Jewett.* Kittery Point,
Me.: Gundalow Club, 1960. P. 155.
HG is listed as a local-color writer.

C137. Fryckstedt, Olov W. *In Quest of America/A Study of
Howells' Early Development as a Novelist.* Cambridge,
Mass.: Harvard U Press, 1958. P. 265 and passim as
indexed.
HG praised *A Modern Instance* as a great novel.

C138. Fujii, Gertrude Sugioka. "The Veritism of HG." Unpublished dissertation, U of Southern California, 1970.
[DAI, 31 (1970), 2914A.]
"The purpose of this study is to delineate the principal elements of veritism, identify its influences, and
show its relationship to G's work and to the development of literary criticism."

C139. Fuller, Henry B. "The Downfall of Abner Joyce," in
Under the Skylights. N.Y.: Garrett, 1969. Pp. 3-139.
Satirical sketch of HG.

C140. Fullerton, B[radford] M. *Selective Bibliography of American Literature 1775-1900.* N.Y.: William Farquhar
Payson, 1932. Pp. 111-112.
Brief summary of HG's career and worth followed by
listing of first editions of *MTR, Folks,* and *CI.*

C141. Fussell, Edwin. *Frontier/American Literature and the
American West.* Princeton, N.J.: Princeton U Press,
1965. P. 439.
Whitman could never keep HG's name straight. He
wrote to HG telling of his love of the West and his
desire for HG to write about it.

C142. Gabriel, Ralph. *The Course of American Democratic Thought.*
N.Y.: Ronald, 1940. P. 255.
HG was a realistic writer who "was a humanitarian"
and who "exposed frontier poverty."

C143. Garson, Helen Sylvia. "The Fallen Women in American Naturalistic Fiction: From Crane to Faulkner." Unpublished dissertation. U of Maryland, 1967. [DA, 28 (1968), 5052A.]

HG, "an optimist, saw woman as strong enough to resist the corrupting influences of the environment."

C144. Garvey, Bernadette M. "HG's Relationship to the Naturalistic Movement." Unpublished dissertation. St. John's (Brooklyn) U, 1942.

Not seen.

C145. Geismar, Maxwell. *The Last of the Provincials*. Boston: Houghton Mifflin, 1947. P. 7 and passim as indexed.

Mencken was not at all impressed with HG's work (7).

C146. ---. *Rebels and Ancestors/The American Novel, 1890-1915*. Boston: Houghton Mifflin, 1953. P. 405 and passim as indexed.

Brief notes concerning HG-Crane relationship and statement that HG was an important influence on the course of the new realistic movement in literature.

C147. Gerber, Philip L. *Theodore Dreiser*. N.Y.: Twayne, 1964. P. 125 and passim.

HG refused to defend Dreiser's *The "Genius"*; he "charged the entire movement with being 'a piece of very shrewd advertising' promulgated by the John Lane Company."

C148. Gibson, Donald B. *The Fiction of Stephen Crane*. Carbondale: Southern Illinois U Press, 1968. Pp. 50-51.

HG accurately judged Crane's *George's Mother* as an experiment of a young author and not much more.

C149. Gilkes, Lillian. *Cora Crane/A Biography of Mrs. Stephen Crane*. Bloomington: Indiana U Press, 1960. Pp. 28, 267-268, and passim as indexed.

Crane's novels were enjoyed by readers "who were addicted to the new realism championed by William Dean Howells and HG."

Mentions correspondence between HG and Cora concerning HG's praise of Crane's work and points out
that in one of his letters Crane expressed great pleasure at having met and become the friend of HG.

---. See also Stallman, R. W., and Lillian Gilkes.

C150. Gohdes, Clarence. *Bibliographical Guide to the Study of
the Literature of the U.S.A.* 3rd. ed. Durham, N.C.:
Duke U Press, 1970. P. 65.
   HG's volumes of reminiscences--*Roadside, Companions,
Contemporaries,* and *Neighbors*--are listed under "Gen-
eral Histories."

C151. ---. "The Later Nineteenth Century," in *The Literature of
the American People,* ed. Arthur H. Quinn. N.Y.: Appleton-Century-Crofts, 1951. Pp. 648-651.
   "Kirkland's efforts to tell the truth, though not all the
truth, supplied encouragement to the most important of
the realistic depicters of the Middle West during the
eighties, namely, HG." *CI* is a "collection of rather
shallow critical essays . . . a volume which indicates the
strong influence exerted upon . . . [HG] by the local
colorists." *Rose* was "honest apprentice work in the
manner of Howells."

Gray, James. See Brodbeck, May, James Gray, and Walter
Metzger.

C152. Greenbie, Marjorie Barstow. *American Saga/The History
and Literature of the American Dream of a Better Life.*
N.Y.: McGraw-Hill, 1939. Pp. 31, 270, 368, 595-596,
601.
   HG's autobiographical works tell "the whole social
history" of the state of Wisconsin. HG was "touched
by the grace of New England, more sweetly articulate
than Howe," and "his protest was divided between the
old protest of the pioneer against debt and land speculation, and the new protest that life is sour till we have
culture equal to material opportunity."

C153. Griffin, Constance M. *Henry Blake Fuller*. Philadelphia: U of Pennsylvania Press, 1939. Pp. 39, 60, 75.
HG ''sounded the approach of naturalism with his book of essays, *CI* (1893).'' He was the figure satirized by Fuller in ''The Downfall of Abner Joyce,'' but he still valued Fuller's judgment ''above any save [that of] Howells.''

C154. Groman, George L. ''Introduction,'' *Political Literature of the Progressive Era*, ed. George L. Groman. [East Lansing]: Michigan State U Press, 1967. Pp. xi-xxii.
HG is the only one of many Populist writers of fiction who is ''remembered today'' (xvii). In *Member*, he ''anticipated the popular Progressive technique of using well-publicized political scandal as a basic plot device. Also, as in much of later Progressive-era fiction, he pictured a political reformer with strong moral convictions who might look forward to a satisfying and successful life.''

C155. Gronewold, Benjamin F. ''The Social Criticism of HG.'' Unpublished dissertation. New York U, 1943.
Not seen.

C156. Hahn, Emily. *Romantic Rebels*. Cambridge, Mass.: Riverside, 1967. P. 94 and passim as indexed.
Howells supported HG's attempts at realism ''when G produced grim stories 'exposing' the drabness of Middle West life.''

C157. Halleck, Reuben Post. *The Romance of American Literature*. N.Y.: American Book, 1934. Pp. 245-246 and passim as indexed.
HG's father's early migrations ''etched the hardships of the wilderness upon his son's youthful mind and made him a realist.'' HG's stories ''display a sterner truth to life than Howells sought''; and ''his stories of crude, cramping communities anticipate the work of Sinclair Lewis and other twentieth-century critical realists.''

Books and Parts of Books

C158. *HG Memorial.* Written by The Federal Writers' Project of the Works Progress Administration in South Dakota. American Guide Series. 2d ed. Mitchell, So. Dak.: South Dakota Writers' League, 1939.

This 33-page pamphlet, originally published in 1936, includes a "Preface" (3-5) by Lisle Reese; "Foreword" (7) by HG; and "HG--A Biographical Sketch" (9-33). The latter emphasizes HG's Dakota connections and includes numerous quoted passages from *Son* and other works drawn from his experiences in Dakota.

C159. *HG/A Son of the Middle Border.* N.Y.: Macmillan, 1927.

This 38-page promotional brochure issued by HG's publishers includes the following:

"HG" (3-7): appreciation of HG, which quotes from citation of honorary degree he received at U of Wisconsin in 1926 and gives preview of *Trail Makers,* soon to be published.

"HG--The Hardy of the West" by Joseph Edgar Chamberlin (9-20): rptd from Boston *Transcript* (see under "Periodicals").

"A Son of the Middle Border" by William Dean Howells (21-33): very abridged version of *N.Y. Times Book Review* piece (see under "Periodicals").

"Three Generations" by Henry B. Fuller (25-28): rptd review of *Daughter* from the *Freeman* (see under Periodicals").

"The G-McClintock Saga" by Carl Van Doren (30-31): rptd review of *Daughter* from *Nation* (see under "Periodicals").

"An English View of the Middle Border" (33-34): rptd review of *Son* from London *Times* (see under "Periodicals").

"Notable Comments" [on *Son*] by Theodore Roosevelt (36-37) and Edwin Markham (37).

C160. Haney, John Louis. *The Story of our Literature/An Interpretation of the American Spirit.* Rev. ed. N.Y.: Scribner's, 1939. Pp. 269-270, 381.

Brief account of HG's career, with mention of several books. Very general.

201

C161. Harkins, Edward F. "HG," in *Little Pilgrimages Among the Men Who Have Written Famous Books*. Boston: Page, 1901. Pp. 247-261.

   Biographical survey essentially. Includes list of literary topics that HG used during his two years of teaching and lecturing in the East after graduating from Cedarville Academy. HG "occupies a unique place in American literature, for not only has he sounded a new, vibrant chord in our literature, but he also has been our one fearless and unchangeable literary impressionist."

C162. Harlow, Alvin F. *Bret Harte of the Old West*. N.Y.: Julian Messner, 1943; rptd, 1963. Pp. 280-281.

   Recounts HG's meeting with Harte in England.

C163. Harris, Elbert Leroy. "HG's Use of the American Scene in His Fiction." Unpublished dissertation. U of Pennsylvania, 1959. [DA, 20 (1960), 3742-3743.]

   Attempt "to find out how HG obtained his knowledge of the American scene, to discover what he knew about it, to explore the extent of his use of it, and to depict how he translated his knowledge into his fiction." Thesis concludes "that during the major portion of his literary career, G was a romanticist, that he was influenced in varying degrees by Howells, Kirkland, Flower, and Fuller; that his environment was a paramount factor in the creation of all his fiction; that the use of the American scene and its many pertinent problems is negligible; that he was indebted to Henry George's *Progress and Poverty* for his social philosophy; that social criticism is poor in the fiction but is good in the unpublished notes."

C164. Hart, James D. *The Oxford Companion to American Literature*. 4th ed. N.Y.: Oxford U Press, 1965. Pp. 306, 974.

   Biographical sketch and list of almost all HG's work with comments tracing movements represented. HG's early efforts combined "objective realism and ethical romanticism." Chronological index concluding volume contains HG dates.

C165. ---. *The Popular Book/A History of America's Literary Taste.* N.Y.: Oxford U Press, 1950. P. 169.
Very brief mention of *Jason Edwards* and *Spoil,* "novels of social inquiry" of 1880's and 1890's containing "proposed specific remedies."

C166. Hartwick, Harry. *The Foreground of American Fiction.* N.Y.: American Book, 1934. Pp. 143, 339-340, and passim as indexed.
HG in *CI* "wanted to smash the old Gods" and to acquire freedom, truth, and individual expression. Hartwick notes HG's connections with Howells, Whitman, and Henry George, and comments on Sinclair Lewis' indebtedness to HG.

C167. *Harvard Guide to American History,* ed. Oscar Handlin et al. Cambridge, Mass.: Belknap Press, 1954; rptd 1963. Pp. 179, 241, 433, 461, 464.
Under "Personal Records" (179-184), HG's autobiographical and literary acquaintance books are listed.
Under "Select List of Historical Novels and Short Stories" (238-243), *MTR, Norsk, Rose,* and *Captain* are listed.
Under "Lands and Agriculture, 1862-1880" (415-416), *Son* and *Boy Life* are listed as source works for a study of the financial problems of the time.
Under "The Farmers' Revolt and National Politics, 1889-1900" (429-432), *Son* is listed as a source work.

C168. Hatcher, Harlan. *Creating the Modern American Novel.* N.Y.: Farrar and Rinehart, 1935. Pp. 13, 277.
HG wrote about the realities of the Middle West.

C169. Hazard, Lucy Lockwood. *The Frontier in American Literature.* N.Y.: Crowell, 1927. Pp. 261-268 and passim as indexed.
HG is the first "actual farmer in American fiction." His natural repugnance to farm life and resentment of it "color the 'realism' with which he puts into his fiction those aspects of farm life which had been most disagreeably real to him." But more significant is his concern with the strength of the men who face great

forces and still survive, as "he sees in the defeat of
his pioneer father the collapse of traditional American
idealisms." HG's work is compared with de Crevecoeur's.
"G and Norris, in telling of the defeat of the farmers on
the last frontier, have viewed the defeat as an economic
tragedy."

C170. ---. *In Search of America.* N.Y.: Crowell, 1930. P. 551 and
passim as indexed.
Mencken judged *Son* to be "amateurish, flat, banal,
and repellent."

C171. Henson, Clyde. *Joseph Kirkland.* N.Y.: Twayne, 1962.
Pp. 93-97 and passim as indexed.
The HG-Kirkland relationship began when HG read
Zury. Kirkland saw HG as one "who wanted to reform
all literature by reconstructing it on a realistic basis,"
and he influenced "G to turn to the writing of fiction
in order to depict actual farm life."

C172. Herne, Julie A. "Biographical Note," in James A Herne,
Shore Acres and Other Plays, ed. Mrs. James A. Herne.
N.Y.: Samuel French, 1928. Pp. ix-xxix.
Brief mention (xviii-xix, xxi-xxii) of HG's friendship
with Herne. HG is credited with bringing about Herne's
"conversion to the Single Tax."

---. See Edwards, Herbert J., and Julie A. Herne.

C173. Herron, Ima Honaker. *The Small Town in American Drama.*
Dallas, Texas: Southern Methodist U Press, 1969.
Passim as indexed.
Multiple insignificant glancing references to HG and
his relationship to other writers of the time. His reaction to Herne's "radical" *Margaret Fleming* is detailed (186).

C174. ---. *The Small Town in American Literature.* Durham, N.C.:
Duke U Press, 1939. Pp. 218-226, 273-277, and passim
as indexed.
Detailed biographical examination. HG "wanted to
tell the truth and call attention to the hard lives of the

prairie folk," but his realism is "a romantic-realism."
HG fell from his early realism to romanticism after
1902 with the publication of *High Trails*. In spite of
lapses, "G at times cultivated a limited realism pic-
turing certain isolated settlements of the Mountain
West. . . ." He always retained realistic touches especially in his presentation of characters.

C175. Hicks, Granville. *The Great Tradition/An Interpretation
of American Literature Since the Civil War*. Rev. ed.
N.Y.: Biblo and Tannen, 1967. Pp. 143-148 and passim
as indexed.
Emphasis is on HG's progress from a highly successful protest writer in his early fiction (they are "the
finest stories yet written of American farm life--direct,
comprehensive, moving, and savagely honest") to the
complacent non-controversial writer of romantic magazine fiction in which "the rebel had vanished," and
autobiographical volumes, "each one a step to greater
comfort and a more impeccable standing." On p. 280,
a comparison is suggested between HG and Glenway
Wescott: like HG, Wescott "knew what the fruits of
pioneering were because he had tasted them," but he
"felt none of G's early desire to transform the conditions he detested" and "felt from the first what G
came soon enough to feel, the desire to escape."

C176. Hicks, John D. "The Development of Civilization in the
Middle West, 1860-1900," in *Sources of Culture in the
Middle West/Backgrounds Versus Frontier*, ed. Dixon
Ryan Fox. N.Y.: Russell & Russell, 1964; 1st pub. by
Appleton-Century, 1934. Pp. 73-101.
Very brief mention of HG (94) as writer produced by
Middle West in latter half of 19th century.

C177. ---. *The Populist Revolt*. Minneapolis: U of Minnesota
Press, 1931. P. 4.
HG named the Mid-West the Middle Border.

C178. Higginson, Thomas Wentworth, and Henry Walcott Boynton.
A Reader's History of American Literature. Boston:
Houghton Mifflin, 1903. Pp. 254-255.

In *MTR* "the vigor of characterization carries one
away from the first moment to the last, and the figures
seem absolutely real." HG's "earlier tales have much
of the ironical compactness of de Maupassant."

C179. Hilfer, Anthony Channell. *The Revolt from the Village/
1915-1930.* Chapel Hill: U of North Carolina Press,
1969. Pp. 18-19, 22, 39, 42-48, 84.
Mention (18-19) of G's story "God's Ravens" as a
"supremely saccharine apotheosis of Midwestern folksi-
ness" but emphasis (42-48) on G as a revealer of "the
drabness and sterility of Midwestern farm and town life"
as seen in *MTR.* Several stories from *MTR* are analyzed
briefly and Hilfer concludes that G "is not a chronicler
of the buried life so much as a life in which the only
emotion, sometimes a quite open one, is that of weary
despair."

C180. Hill, Eldon C. "A Biographical Study of HG from 1860 to
1895." Unpublished dissertation. Ohio State U, 1940.
[Ohio State University--*Abstracts of Doctoral Dissertations*, No. 34 (1940), 215-220.]
Not seen.

C181. ---. "Garland, [Hannibal] Hamlin," in *The Reader's En-
cyclopedia of American Literature.* N.Y.: Crowell, 1962.
Pp. 372-374.
Extensive summary of HG's life and career.

C182. [Hippensteel, H. S.] "HG," in *Wisconsin Authors and their
Works*, ed. Charles Ralph Rounds. Madison, Wis.: Parker
Educational Co., 1918. Pp. 1-2.
Brief sketch of HG's life and career as preface to se-
lections from his work.

C183. Hoffman, Daniel G. *The Poetry of Stephen Crane.* N.Y. and
London: Columbia U Press, 1957. Pp. 5, 39, 176.
HG asserted that Crane's poetry seemed to be a case
of "automatic writing." "The Reformer" was probably
"written at HG's suggestion, for the more established
writer had sent some of Crane's newspaper sketches to
B. O. Flower for republication...."

C184. Hoffman, Frederick J. *The Modern Novel in America 1900-1950*. Chicago: Henry Regnery, 1951. P. 7.
In writing of James, Hoffman states that "HG had insisted that a novelist could do no more or less than portray truthfully and honestly conditions which a politician might conceivably move to remedy or improve."

C185. ---. *The Twenties/American Writing in the Post War Decade*. N.Y.: Free Press, 1965. Passim as indexed.
The young Bohemians of the twenties were no longer directed by HG's veritism (41).

C186. Hofstadter, Richard. *The Age of Reform*. N.Y.: Knopf, 1955. Pp. 186, 197, and passim as indexed.
Connects muckrakers and realistic novelists: "Now, while novelists were replacing a literature bred out of other literature with a genre drawn from street scenes and abattoirs or the fly-specked rural kitchens of HG's stories, the muckrakers were replacing the genteel travel stories and romances of the older magazines with a running account of how America worked."

C187. ---. *Social Darwinism in American Thought/1860-1915*. Philadelphia: U of Pennsylvania Press, 1944. P. 21.
Very brief mention of Herbert Spencer's influence on HG.

C188. Holaday, Clayton A. "Joseph Kirkland: Biography and Criticism." Unpublished dissertation. Indiana U, 1949. Not seen.

C189. Holloway, Jean. *Edward Everett Hale/A Biography*. Austin: U of Texas Press, 1956. P. 213.
Quotes from *Son* concerning HG's meeting Hale and receiving assistance from him when he first came to Boston.

C190. [---.] "G,H," by JMH, in *Encyclopaedia Britannica*. Chicago: Encyclopaedia Britannica, 1966. IX, 1146.
Brief summary of HG's life and writing career.

C191. ---. *HG/A Biography*. Austin: U of Texas Press, 1960.

Intention is to "present in chronological sequence the genesis and composition of G's various works and the critical reactions of his contemporaries, including only sufficient references to modern controversies to give point to the narration."

C192. Holman, C. Hugh, comp. *The American Novel Through Henry James*. Goldentree Bibliographies. N.Y.: Appleton-Century-Crofts, 1966. Pp. 30-31.
Listing of primary and secondary materials related to HG. Twenty-five critical essays (including two by HG) are included.

C193. Horton, Rod W., and Herbert W. Edwards. *Backgrounds of American Literary Thought*, 2d ed. N.Y.: Appleton-Century-Crofts, 1967. Pp. 258, 282.
Brief mention of HG as critic (282) and as fictionist (258) who "was a trail-blazer who enabled subsequent writers to portray life in America with far greater strength and veracity than formerly."

C194. Hough, Robert L. *The Quiet Rebel/W. D. Howells as Social Commentator*. Lincoln: U of Nebraska Press, 1959.
P. 113 and passim as indexed.
Howells supported HG's *MTR*, which was "a realistic though austere picture of life on the prairie farms of the Midwest."

C195. Howard, Leon. *Literature and the American Tradition*. Garden City, N.Y.: Doubleday, 1960. P. 227-228.
Of all the realists, HG "was the most acutely conscious of the economic forces which made life, as he had known it, on the western plains, so drab." He was an "ardent Spencerian" and was greatly influenced by the single-tax system of George. His stories had "a vividness of realistic detail"; however "there was no great power in G's thought, and he was easily diverted to the artificial romances which became so popular at the end of the century."

C196. Howells, Mildred, ed. *Life in Letters of William Dean Howells*. 2 vols. N.Y.: Russell & Russell, 1968.

Both vols., passim as indexed.
Letters from Howells to HG on various subjects, mostly literary, are reprinted. HG is also mentioned in other letters.

C197. Howells, William Dean. "Introduction," *Main-Travelled Roads*. N.Y. and London: Harper, 1899. Pp. 1-6.
[Rptd from *Harper's*, 83 (Sep 1891), 638-642. See under "Periodicals."]

C198. ---. *Literature and Life*. Port Washington, N.Y.: Kennikat Press, 1968; originally pub. by Harper, 1902. Pp. 176, 186, 296.
Howells describes HG as Chicago-centered writer of "genuine and original gift," as zealous follower of Henry George's Single Tax agitation, and as writer of Northwest who "expressed the sad circumstances . . . in his pathetic idyls, colored from the experience of one who had been part of what he saw."

C199. Hubbell, Jay B. "HG--1860-1940," in *American Life in Literature*. Rev. ed. 2 vols. N.Y.: Harper, 1949. II, 378-380.
Biographical summary precedes "Up the Coolly." HG "is a reformer, not a sentimentalist. Artistically, his work is too often clumsy, even crude; but his fundamental honesty and his depth of feeling enable him to write with force and vividness and sometimes with beauty."

C200. ---. *The South in American Literature 1607-1900*. Durham, N.C.: Duke U Press, 1954. Pp. 407n, 847.
HG read Moncure Conway's *Autobiography* and in *Contemporaries* expressed his feeling that writers romanticized the South.

C201. Hutton, Graham. *Midwest at Noon*. Chicago: U of Chicago Press, 1946. P. 219.
Very brief mention of HG.

C202. Inge, M. Thomas, ed. *Agrarianism in American Literature*. N.Y.: Odyssey, 1969. Pp. 108-109, 383.

.Includes (108-109) comment on the political background of ''Under the Lion's Paw'' and (383) a biographical note on G.

C203. *Iowa/A Guide to the Hawkeye State.* Compiled and Written
by the Federal Writers' Project of the Works Progress
Administration for the State of Iowa. American Guide
Series. N.Y.: Hastings House, 1949. Pp. 132-133, 373.
  Brief biographical sketch. *Boy Life* is a ''sincere and
vivid account'' of HG's early years. *MTR* ''set a new
standard of realism in the treatment of American farm
life on the Frontier.'' *Son* contains some of HG's
''finest writing.''

C204. Izzo, Carlo. *Storia Della Letteratura Nord-Americana.*
Milan: Nuova **Acoademia**, 1957. Pp. 401, 428, 450-
454, 458, 465, 515.
  Summary (450-454) of HG's life and career, with brief
paragraph on major works.

C205. Johnson, Jane. ''Introduction,'' *Crumbling Idols.* Cambridge,
Mass.: Belknap Press, 1960. Pp. ix-xxviii.
  In *CI* we see ''G as an impassioned propagandist but
not as a wholly original thinker.'' HG belongs to the
''gentler school of realism'' where heroic people exist
in hopeless hardship. His position on realism was much
like that of Howells and those who ''felt that the truthful depiction of American life presented a scene more
healthy, fortunate, and moral than other literatures af-
forded.'' For HG ''it was the responsibility of the novelist to depict not only society's wrongs but also man's
finer nature struggling toward an inevitably brighter day.''
The influence of Whitman on HG is also indicated.
Textual note, xxix-xxxi.

C206. Johnson, Merle. *High Spots of American Literature/In Three
Parts/Part I.* N.Y.: Bennett Book Studios, 1929. P. 35.
  Pioneer Mother (1922) and *MTR* (1891 ed.) are listed.

C207. Jones, Howard Mumford. *Guide to American Literature and
Its Backgrounds Since 1890.* Cambridge, Mass.: Harvard
U Press, 1959. Pp. 147-148, 212.

HG was a "soft naturalist" as opposed to Bierce,
Crane, and Dreiser. *CI* is "an imperfect theory of
fictional naturalism." Lists HG's works which are
naturalistic in part and which "seek improvement in
the social and political order" *(MTR, Spoil, Folks,
Rose,* and *Jason Edwards)* and those which are examples of 20th-century autobiography *(Son, Daughter,
Trail Makers,* and *Back-Trailers).*

C208. ---. "Realism in American Literature," in *The American
Story/The Age of Exploration to the Age of the Atom,*
ed. Earl Schenck Miers. N.Y.: Channel Press, 1956.
Pp. 275-279.
Brief mention of HG as realist associated with Howells
and Norris. HG and Norris give importance to "sexual
energy," an element that Howells "tended to soft-pedal."

C209. ---. *The Theory of American Literature.* Ithaca, N.Y.:
Cornell U Press, 1965. Pp. 124-125.
HG's views on literary independence and American
literary history are quoted.

C210. Kaplan, Justin. *Mr. Clemens and Mark Twain/A Biography.*
London: Jonathan Cape, 1967. Pp. 260, 354-355.
HG held a high opinion of Twain as opposed to Cable
with respect to their performances. HG met with Twain
and Harte in England.

C211. Karolides, Nicholas J. *The Pioneer in the American Novel,
1900-1950.* Norman: U of Oklahoma Press, 1967. P. 275.
HG had little influence on frontier fiction of the first
two decades.

C212. Kazin, Alfred. *On Native Grounds.* N.Y.: Harcourt, Brace,
1942. Pp. 16-17, 36-38, and passim as indexed.
HG was a "vigorous pioneer realist," and it is to
HG and other "primitive realists . . . that contemporary
literature in America owes the paramount interests that
have dominated it for fifty years, and the freedoms it
takes for granted." *CI* was HG's "naturalist manifesto,"
and HG was one of the first to create "a modern literature of protest in America."

However, HG "identified himself with realism so completely" that one often forgets that he "had a dreary mind and pedestrian talent." He was more concerned with actions than with art and saw realism as "a guide to action" and as something "utterly remote from its possibilities as a craft, or even as a philosophy of letters." Nevertheless, his importance to American letters is not to be overlooked.

C 213. Keiser, Albert. "Travelling the White Man's Road," in *The Indian in American Literature*. N.Y.: Oxford U Press, 1933. Pp. 279-292.
    This book is dedicated to HG and discusses *American Indian*. HG dealt realistically and sympathetically with Indian problems. His knowledge came from direct experience. HG is a "realist who desires to complete the history of the border" and believes that "truth and moderation alone can paint the picture worthy of a great and magnificent subject, the passing of a once powerful race."
    HG's "most systematic fictional study of the red man trying to walk the white man's road under difficult circumstances is found in *Captain*, 1902, a powerful novel and quite generally accepted by reviewers as a truthful presentation of life on an Indian reservation in the nineties."

C 214. Kindilien, Carlin T. *American Poetry in the Eighteen Nineties*. Providence, R.I.: Brown U Press, 1956. Pp. 137-142 and passim as indexed.
    Biographical approach to the realistic themes in HG's poetry. Although *Songs* is somewhat diluted by "sentimental hack work," the realistic emphasis serves to make it the "finest volume of poems written about the region in the nineties."

C 215. Kirk, Clara Marburg. *W. D. Howells and Art in His Time*. New Brunswick, N.J.: Rutgers U Press, 1965. Pp. 211-215, and passim as indexed.
    HG accepted as his literary guide Howells' *Criticism and Fiction*. Both men believed that "art and literature belong to the common man, and that they must come to

grips with truth, no matter how many idols crumbled in the quest.''
Summarizes HG's ideas on realism, veritism, and impressionism.

C216. ---, and Rudolf Kirk. *William Dean Howells.* N.Y.: Twayne, 1962. Pp. 114, 123, 124, 130, 131, 135, 142, 154, 211, 212.
Scattered brief mention of HG's comments on Howells, his association with Howells, and other points of contact between the two men and their work.

Kirk, Rudolf. See Kirk, Clara M., and Rudolf Kirk.

C217. Knight, Grant C. *American Literature and Culture.* N.Y.: Long and Smith, 1932. Pp. 354-356, 396.
The best story in *MTR* is "Up the Coolly." *Rose* ''proved too shocking for the nineties but was followed by others like *Captain* (1902) which could offend no one but which will leave no mark upon American letters.''

C218. ---. *The Critical Period in American Literature.* Chapel Hill: U of North Carolina Press, 1951. Pp. 48-62, 101-105, and passim as indexed.
MTR ''did not break utterly with the Genteel Tradition-- G was never to do that--but it did inch closer to such a rupture than any other important American writing had come by that date.'' In ''Up the Coolly,'' a story in *MTR*, HG rejected ''all temptations to compromise with romanticism,'' and he ''proved himself a genuine realist by bringing 'Up the Coolly' to an unorthodox but satisfying end.'' *CI* is very much like Howells' *Criticism and Fiction*.

C219. ---. *The Strenuous Age in American Literature.* Chapel Hill: U of North Carolina Press, 1954. P. 27, 224, and passim as indexed.
Later in his career HG abandoned ''his *MTR* themes and became allied with a group of more romantic midwestern writers like Octave Thanet, William Allen White, and Booth Tarkington.'' HG's veritism prepared the way for the sociological emphasis in American literature.

213

C220. Kolb, Harold H., Jr. *The Illusion of Life/American Realism as a Literary Form.* Charlottesville: U Press of Virginia, 1969. Pp. 11, 141-142.
Brief mention (142) of *MTR* with emphasis on the non-specific and epic nature of the volume.

C221. Kramer, Dale. *Chicago Renaissance.* N.Y.: Appleton Century, 1966. P. 7.
"The trouble with Fuller and G as possible leaders of a peculiarly Midwestern or even Chicago movement was that neither was a wholehearted realist either as an artist or as an individual."

C222. Kramer, Sidney. *A History of Stone & Kimball and Herbert S. Stone & Co. With a Bibliography of their Publications-1893-1905.* Chicago: Norman W. Forgue, 1940. Pp. 11, 17-19, 46, 66, 71-72, 88-89, 197-198, 207, 233-234.
HG's books "were the rock on which the firm [of Stone & Kimball] was securely founded." They published *MTR* (1893 ed.), *CI* (1894), *Rose* (1895), *Folks* (1895). How HG came to have them publish his books is explained. HG is quoted passim about Stone & Kimball; and his books are listed and bibliographically described in the bibliography appended to this book.

C223. Kranendonk, A. G. Van. *Geschiedenis Van De Amerikaanse Literatur.* Amsterdam: Van Oorschot, 1946. Pp. 310-318.
Very brief general mention.

C224. Krause, Sydney J. *Mark Twain as Critic.* Baltimore, Md.: Johns Hopkins Press, 1967. Pp. 17, 262.
Very brief mention of HG, who had a common interest with Twain in realism.

C225. Labrie, Rodrique Edward. "American Naturalism: A View From Within." Unpublished dissertation. Pennsylvania State U, 1964. [DA, 26 (1965), 1044.]
Study traces the evolution of American naturalism as seen in "the critical writings, autobiographical works, and personal correspondence" of HG, Crane, Norris, and Dreiser.

C226. Lawton, William Cranston. *American Literature.* N.Y. and Chicago: Globe School Book, 1902. P. 333.
"The fierce and all but pessimistic realism of HG has its truthful side, and even its artistic power, also; but we must trust that the future will justify the more hopeful pictures of Miss French."

C227. Leary, Lewis. *Articles on American Literature/1900-1950.* Durham, N.C.: Duke U Press, 1954. P. 118.
Listing of articles about HG.

C228. ---, with the assistance of Carolyn Bartholet and Catharine Roth. *Articles on American Literature/1950-1967.* Durham, N.C.: Duke U Press, 1970. Pp. 224-226.
Listing of periodical articles on HG.

C229. Leisy, Ernest E. *The American Historical Novel.* Norman: U of Oklahoma Press, 1950. Pp. 192-193 and passim as indexed.
Mentions Kirkland's influence on HG and says that *Son* is "the first psychological synthesis of personal and general conditions in the western half of the Mississippi Valley." In *Son* HG caught "not only the material facts, but the spirit of the time, the place, and the people." If the book has a defect, it is its "obstinate romanticism."

C230. ---. *American Literature/An Interpretative Survey.* N.Y.: Crowell, 1929. Pp. 205-206.
HG was "a leader in opposing the tradition of reticence and optimism, though hardly a naturalist...." *MTR* is "a collection of iconoclastic short stories in which he applied the method of the French and Russian realists to the country of corn and wheat-raising and to the rural customs he so well knew." *Son* is a "graphic 'document' of rural life."

C231. Lenehan, William T. "Techniques and Themes in Early English and American Naturalistic Novels--A Study of the Early Novels of George Gissing, George Moore, W. Somerset Maugham, HG, Stephen Crane, and Frank Norris." Unpublished dissertation. U of Oklahoma,

1964. [DA, 25 (1964), 452-453.]

HG, "who early rejected Zola as a model, vacillated between his desire to write an artistic novel and his desire to rectify the economic evils of America, thus exhibiting in his early novels the general uncertainty of the American writers concerning the purpose of the novel."

C232. Lewis, Lloyd, and Henry Justin Smith. *Chicago/The History of its Reputation.* N.Y.: Harcourt, Brace, 1929. Pp. 232, 327.

On the subject of Chicago culture, HG, "the very radical, almost shocking author of *Rose,*" attracted the esteem of Howells and others. HG was one of several writers about Chicago whose "genius was knocking at the gates" of literature.

C233. Lewis, Sinclair. *The Man From Main Street/Selected Essays and Other Writings 1904-1950,* ed. Harry E. Maule and Melville H. Crane. Assisted by Philip Allan Friedman. N.Y.: Random House, 1953. Pp. 15-16, 58, 105, 172, 175, 176, 180.

Notes Howells' influence on HG, who "should in every way have been greater than Howells but who under Howells' influence was changed from a harsh and magnificent realist into a genial and insignificant lecturer." Laments that HG, "who wrote two most valiant and revelatory works of realism, *MTR* and *Rose,*" became a conservative who rejected numerous new, young writers and literary movements. Lewis also says that HG "would not be pleased but acutely annoyed to know that he made it possible for me to write of America as I see it . . . ." Lewis praises Willa Cather's pictures of the West over HG's, but calls HG one of the American masters of the short novel.

C234. Lewisohn, Ludwig. *The Story of American Literature.* N.Y.: Modern Library, 1939. Pp. 314, 317, 330.

[Originally published in 1932 as *Expression in America,* with same pagination.] Only brief references. Reminiscence of HG stalking, "in sombrero and riding-boots," into the graduate students' club at Columbia.

C235. *A Library of Literary Criticism/Modern American Literature,* ed. Dorothy Nyren. 3rd ed. N.Y.: Frederick Ungar, 1964. Pp. 199-201.
Brief excerpts from nine critiques of HG.

C236. Lieberman, Elias. *The American Short Story/A Study of the Influence of Locality in Its Development.* Ridgewood, N.J.: The Editor, 1912. Pp. 7, 51-58.
HG's *MTR* is a study of a new type of Western man no longer concerned with the soil. Three stories from *MTR*--"Branch Road," "Up the Coulee," and "Among the Corn Rows"--are analyzed. "Up the Coulee" is "another story of life in the Mississippi Valley over which there hangs a Homeric gloom, the gloom of the irretrievable and the fated." HG's power "lies in a species of vivid realism . . . . Not only has the locality had an influence upon the author" but "it has seared its drear hopelessness into his brain."

Lillard, Richard G. See Coan, Otis W., and Richard G. Lillard.

C237. Linson, Corwin K. *My Stephen Crane.* Syracuse, N.Y.: Syracuse U Press, 1958. Passim as indexed.
Crane's passion for realism "accounted for his respect for the crystal sincereity of Howells and G."

C238. Liptzin, Sol. *The Jew in American Literature.* N.Y.: Block, 1966. P. 71.
Jewish peddlers and salesmen were no longer mere stereotypes, and novelists were having problems presenting them in their work. "The Jewish salesman, depicted by HG in *Rose,* 1895, was chubby-faced and no longer gaunt, smiling and no longer filled with resentment, a New Yorker by birth but equally happy amidst Chicago's hustle."

C239. *Literary History of the United States/History,* ed. Robert E. Spiller, Willard Thorp, Thomas H. Johnson, and Henry Seidel Canby. 3rd ed., rev. N.Y.: Macmillan, 1963; 1st ed. in 2 vols. and *Bibliography,* 1948. Passim as indexed.

In "Toward Naturalism in Fiction" (1016-1038),
Robert E. Spiller discusses HG as a writer in whom one
"can discover many phases of naturalism" by examining his "harsher forms of realism." In the case of HG,
"The Oedipus complex was ... no deep source of buried
tragedy; it shaped the life of a family and created a
chronicler." Brief comments on several of HG's works.
The 1st ed. *Bibliography* provides an extended list of
works by and about HG.

C240. *Living Authors/A Book of Biographies*, ed. Dilly Tante
[pseud. for Stanley J. Kunitz]. N.Y.: Wilson, 1937.
Pp. 141-142.
Brief biographical sketch.

C241. Loggins, Vernon. *I Hear America....* N.Y.: Crowell; 1937.
Pp. 28, 29, 117, 197, and passim as indexed.
Realism would have developed in America "without
Russian, French, and English naturalists," since "the
progress of science made inevitable such austere books
of the eighties and nineties" as *MTR*. HG's works reflect "a decided sympathy for the proletariat."

C242. Lovett, Robert Morss. *All Our Years*. N.Y.: Viking, 1948.
Pp. 103-104, 127-128, 198.
HG made a major contribution to the establishment of
Chicago as a literary center. An anecdote is told about
HG as chairman of the committee, on which S. P. Sher-
man and Lovett himself served, for the Pulitzer Prize.
Sherman and Lovett suggested Lewis' *Main Street* for
the award and were quite shocked when HG announced
that the award was to go to Edith Wharton for *Age of
Innocence*.

C243. Lowe, Orton. *Our Land and Its Literature*. N.Y. and
London: Harper, 1936. Pp. 45-46 and passim as indexed.
MTR mentioned as local-color book which sets down
"the hardships and drabness of the Middle Border in a
frank and unconventional manner."

C244. Luccock, Halford E. *Contemporary American Literature and Religion.* N.Y. and Chicago: Willett, Clark, 1934. P. 93.

> HG's realistic period, which produced *MTR* and *Rose*, "did not seriously upset the accepted convention" of romanticism.

C245. Ludeke, Henry. *Geschichte Der Amerikanischen Literatur.* Bern: Francke Verlag, 1952. Pp. 435-436.

> Brief survey of G's career.

C246. Ludwig, Richard M. *Literary History of the United States/ Bibliography Supplement.* N.Y.: Macmillan, 1959. P. 129.

> This updating of HG listing in LHUS, Vol. III, includes reprints, correspondence and biography, and criticism.

C247. Lyon, Peter. *Success Story/The Life and Times of S. S. McClure.* N.Y.: Scribner's, 1963. Passim as indexed.

> HG and Booth Tarkington met through a mutual interest in *McClure's*. McClure's attempt to revise *Grant* was main reason for the falling out of HG and McClure.

C248. McAleer, John J. *Theodore Dreiser.* N.Y.: Barnes and Noble, 1968. P. 76.

> HG's work "has been diminished by time."

C249. McComb, E. H. Kemper, ed. *A Son of the Middle Border.* N.Y.: Macmillan, 1923.

> This edition is "for school use." It includes "To My Young Readers" by HG (vii-viii), "To the Boys and Girls Who Read This Volume" by the editor (ix-x), a "Chronological List of Books by HG" (xi), "To Teachers" by the editor (xiii), "Notes" on the text (469-474), and "Questions" (475-478).

C250. McDowell, Frederick P. W. *Ellen Glasgow and the Ironic Art of Fiction.* Madison: U of Wisconsin Press, 1960. Pp. 4, 20, 24.

> Miss Glasgow's "deepest American affinities were

with realists like G and Norris." HG's impressions
of Miss Glasgow after visiting her in Richmond in
1898 are noted.

C251. McElderry, Bruce R., Jr. "Introduction," *Boy Life on the
Prairie*. Lincoln: U of Nebraska Press, 1961. Pp. v-
xvi.
[Rptd from *Educational Leader*, 22 (1 Apr 1949), 5-
16. See under "Periodicals."]

C252. ---. "Introduction," *Main-Travelled Roads*. N.Y.: Harper,
1956. Pp. ix-xix.
A biographical sketch "explains why ... [HG] wrote
the book." The stories in *MTR* "are most valuable,
no doubt, as a fictional record of midwest farm life as
it was in the 1880's and 1890's, but the record is set
down with insight and skill."
Much of this introductory essay centers on HG's other
works and attempts to defend HG against attacks on his
decline from realism. *Boy Life* is "a neglected classic
of nineteenth century childhood." A "fair examination
will show that after 1891 G's achievement is more varied
and useful than has commonly been thought." Between
1900 and 1915, he wrote about the Far West; most of
these stories "are hampered by the popular stereotypes
of conventional romance, but there is no doubt that G
knows the country and the people he describes." *American Indian* rises above journalism, and in literary insight it compares with *MTR*. "A Bibliographical Note"
(xix-xx).

C253. ---. "The West," in *The Realistic Movement in American
Writing*, ed. Bruce R. McElderry, Jr. N.Y.: Odyssey,
1956. Pp. 305-306.
Brief mention (306) of HG emphasizes his being influenced by Eggleston, Howe, and Kirkland.

C254. McGall, Edith. "HG, Boy of the Prairie," in *Frontiers of
America/Pioneering on the Plains*. Chicago: Children's
Press, 1962. Pp. 7-79.
This book appears to be a fictionalized biography of
HG, written for children.

C255. McKeehan, Irene Pettit. "Colorado in Literature," in
Colorado/Short Studies of Its Past and Present. Univ.
of Colorado Semicentennial Publications. Boulder: U
of Colorado, 1927. Pp. 141-202.
Brief mention of G (168-169) as writer not a Coloradoan
but who has used the state as a subject in ten of his books.

C256. McMurray, William. *The Literary Realism of William Dean
.Howells.* Carbondale, Ill.: Southern Illinois U Press,
1967. Pp. 111-114.
Brief discussion of HG's relation with Howells.

C257. Maillard, Denyse. *L'Enfant Américain Au XXe Siécle/
D'Apres Les Romanciers Du Middle-West.* Paris: Nizet
& Bastard, 1935. Pp. 19-21, 23, 34, 51, 67, 91-94,
110-111, 134-135, 153-154, 156, 160-163, 167, 173-
174, 182, 195, 217, 224, 234, 248-250, 253.
Considerable mention throughout of HG's pictures of
Middle-Western life, with emphasis on the Middle Border
books and *Rose.*

C258. Mane, Robert. *HG/L'Homme Et L'Oeuvre (1860-1940).* Paris:
Didier, 1968.
The most extensive work on HG published to date,
this volume is both a detailed biography and a critical
study. All of HG's works are discussed, and extensive
bibliographies of writings by and about HG are included.

C259. Mann, Arthur. *Yankee Reformers in the Urban Age.* Cambridge, Mass.: Belknap Press, 1954. Pp. 157-158, 167-
169, 172-174, and passim as indexed.
HG knew Solomon Schindler through the American
Psychical Society and carried on, in the pages of the
Arena, a debate with him on the subject of socialism
versus individualism. HG was an expert for the *Arena*
and suggested to Flower the hiring of W. A. McCrackon
as specialist in government and politics. Brief reference to HG's Boston days and to some of his works.

C260. Marble, Annie Russell. *A Study of the Modern Novel/Brit-
ish and American Since 1900.* N.Y.: Appleton, 1928.
Pp. 220-225.

HG is classified among novelists of history and romance "because he has chosen scenes of history,
epochs of vital moment in national life." Only three
of his works "will be rated among the significant books
of modern fiction": *Captain*, "written with verve and
graphic setting," *Son* and *Daughter*.

C261. Marchand, Ernest. *Frank Norris/A Study*. N.Y.: Octagon
Books, 1964. Pp. 29, 216, 231-232.
HG and Norris were attacked by critics for crying
out against the literary traditions of the Eastern states
and then going farther East to France and Zola for
their model.

C262. Marsh, Philip. *American Literature/A Concise History*.
Austin, Tex.: Steck, 1950. Pp. 79, 82-83.
Brief summary of HG's life and career: "His work
lacks polish and depth, but has the ring of sincerity
and truth."

C263. Martin, Jay. *Harvests of Change/American Literature 1865-
1914*. Englewood Cliffs, N.J.: Prentice-Hall, 1967.
Pp. 111, 124-132, and passim as indexed.
The so-called fathers of realism--Eggleston, Howe,
Kirkland, HG--were "realists only because their myths
had been shattered by experience. As soon as the
shock of their disillusion was dissipated, they usually
either reoriented their value-schemes in accordance
with new systems of myth and romance, or eliminated
the personal shock of repeated recognition by resort-
ing to the objectivity of historical research and writing."
HG's work has "the double vision of all regional
literature. The depth of the writer's romanticism drives
him to realism, in a rage to reorder his anti-romantic
age. Contrary to the claims of many critics that G fell
into romance after an earlier recognition of social problems in the West, it is clear that from the very beginning of his career both impulses are present and operate
sometimes simultaneously, sometimes separately in his
work." HG's trip back West in 1887 perhaps caused G
to be "shocked into realism." "Up the Coulee" and

"A Prairie Heroine" are stories that "best record both the loss of the agrarian myth and the consequent yearnings for a better life that these Westerners believed existed in the cultured, affluent East."

HG was a realist for only three years (1888-1891). "Although his style remained uniformly realistic in fidelity to fact and detail," he was really "a maker and follower of myth and romance." *Boy Life* is a romantic, myth-following book. *Goldseekers* shows HG's desire to recapture the frontier life of his boyhood. The Middle Border series kept "alive the myth he had once, briefly, been compelled to reject."
[Brief comments on all of HG's works, including his books on spiritualism which are related to myth-making.]

C264. *Massachusetts/A Guide to Its Places and People*. Written and compiled by the Federal Writers' Project of the Works Progress Administration for the State of Massachusetts. American Guide Series. Boston: Houghton Mifflin, 1937. P. 107.

HG came to Boston in 1885 seeking literary giants. *Son* "contains many valuable indications of intellectual currents of the 1880's in Massachusetts."

C265. Matthiessen, F. O. *American Renaissance*. N.Y.: Oxford U Press, 1941. P. 603.

As HG talked to Whitman "enthusiastically about the local color school of Cable, Harris, and Mary Wilkins as the forerunner of powerful native art, Whitman took strenuous exception." Whitman thought these writers did not seem content with the normal man.

C266. ---. *Theodore Dreiser*. N.Y.: William Sloane, 1951. Pp. 58, 104, and passim as indexed.

Dreiser admired *MTR*, and HG admired *Sister Carrie*.

C267. May, Henry F. *The End of American Innocence/A Study of the First Years of Our Own Time/1912-1917*. N.Y.: Knopf, 1959. Pp. 89, 104-105.

CI calls for a fresh "truly Western Chicago literature, at once realistic and full of idealism." May discusses HG's activities in Chicago and his subsequent move

223

back East to New York.

C268. Mencken, H. L. "HG," in *A Mencken Chrestomathy/Edited and Annotated by the Author.* N.Y.: Knopf, 1949. Pp. 498-500.

A reprint with slight alteration of the item immediately following. In headnote Mencken tells of his initial attack on HG and of HG's "revenge" in *Contemporaries.* Mencken concludes, "He was greatly overestimated in his lifetime, mainly because of his energy and effrontery as a literary politician. His actual talents were very meagre, and he was shabby and devious as a man" (498).

C269. ---. "Six Members of the Institute/A Stranger on Parnassus," in *Prejudices/First Series.* N.Y.: Knopf, 1919. Pp. 134-138.

In a typically satiric vein, Mencken asserts that HG "has no more feeling for the intrinsic dignity of beauty, no more comprehension of it as a thing in itself, than a policeman" (135). HG was only a preacher and pedagogue. His worst effort was *Forester's Daughter.* *Shadow World* is "a record of his communings with the gaseous precipitates of the departed" (137). At first judging *Son* "third-rate" without a trace of "charm," Mencken relents by concluding it is "an honest book."

C270. *Merle Johnson's American First Editions,* ed. Jacob Blanck. 4th ed. N.Y.: Bowker, 1942. Pp. 200-203.

Includes listing of limited editions and private printings of HG works.

C271. Metcalf, John Calvin. *American Literature.* Atlanta, Ga.: Johnson, 1914. P. 397.

Biographical sketch. HG "is a realist, and his stories reproduce the somewhat prosaic life on the vast stretches of the region of which he is native." But "realist though he is, HG has come more and more to mingle the softening atmosphere of romance with pictures of the daily grind of life."

Metzger, Walter. See Brodbeck, May, James Gray, and Walter Metzger.

C272. Meyer, Roy W. *The Middle Western Farm Novel in the 20th Century.* Lincoln: U of Nebraska Press, 1965. Pp. 26-27, 30-38, and passim as indexed.

Recognizes Howe's influence on HG. The significance of *MTR* in the history of the farm novel is that HG "handled his materials in a thoroughly realistic fashion." He was "the first authentic farm novelist." In his analysis of the psychological effects of a Dakota winter on the settlers (*Ranch*), especially the women, G anticipated Rolvaag . . . . "

C273. Michaud, Regis. *The American Novel To-Day/A Social and Psychological Study.* Boston: Little, Brown, 1928. P. 200n.

In his discussion of realism Michaud refers to HG's *CI*, which "frankly put the case of realism versus sentimentalism before the public. He quoted Mistral and the French Felibres, as well as Taine and the critic Veron in support of his plea for what he called *provincialism*."

C274. Miller, James McDonald. *An Outline of American Literature.* N.Y.: Farrar and Rinehart, 1934. Pp. 263-265 and passim as indexed.

HG was "one of the first to revolt against the smiling optimism of the Gilded Age."

C275. Millgate, Michael. *American Social Fiction/James to Cozzens.* N.Y.: Barnes and Noble, 1964. P. 128.

HG's *MTR*, along with Howe's *The Story of a Country Town*, "anticipate[s] the inversion of the success theme found in *An American Tragedy*."

C276. Milne, Gordon. *The American Political Novel.* Norman: U of Oklahoma Press, 1966. Pp. 36-38 and passim as indexed.

Spoil, as a document, shows that HG's solution to political corruption in government was to back "the Populists, urging a revolt, led by the farmer, against land monopoly." HG followed the fictional technique of Mrs. Humphrey Ward, an English writer of political novels.

225

C277. Mitchell, Marvin O. "A Study of the Realistic and Romantic Elements in the Fiction of E. W. Howe, Joseph Kirkland, HG, Harold Frederic, and Frank Norris (1882-1902)." Unpublished dissertation. U of North Carolina, 1953. [Not included in *Dissertation Abstracts* and not available on microfilm.]

C278. Monroe, Harriet. *A Poet's Life/Seventy Years in a Changing World*. N.Y.: Macmillan, 1938. Pp. 174, 198.
Fuller's "The Downfall of Abner Joyce," containing the satirical sketch of HG, is "a masterpiece in that kind."

C279. Morgan, Anna. *My Chicago*. Chicago: Ralph Fletcher Seymour, 1918. Pp. 44-45, 163, 188.
Before the curtain rose for the production of "The Master Builder" (21 Mar 1896), HG remarked that Chicago, not Ibsen's play, was on trial. Barrett Eastman of the *Tribune* "roasted" him for the comment. Morgan, expressing admiration for HG and her other literary friends, commends him for founding The Cliff Dwellers.

C280. Morgan, H. W. "HG: The Rebel as Escapist," in *American Writers in Rebellion/From Mark Twain to Dreiser*. N.Y.: Hill and Wang, 1965. Pp. 76-103.
Extended biographical study. *MTR* put HG in "the front rank of realistic writers"; its "style made it a major contribution to Realism and bore in it the seeds of a Naturalism that others developed."
Morgan traces reasons for HG's decline and suggests that his veritism "would not be Naturalism or deterministic; nor did he propose any greater frankness than Howells already offered. Already he betrayed an aversion to sex and the sordid that turned his later work to romance." Secondly, he was "always interested in people rather than ideas, [and] he was stranded when the types he knew disappeared." Furthermore, "His imagination could not make the leap from personal to universal experience."

C281. Morris, Lloyd. *Postscript to Yesterday/America/The Last Fifty Years*. N.Y.: Random House, 1947. Pp. 107, 109, 254.

HG discovered Crane and was admired by William Allen White.

Murphy, Ella M. See Vogel, Stanley M., and Ella M. Murphy.

C282. Nelson, John Herbert. *The Negro Character in American Literature*. Lawrence, Kan: Dept. of Journalism Press, 1926; rptd, 1968. P. 128.
HG was one of many writers to use the Negro in his works as "either an amusing menial or else a stock figure useful in the action, or both."

C283. Neumann, Edwin J. "HG and the Mountain West." Unpublished dissertation. Northwestern U, 1951. [*Northwestern University--Summaries of Doctoral Dissertations*, XIX (1951), 31-34.]
Not seen.

C284. Newcomer, Alphonso Gerald. *American Literature*. Chicago and N.Y.: Scott, Foresman, 1901; 1913. Pp. 306, 322.
HG is mentioned along with several other writers: "While one of these writers has fancy, and another technique, and another strength, and another humor, it is too early to say that any of them have brought the right combination of powers to their task, and the scenes and characters which they have more or less faithfully portrayed still await the final delineation."

C285. Norris, Frank. *The Literary Criticism of Frank Norris*, ed. Donald Pizer. Austin: U of Texas Press, 1964. Pp. 38, 99, 111, 193.
Scattered brief mention of HG, mostly in Pizer's introductions and notes. Only observation on HG of any substance by Norris is remark about him and Edith Wharton: "Their conceptions of art are as different as the conditions of life they study in their books."

C286. Nuhn, Ferner. "Pure Lines and Poor Relations," in *The Wind Blew From the East/A Study in the Orientation of American Culture*. N.Y.: and London: Harper, 1940; 1942. Pp. 73-86.

HG is compared to Henry James on the theme of the East versus the West (79-86). "A budding author, like young G, could not for long be true to his 'vulgar but heroic' literary material and to the overgenteel literary mode. For a time he held the two in a precarious balance--then the one, the gentility, won out."

C287. O'Brien, Edward J. *The Advance of the American Short Story*. N.Y.: Dodd, Mead, 1923. Pp. 14, 163-164, 216-217, and passim as indexed.
HG's aim is "precise photography of significant moments, and it must be confessed that his art hardly transcends his material." *MTR* is "the touchstone of a period" presenting to readers "our characteristic regionalism at its best." In HG's work there is a combination of "the Anglo-Saxon racial memory and the later experience of conflict with nature while wresting from destiny a new and untamed land."
William Allen White and Frances Gilchrist Wood remind one of HG.

C288. O'Connor, Richard. *Bret Harte*. Boston: Little, Brown, 1966. Pp. 292-293.
HG's meeting with Harte in London is described. HG was "a very serious, rather priggish young Westerner who carried the banner for naturalism."

C289. O'Donnell, Thomas F., and Hoyt C. Franchere. *Harold Frederic*. N.Y.: Twayne, 1961. Passim as indexed.
Brief mention. Notes that the realism of HG and Frederic was not widely accepted by the reading public in the 1890's (150).

C290. O'Neill, Edward H. *A History of American Biography/1800-1935*. N.Y.: Russell & Russell, 1968. Pp. 57-58.
Brief discussion of *Grant*. HG tried to be objective; but his political bias favored Grant, and it shows up in the book. "With all its faults, G's biography is the best one written of...[Grant] in the nineteenth century and perhaps in the twentieth."

C291. Orians, G. Harrison. *A Short History of American Literature*. N.Y.: Crofts, 1940. Pp. 243-246, 254, 264-265.
     HG's work is analyzed in outline form under several categories: his theory of veritism; his introduction of the farmer in literature ("What his stories lacked in literary imagination or in structural excellence, they partly supplied in abundance of social fact"), with specific brief analysis of *Rose*; HG as proponent of local color who "refused to inject an element of optimism into his tales"; and HG as writer of Western romantic fiction during the decade 1900-1910.

     Oxford Companion to American Literature. See Hart, James D.

C292. Paden, Erma Elizabeth. "HG as a Reformer From 1887 to 1895." Unpublished M.A. thesis. Duke U, 1951.
     Not seen.

C293. Pancoast, Henry S. *An Introduction to American Literature*. N.Y.: Holt, 1898. Pp. 385, 398.
     Brief mentions of HG, along with others, as Western writers.

C294. Parker, Jean Hill. "HG as a Pioneer." Unpublished M.A. thesis. U of Southern California, 1938.
     Not seen.

C295. Parrington, Vernon Lewis. "The Development of Realism," in *The Reinterpretation of American Literature/Some Contributions Toward the Understanding of Its Historical Development*, ed. Norman Foerster. N.Y.: Russell & Russell, 1959. Pp. 139-159.
     [Pp. 141, 149-154 deal specifically with HG.] HG's realism "emerged from the economic maladjustments that bred Populism." In *MTR*, HG's "great contribution to American realism," *Folks* and *Rose*, he "reached a height of mordant realism he never afterwards attained." HG was not "a confirmed realist, with a single-hearted devotion to objective presentation," but was "at heart...a romantic, with a longing for a

beautiful life,'' and hence he turned to romance in his later work.

C296. ---. *Main Currents in American Thought.* 3 vols. N.Y.: Harcourt, Brace, 1930. III, xi, 288-300.

HG is really more of a "thwarted Romantic" than a realist, "an idealist of the old Jeffersonian breed, an earnest soul devoid of humor, who loves beauty and is mightily concerned about justice ...." The originality of his work, "that sets it apart from other studies of the local-color school, sprang from the sincerity of his reaction to environment."

HG will be remembered for *Rose, Son, MTR* and *CI. MTR* and *Folks* "constitute a landmark in our literary history, for they were the first authentic expression and protest of an agrarian America then being submerged by the industrial revolution." HG's social consciousness and his link with Henry George and others dissipated his powers as a creative artist.

C297. Pattee, Fred Lewis. "The Aftermath of Veritism--A Letter From the Sabine Farm to HG," in *Tradition and Jazz.* N.Y. and London: Century, 1925. Pp. 103-127.

A delightful chapter in epistolary form directed to HG reminding him of his youthful days of radicalism, reviewing in some detail the growth of the realistic movement, and suggesting that HG be less harsh on the new writers who are crumbling idols as he and others so admirably tried to do some thirty or forty years ago.

C298. ---. *The Development of the American Short Story.* N.Y.: Harper, 1923. Pp. 313-317 and passim as indexed.

HG, Mary Wilkins, and Crane went beyond "the selective realism" of Howells and Harte. The distinction of the stories in *MTR* "lies in their genuineness and their spontaneous freshness." Most of HG's stories "fall short of real greatness as literature" because of their documentary intent; but a few like "Among the Corn Rows" are "universal and timeless."

C299. ---. *The Feminine Fifties.* Port Washington, N.Y.: Kennikat
Press, 1966. P. 63.
   Alice Cary's *Clavernook* "was the first piece of HG-
like realism to come out of the Middle Border lands,
and it came some ten years before HG was born."

C300. ---. *A History of American Literature Since 1870.* N.Y.:
Century, 1915; N.Y.: Cooper Square, 1968. Pp. 24,
106, 307, 321, 372-377, 383, 400, 431.
   HG is not "a mere teller of tales. The Scotch and
Yankee elements within him made of him a preacher,
a man with a message." His novels are not as successful as his stories because he "lacks power of construction and ability for extended effort." His "best long
novel" is *Rose*: but *Money Magic*, while it "has a certain sense of power connected with it," lacks "the
final touch of actual life." *Son*, however, "has a value
above all his novels, above all else that he has written,"
except for *MTR*.

C301. ---. *The New American Literature 1890-1930.* N.Y.: Century,
1930. Pp. 23-27 and passim as indexed.
   HG was influenced by Kirkland and Howe. He recorded
the condition of his home "with angry pen--not too angry,
since at heart he was a romanticist dealing with the
lands of his boyhood...." HG's veritism was another
name "for the 'naturalism' of France and of the school in
England which was to follow Thomas Hardy." HG wanted "his West free, original, autochthonic; but he would
have it study European 'expressionism' and 'symbolism'
and the older rules of art." *Rose* was so veritistic that
it "was ruled out of public libraries as unsafe reading."
There are two kinds of autobiography: Howells' realistic
presentation of self; and HG's "five volumes at present
romanticizing the Middle Border and its central figure
HG."

C302. Patterson, Cecil L. "Methodism and Moral Conflict in the
Novels of Twain, Howells, G and Others." Unpublished
dissertation. U of Pennsylvania, 1956.
   Not seen.

C303. Payne, Leonidas Warren. *History of American Literature.*
Chicago and N.Y.: Rand McNally, 1919. Pp. 365-366.
In HG (listed under heading of "Minor Western Writers
of Fiction") "we find the hard realism of the Middle
West farm life voicing itself." *Rose* and *Eagle's Heart*
are "typical Western novels." *Son* is "one of the most
valuable of all Mr. G's books" because "it gives a
truthful and satisfying picture of life in the Middle and
Far West--of the whole of America, in fact--and at the
same time it is as entertaining as a novel."

C304. Perry, Bliss. *A Study of Prose Fiction.* Boston: Houghton
Mifflin, 1902. Pp. 159, 348.
HG wrote of farming and of the Northwest.

C305. Pierce, Bessie Louise, ed. *As Others See Chicago/Impres-
sions of Visitors, 1673-1933.* Chicago: U of Chicago
Press, 1933. Pp. 377, 444.
HG is listed among Chicago writers, 1893-1933.

C306. Pilkington, John, Jr. *Henry Blake Fuller.* N.Y.: Twayne,
1970. Passim as indexed.
Numerous mentions of G and his close friendship with
Fuller, especially in relation to Chicago as the new
cultural center of the 1890's. Pilkington also relies
on HG's diaries for a first-hand view of Fuller. Fuller's
satire on G, "The Downfall of Abner Joyce," is also
discussed, suggesting that G remained a close friend
of Fuller, in spite of the satire.

C307. Pinchot, Gifford. "Introduction," *Cavanagh.* N.Y.: Harper,
1910. Pp. vii-viii.
Letter to HG praises *Cavanagh* for its "sympathetic
understanding of the problems which confronted the
Forest Service."

C308. Pizer, Donald. "The G-Crane Relationship," in *Realism
and Naturalism in Nineteenth-Century American Literature.* Carbondale: Southern Illinois U Press, 1966.
Pp. 114-120.
[Rptd from *Huntington Library Quarterly*, 24 (Nov
1960), 75-82. See under "Periodicals."]

C309. ---. "HG: A Critical Study of His Early Work and Career
(1884-1895)." Unpublished dissertation. U of California at Los Angeles, 1955.
Not seen. Basis of Pizer's *HG's Early Work and Career* (see below).

C310. ---. "HG and Stephen Crane: The Naturalist as Romantic
Individualist," in *Realism and Naturalism in Nineteenth-Century American Literature.* Carbondale: Southern
Illinois U Press, 1966. Pp. 88-98.
[Rptd from *American Quarterly,* 10 (Winter 1958), 463-475. See under "Periodicals."]

C311. ---. "HG's *A Son of the Middle Border,*" in *Essays in American and English Literature Presented to Bruce Robert McElderry,* ed. Max F. Schulz, William D. Templeman,
and Charles R. Metzger. Athens: Ohio U Press, 1967.
Pp. 76-108
[Rptd from *South Atlantic Quarterly,* 65 (Autumn 1966),
448-459. See under "Periodicals."]

C312. ---, ed. *HG's Diaries.* San Marino, Calif.: Huntington Library, 1968.
In "Introduction and Editorial Note" (xi-xv), Pizer
gives the background and circumstances of composition
of the diaries. He briefly introduces the various categories of material: "Social and Literary Experiences,"
"Reflections on Life and Career," "The G Family,"
"Psychic Interests," "Literary Work," "Personalities,"
"Political Figures and Events," "The American Institute and The American Academy," "American Life and
Its Problems," and "American Places."

C313. ---. *HG's Early Work and Career.* Berkeley and Los Angeles:
U of California Press, 1960.
Detailed examination and analysis of HG's life and
works between 1884 and 1895. Emphasis on HG as,
successively, local colorist, social reformer, theater
reformer, Populist, arts reformer, and impressionist.

C314. ---. "Introduction," *Main-Travelled Roads.* Charles E.

Hamlin Garland

Merrill Standard Editions. Columbus, Ohio: Charles E.
E. Merrill, 1970. Pp. v-xvii.

Brief summary of HG's life up to his Western trip in
the summer of 1887 and the journal he kept during this
trip. The journal shows him to have a "two-fold vision
of western life," for he is both the " 'insider' who knows
the truth about farm life and who therefore implicitly
despises the bucolic as a literary convention" and the
" 'outsider' who is aware of the rich life, the 'beauty,'
which is both unknown and unavailable to the farmer."
MTR also shows the influence of HG's reading of Henry
George in that HG attributed "all economic and social
deprivation to the evils of land speculation." "Under
the Lion's Paw" and "Up the Coulé" are examined
specifically for evidence of George's theories which in-
form *MTR* in "two oblique but important ways": one is
"in his dramatization of the mortgage as the major
source of fear in western life"; the other is "in the
tone of indignation which characterizes his depiction
of the hardships and bleakness of western life, a tone·
which emerges out of his conviction that these conditions
are the product of an unjust land system rather than at-
tributable either to the farmers or to the land."

The stories in *MTR* show HG's strengths and weaknesses. They show the great difficulty he had with plot and
several are marred by "inept narrative devices" and/
or "melodramatic and sentimental touches." But the
book as a whole is "artful and moving" for several reasons. One is HG's use of the road metaphor. HG "not
only used the road image [introduced in the title, pur-
sued in the dedication and preface, and maintained in
the epigraphs to each story] as an overt linking device
in the collection as a whole but also structured each
story around a physical move from one place to another."
Of further significance is the fact that "this move in
every story is a return."

Another unifying element in the book is its use of three
different sorts of "pictorial images." One "juxtaposes
the beauty of nature (a spring morning, a summer day,
a sunset) and the ugliness and toil of farm activities";
another "focuses on a man and a woman"; and a third is
that of "social gatherings," scenes which usually have

"a cheerful cast, though the reality or memory of intense labor is always present."

Thus, *MTR* is important both as an "historical document" which "portrays more vividly than any work of its time the physical and social conditions which led to the Populist revolt," and as art in which "road and picture, rather than plot, constitute the permanently moving."

C315. ----. "Introduction," *Rose of Dutcher's Coolly.* Lincoln: U of Nebraska Press, 1969. Pp. vii-xxiv.

A close examination of all aspects of *Rose.* None of HG's more important works (*MTR, CI,* and *Son*) are novels, which points up the fact "that he was not entirely at home as a novelist and that his longer fiction is of little permanent value." *Rose* is an exception. Focused on escape and guilt, it treats a favorite HG theme. Specifically it is HG's attempt to deal with the currently popular woman problem, already treated by both Hardy and Ibsen. HG's approach differs from theirs in that "he wished to bring alive the themes that sexual knowledge and experience are inseparable from growing up on a farm, and that such knowledge and experience could be a source of moral and emotional development rather than a cause of social catastrophe." HG was bitterly disappointed with the preponderance of negative reviews of the book and never again dealt with such controversial themes. HG's treatment of sex is ultimately conventional as opposed to that found in Zola and Norris. *Rose* is compared with Dreiser's *Sister Carrie.*

This text also contains "A Selected Bibliography" (xxv-xxvi), a note on the 1899 edition of *Rose* (xxvii-xxxiii), and a note on the text (404).

C316. Poirier, Richard. *A World Elsewhere.* N.Y.: Oxford U Press, 1966. P. 38.

The irony involved in finding or fighting a verbal struggle to embody new passions and ideas is a convention itself and is as much a part of Cooper and Emerson as of HG and Hemingway.

C317. Policardi, Silvio. *Breve Storia Della Letteratura Americana.*
    Milan: Varese Cisalpino, 1951. Pp. 206-208.
    Summary of HG's career and life.

C318. Pollard, Percival. *Their Day in Court.* N.Y. and Washington:
    Neale, 1909. Pp. 186, 230-236, 276, 373.
    HG is taken severely to task (230-231) for his attempts
    to reproduce English speech which result in "pure non-
    sense": "Time and again Mr. G, who for years preached
    naturalism and sincerity to all the rest of us, wrote, as
    the speech of Englishmen, such sounds as no human
    being in either Old or New England ever evolved. So
    doing, he made valueless all the theories he had been
    preaching so many years. Why could he not have stuck
    to his plows and other Western implements? He was at
    home there; he put simple and true art into his treatment
    of that material; why could he not have left alone the
    things he was ignorant of?" Also included is an extended
    appreciation of Fuller's satirical sketch on HG (231-236).

C319. Preston, Wheeler. "G,H," in *American Biographies.* N.Y.:
    Harper, 1940. P. 360.
    Biographical sketch.

C320. Pritchard, John Paul. *Criticism in America.* Norman: U of
    Oklahoma Press, 1956. Pp. 166, 187, 197-198.
    Howells' praise of HG for putting "his faith in the
    good he sees as well as in the evil" (166) is mentioned.
    Brief references to HG as veritist (187) and as early
    regionalist (197-198).

C321. Quantic, Diane Dufva. "Anticipation of the Revolt From
    the Village in Nineteenth Century Middle Western Fic-
    tion: A Study of the Small Town in the Works of Edward
    Eggleston, E. W. Howe, Joseph Kirkland, HG, William
    Allen White, Zona Gale, and Willa Cather." Unpublish-
    ed dissertation. Kansas State U, 1971. [DAI, 32 (1972),
    5198A.]
    "In the 1890's, HG wrote several pessimistic stories
    about the cultural and intellectual sterility of the Mid-
    western small town."

C322. Quinn, Arthur Hobson. *American Fiction/An Historical and Critical Survey.* N.Y.: Appleton-Century, 1936. Pp. 454-459 and passim as indexed.

    HG's "tragic stories are the best." In his earlier novels, "G the reformer overshadowed G the artist." But in *Norsk*, "the characters are individualized, and the distinction between the loves of the two men for the girl is quite well drawn." In *Rose*, HG is again "a realist," and the "incident of the captain sailing his ship on the rocks in order that he might remain in control until the very end represents G's style at its best."

    The essays in *CI* now "have a certain historical interest because they reveal the strength and weakness of the provincial point of view." HG failed to see that "the very 'universality' against which he was inveighing was the reason for the superiority of his early work to the fiction that came from him after 1900." *Cavanagh* is "probably the best" of his Far West novels.

    His four autobiographical volumes, after his excursions into the idealistic romance of the Far West, "form an epic of migration, of struggle and discouragement, of the conquest of unfriendly nature, and of human indifference which no historian of literature or of life may neglect."

C323. ---. *A History of the American Drama From the Civil War to the Present Day.* Rev. one-vol. ed. N.Y.: Crofts, 1936. I, 138, 140, 141, 158; II, 12.

    First four references deal with HG's support of and enthusiasm for James A. Herne. Last reference is brief mention of trip to Rocky Mountains which HG took in 1901 with William Vaughn Moody.

C324. ---. *The Soul of America/Yesterday and Today.* Philadelphia: U of Pennsylvania Press, 1932. Pp. 40, 105.

    Trail Makers presents real life in the early West. Both *Trail Makers* and *MTR*, as well as *Son*, reveal the feeling of the early pioneers, the hardships of the women, and their endurance.

C325. Randel, William P. *Edward Eggleston.* N.Y.: Twayne, 1963. Pp. 147, 150.

Eggleston met HG at the Cosmos Club in Washington. HG expressed admiration for *The Hoosier School-Master* and indicated that it had been a major influence on his writing career.

C326. ---. *Edward Eggleston/Author of The Hoosier School-Master.* Gloucester, Mass.: Peter Smith, 1962. Pp. 207, 221; orig. pub., N.Y.: King's Crown, 1946.

HG was linked with Eggleston in a Minneapolis *Journal* editorial which censured them both for abandoning the West.

C327. Rankin, Thomas E., and Wilford M. Aikin. *American Literature.* N.Y.: Harcourt, Brace, 1922. Pp. 231, 233-234, 236.

HG is one of "the leading short story writers since 1890." His work "cannot be said to have in high degree the quality of literary elegance, but in the short stories it has the quality of convincingness, and much of it is very entertaining." Mary Wilkins Freeman is "more evenly somber" than HG.

C328. *The Reader's Encyclopedia,* ed. William Rose Benét. 2d ed. N.Y.: Crowell, 1965. Pp. 382-383.

Brief summary of HG's career.

C329. Reamer, Owen J. "HG: Literary Pioneer and Typical American." Unpublished dissertation. U of Texas, 1951. Not seen.

C330. Rees, Robert A., and Earl N. Harbert, eds. *15 American Authors Before 1900/Bibliographic Essays on Research and Criticism.* Madison: U of Wisconsin Press, 1971. Pp. 109, 112, 117, 121, 314, 322, 323.

Scholarship and criticism on G is mentioned and described in chapters on Crane (Donald Pizer) and Norris (William B. Dillingham).

C331. Regier, C. C. *The Era of the Muckrakers.* Chapel Hill: U of North Carolina Press, 1932. Pp. 18, 46, 161.

Brief mention of HG, primarily as Populist and as realist.

C332. Rewald, John. *The History of Impressionism.* Rev. ed.
N.Y.: Museum of Modern Art, 1961. P. 610.
In his bibliography Rewald lists *CI* and notes that
its chapter on impressionism is "probably the first
all-out defense of the movement to be written in English."

C333. Rideout, Walter B. *The Radical Novel in the United States,
1900-1954.* Cambridge, Mass.: Harvard U Press, 1956.
P. 289.
HG is part of a whole tradition of social protest novel-
ists including, among others, Twain and Harriet Beecher
Stowe.

C334. Robinson, Cecil. *With the Ears of Strangers.* Tucson: U of
Arizona Press, 1963. Pp. 140-141, 165.
HG's treatment of the Far West followed the early
"bitter realism of his middle border stories." In
"Delmar of Pima," HG romanticized a Mexican character giving him "virtues that Anglo-Saxons usually reserve for themselves[:] modesty, courage, and chastity."

C335. Rosati, Salvatore. *Storia Della Letteratura Americana.*
2d ed. Turin: *ERI,* 1967. Pp. 186-187, 209.
Brief summary of HG's life and writing career.

C336. Rose, Edward J. *Henry George.* N.Y.: Twayne, 1968. Pp.
19, 137, 151, 155, 158, 159, 163.
Brief scattered references to the G-George relationship,
with emphasis on G's high opinion of George.

C337. Ross, Danforth R. *The American Short Story.* Minneapolis:
U of Minnesota Press, 1961. Pp. 26-27.
HG was "one of the first American writers to take a
tentative step toward naturalism"; he "called himself
a veritist, a realist who pushes deeper toward truth
than the ordinary realist." "'The Return of a Private'
is weak aesthetically in that it achieves its theme
didactically rather than through suggestion. It falls
short of naturalism in that the soldier is not so much a
victim of an economic system as of injustice. He is
viewed as morally good, his fellow men as morally bad.

A more searching naturalist would examine the environment that has produced the fellow men" (27).

C338. Rubin, Louis D., Jr. *The Curious Death of the Novel.*
Baton Rouge: Louisiana State U Press, 1967. P. 102.
HG was one of the remaining literati when Mencken came on the scene in the 1900's.

C339. Schieber, Alois John. "Autobiographies of American Novelists: Twain, Howells, James, Adams, and G." Unpublished dissertation. U of Wisconsin, 1957. [DA, 17 (1957), 2261.]
HG's ideas on life and art were influenced by Spencer, George, and Taine. His "early idealistic notions of farming reform gradually gave way to conventional ideas on politics, society, and wealth."

C340. Schneider, Robert W. *Five Novelists of the Progressive Era*.
N.Y.: Columbia U Press, 1965. Passim as indexed.
Mention of HG and his friendships with Howells, Crane, and Norris.

C341. Schorer, Mark. "Afterword," *Main-Travelled Roads*. N.Y.:
New American Library, 1962. Pp. 259-269.
HG was "influenced by the realism of William Dean Howells and the local colorists...." HG's veritism differs from Howells' realism in that HG emphasized impressionism, the importance of the individual artist's vision. The theme of the return is seen in "Up the Coulee," "A Branch Road," and "God's Ravens." This "theme of the return to his rural past was, in large part, the theme of G's life." The "most impressive subsidiary theme in the entire collection...is the theme of the irrelevance of romantic love." Although HG "recognized that brutality and connivance and cold selfishness do exist in human nature, something instinctive in him made it impossible for him to accept these qualities as essential in human nature."

C342. ⊢--. *Sinclair Lewis/An American Life*. N.Y.: McGraw-Hill, 1961. Pp. 60, 229-230, 248, 250, 269, 274, 286, 287, 299, 327.

Brief random mention of HG's influence on Lewis
(especially in *Main Street*), Lewis' enthusiasm for *Son*,
HG's dislike of *Main Street* (he urged Henry Seidel
Canby of the *Literary Review* of the N.Y. *Evening Post*
to take a public position against it), and his rather para-
doxical vote for it as a member of the 1921 Pulitzer
Prize committee.

Seagle, William. See Ernst, Morris L., and William Seagle.

C343. Sherman, Stuart P. *The Genius of America/Studies in Behalf
of the Younger Generation.* N.Y. and London: Scribner's,
1923. Pp. 219.
MTR is a realistic work which belongs to what Van
Doren, in *Contemporary American Novelists*, calls "the
revolt from the village."

C344. Shumaker, Arthur W. *A History of Indiana Literature.* Indianapolis: Indiana Historical Bureau Society, 1962. Pp.
306, 357-358.
HG, "an exponent of realism," debated the realism-
romanticism issue with Mrs. Catherwood in Chicago in
1893. Catherwood "defended [her] point of view effectively."
HG supported Booth Tarkington in his dealings with
McClure's.

C345. Silveira, Brenno. *Pequena Historia Da Literatura Norte-
Americana.* Sao Paulo: Martins, 1943. Pp. 164-168.
Brief summary of HG's career.

C346. Simonson, Harold P. *Zona Gale.* N.Y.: Twayne, 1962.
Pp. 15, 24, 47, 53, 70, 86, 98, 99, 111.
Brief random mention of HG's comments on Zona Gale,
the relationship of their works, and their few personal
contacts.

C347. Smily, Roger E. "An Index to the Autobiographical Works
of HG." Unpublished M.A. thesis. Pennsylvania State
U, 1938.
Not seen. Pizer calls it faulty but useful.

C348. Smith, Bernard. *Forces in American Criticism.* N.Y.: Harcourt, Brace, 1939. Pp. 164-165, 178-181, 184, 230, and passim as indexed.

HG's critical ideas were animated by concepts of "Democracy, individualism, and the inevitability of progress . . . . " HG's interpretation of realism was "inherently romantic"; "there was no contradiction between G's optimism and his insistence that novelists be honest with their subjects . . . . It was an optimism founded on the admission of unpleasant facts." HG wanted literature to arouse men "to fight for the establishment of a just and beautiful order," and "cynicism and nostalgia had no place in G's scheme . . . " as they did in Twain's.

Smith, Henry Justin. See Lewis, Lloyd, and Henry Justin Smith.

C349. Smith, Henry Nash. *Virgin Land/The American West as Symbol and Myth.* Cambridge, Mass.: Harvard U Press, 1950; rptd Vintage Books, 1957. Pp. 284-290 and passim as indexed.

Relates HG and Markham's "Man with the Hoe." Smith moves away from Parrington's view that HG and Kirkland were important because they attributed "the bitterness of the frontier to the development of realism in fiction." He sees them as a culmination of a way of looking at Western farm life. *MTR* owes "more to Howe's melancholy than to Kirkland's rather cold fidelity to linguistic fact or his use of a tall tale tradition." HG was "seldom able to integrate his theories with the materials he had gathered by personal experience and observation. The radical ideas occur as concepts. They are seldom realized imaginatively--perhaps never fully except in 'Under the Lion's Paw.' " HG's "strength lay in a simple humanitarian sympathy that was enitrely congruous with the sentimental tradition."

C350. Smith, Herbert F. *Richard Watson Gilder.* N.Y.: Twayne, 1970. Pp. 91-103 and passim as indexed.

Detailed and valuable analysis of the Gilder-HG relationship. After examining correspondence closely,

Smith concludes that Gilder did not try to turn HG away from "writing stories of social protest" but was more concerned with "literary effectiveness." This is an attempt to vindicate Gilder from recent critical attacks on him as a corrupter of HG.

C351. Smith, Martha Stribling. "A Study of the Realistic Treatment of Psychic Phenomena in Selected Fiction of William Dean Howells, HG, Henry James, Frank Norris, and Theodore Dreiser." Unpublished dissertation. U of North Carolina, Chapel Hill, 1972. [DAI, 33 (1972), 1743A-1744A.]

The evidence indicates that HG "was deceived by the mediums whom he was investigating because of his own psychological involvement. His interpretation of reality in his fiction is consequently distorted." *Tyranny* and *VO's Discipline* are discussed.

C352. Snell, George. *The Shapers of American Fiction/1798-1947*. N.Y.: Dutton, 1947. Pp. 200, 224.

HG's debts to Howells, Twain, Howe, and De Forest are mentioned. "G's work was an extension of the local colorists' methods, in that it showed signs of the French naturalists' influence and spoke forthrightly of many things Howells would have excluded from his own novels."

C353. Solomon, Eric. *Stephen Crane/From Parody to Realism*. Cambridge, Mass.: Harvard U Press, 1966. Pp. 11, 178.

Brief reference to HG as early mentor of Crane (11) and as a pre-Crane portrayer of realistic small town life (178).

C354. ---. *Stephen Crane in England*. Columbus: Ohio State U Press, 1964. Pp. 7, 11, 12, 26, 58, and passim as indexed.

Notes on the HG-Crane relationship, which is called, from HG's point of view, "avuncular and condescending."

C355. Spayd, Barbara Grace. "Introduction: HG," *The Long Trail*. N.Y.: Harper, 1935. Pp. xiii-lxvii.

Detailed and extended account of HG's life to date. This edition also includes a "Preface" (ix-xii), the text of "The Return of a Private," and "Suggestions for Study" (305-332).

C356. Speake, Clara E. "Iowa Dialect in the Work of G and Quick." Unpublished M.A. thesis. U of Iowa, 1926.
Not seen.

C357. Spencer, Benjamin T. *The Quest for Nationality/An American Literary Campaign.* Syracuse, N.Y.: Syracuse U Press, 1957. Pp. 253, 259, 287, 292, 322, and passim as indexed.
HG, Eggleston, Riley, Howells, and a host of local colorists "found no incompatibility in holding at once to a national literary end and local means." HG's "doctrine of 'veritism'. . . was essentially local realism"--"a somewhat pretentious and naive version of realism."

C358. ---. "Regionalism in American Literature," in *Regionalism in America*, ed. Merrill Jensen. Madison: U of Wisconsin Press, 1951. Pp. 219-260.
HG is discussed, pp. 230-231, 237-242. Largest section is devoted to a summary of major ideas in *CI* and their implications for the writers who came after HG.

C359. Sper, Felix. *From Native Roots/A Panorama of Our Regional Drama.* Caldwell, Idaho: Caxton Printers, 1948. P. 189.
Brief mention of "Wheel" which "stripped away the false glamor from the barren existence in the Boomtown of 1884." Calls "Wheel" "probably the first" thesis play "to be written in this country" and notes that "the action is loose and episodic and definitely contrived to prove a set of premises."

C360. Spiller, Robert E. *The Cycle of American Literature.* N.Y.: Macmillan, 1956. P. 201 and passim as indexed.
"In the faltering insights of this son of the prairie, American naturalism found its first unqualified state-

ment and illustration in fiction." The movement of
realism to the harsher aspects of naturalism brought
with it a certain pessimism which was "making its
inroads without benefit of fresh insights or more flex-
ible methods of expression." "Even the serious work
of Howells, James, Crane, G, and London could not
break into the close knit frame of British-American
romantic values, built up in a century of expanding
political power and unlimited economic resources."

C361. ---. "Introduction," *Crumbling Idols*. Gainesville, Fla.:
Scholars' Facsimiles and Reprints, 1952. Pp. i-viii.
HG "recognized, as Howells did not always, the in-
adequacy of a literary philosophy that left the artist a
passive recorder of objective facts." He wanted "the
faithful recording of *truth* rather than mere fact." Realism and veritism in literature differ as do realism and
impressionism in art, and "much of the value of G's
essay lies in his comparative treatment of the movement
in the two arts." Furthermore, "G's plea for impressionism in literature and art ... was answered by the
tales of Stephen Crane and Henry James with much more
artistry than he himself could manage, but no one at
that time defined the issue as sharply as he did." Later
"the subjective symbolism of O'Neill, Eliot, Hemingway,
and Faulkner created a literary movement that went far
beyond anything the young G dreamed, even though it
followed, in the main, the path which his book suggested."
Concludes with interesting note on the actual printing
of *CI* by Stone and Kimball and a description of the appearance of the book.

C362. ---. *The Third Dimension*. N.Y.: Macmillan, 1946; rptd 1965.
P. 108.
HG's veritism as expounded in *CI* is quite important because "committed as ... [HG] was to the descriptive
techniques of the new realism and inadequate as he was
an artist, by this essay he became one of the first Americans of this period to suggest an aesthetic answer to
the moral dilemma of the American artist. In a brief moment of insight, he saw the artist as sovereign over the
small island of his own consciousness and as legislator

245

in the realms of color and form if not in those of good and evil.''

---. ''Toward Naturalism in Fiction.'' See *Literary History of the United States/History.*

---, Willard Thorp, Thomas H. Johnson, and Henry Seidel Canby, eds. *Literary History of the United States.* See *Literary History of the United States.*

C363. Stallings, Frank L., Jr. ''B. O. Flower and *The Arena:* Literature as an Agent of Social Protest.'' Unpublished dissertation. U of Texas, 1961.
Not seen.

C364. Stallman, R. W. *Stephen Crane.* N.Y.: Braziller, 1968. Pp. 34, 76-77, 87-109, 215, and passim as indexed.
Detailed examination of the HG-Crane relationship.

C365. ---, and Lillian Gilkes, eds. *Stephen Crane/Letters.* N.Y.: New York U Press, 1960. Pp. 14, 16, 29, 35-36, 41, 59-60, 126, 152, 308-309, 318-319, 334, and passim as indexed.
Reprints letters by HG and by Crane dealing with the HG-Crane relationship.
Also reprints letters which merely mention HG.

C366. Stanton, Theodore, ed. *Manual of American Literature.* N.Y.: Putnam's, 1909. Pp. 229-230, 447.
Brief summary of HG's career and achievement (229-230). *Rose* is his ''best novel,'' and he has ''for the most part wisely obeyed his own dictum, to write only of what one knows; his later work shows a notable increase in vigour and grasp of the story-teller's art.''
HG is also listed (447) as contributor to *Century Magazine.*

C367. Starke, Aubrey Harrison. *Sidney Lanier.* N.Y.: Russell & Russell, 1964. Pp. 357-358 and passim as indexed.
HG's early poetry ''does reveal the influence of Lanier.'' HG is supposed to have said that Lanier had ''come to him unheralded and unknown, exalted him, transformed

him, and taught him the essential lesson of life as of art, the lesson of freedom within the law.''

C368. Stegner, Wallace, ed. *The American Novel/From James Fenimore Cooper to William Faulkner.* N.Y.: Basic Books, 1965. Pp. 93, 145, 167, 169.
Glancing references to HG in several essays.

C369. Stewart, George R:, Jr. *Bret Harte/Argonaut and Exile.* Boston and N.Y.: Houghton Mifflin, 1931. P. 319.
HG met Harte in London and suggested that this outwardly bitter man return to America.

C370. Stone, Albert E. *The Innocent Eye.* New Haven, Conn.: Yale U Press, 1961. Pp. 101-102.
Brief mention of HG's love of Beadle's dime novels, which he read voraciously.

C371. Stovall, Floyd. *American Idealism.* Norman: U of Oklahoma Press, 1943. Pp. 126-128.
HG was the ''most prominent'' of the ''new realists'' and ''not a literary man by natural inclination though he was by profession; his greatest enthusiasms were humanitarian, and the best of his early years were devoted to the ideal of righting wrongs and building a more equitable social order.''

C372. Sullivan, Mark. *Our Times/The United States 1900-1925.* Vol. I: *The Turn of the Century 1900-1904.* N.Y.: Scribner's, 1926. Pp. 144-146; Vol. IV: *The War Begins.* N.Y.: Scribner's, 1932. Pp. 208, 210.
Vol. I praises *Son*: it ''not only is one of the fine American books of its time in all respects; as an intimate, a sometimes poignantly personal, story of a typical American family that made two . . . migrations in one generation--as such, it is the truest and best of histories.''
In Vol. IV, HG is quoted as asserting that New York was the cultural capital of the United States.

C373. Swanberg, W. A. *Dreiser.* N.Y.: Scribner's, 1965. Pp. 113, 117, 166, 208, 426.

HG admired *Sister Carrie*, met Dreiser in Chicago and admitted to him that he too felt a tendency "to veer from realism" in order to get away from social animosity. HG later came to dislike Dreiser's work because of its sexual realism, a dislike manifested in his opposition to having the Authors' League of America give Dreiser money to help him in *The Genius* controversy.

C374. Tarkington, Booth. "HG," in *Commemorative Tributes of the American Academy of Arts and Letters 1905-1941*. Freeport, N.Y.: Books for Libraries Press, 1968; orig. pub. by the American Academy of Arts and Letters, 1942. Pp. 399-402.

Brief and appreciative rather than critical assessment of HG. Emphasizes his interest in psychic research.

C375. Taylor, Walter Fuller. "Economic Unrest in American Fiction, 1880-1901." Unpublished dissertation. U of North Carolina, 1930.

Not seen. Basis of Taylor's *The Economic Novel in America* (see below).

C376. ---. "HG," in *The Economic Novel in America*. N.Y.: Octagon Books, 1964; orig. pub. by U of North Carolina Press, 1942. Pp. 148-183 and passim as indexed.

HG retained scattered idyllic memories of his childhood in Wisconsin, but the harsh life of the Iowa prairie taught him that "the satisfaction of work might be outweighed by its tortures." Later experiences validated such conclusions, and he crystallized his philosophical, aesthetic, and economic notions into an all-encompassing view of life. Veritism became an ethical as well as an aesthetic principle, and his observation of economic privation for certain classes in America provided the subject matter for much of his fiction.

C377. ---. *A History of American Letters*. N.Y.: American Book, 1936. Pp. 236, 238, 251, 303-307, and passim as indexed.

HG and Norris had a "heavier-handed naturalism" than did Howells. In *MTR* and *Folks* "American realism first escaped completely from the restraints of the

genteel tradition...." HG's *Son* is "no less than the
record of an era in American history," and in it "the
bitterness of these early stories is now subdued in
the mellow light of historical perspective." HG is
"thought to have been influential in awakening Moody's
(W. V.) interest in the Rocky Mountain West."

C378. ---. *The Story of American Letters*. Chicago: Regnery, 1956.
Pp. 275-279 and passim as indexed.
In *MTR* "American realism had already entered a new
phase, and had conquered for our literature a new area
of life." It and *Folks* were the first instances of American realism escaping "completely from the restraints
of the genteel tradition...." In all of these stories
"our realism began its exploration of those ruder, cruder,
and even repulsive phases of life which make up such a
regrettably large proportion of the human story."

C379. Thompson, Lawrance, ed. *Selected Letters of Robert Frost.*
N.Y.: Holt, Rinehart and Winston, 1964. Pp. 265-266.
Letter dated 4 Feb 1921 from Frost to HG concerning
HG's invitation to Frost to attend memorial service for
Howells at N.Y. Public Library on 1 Mar 1921.

C380. Thompson, Slason. *Eugene Field/A Study in Heredity and
Contradictions.* 2 vols. N.Y.: Scribner's, 1901. I,
155; II, 259-260.
Material concerns HG's published interview with
Field. HG was apparently annoyed with Field and wrote
an imaginary sketch; "the whole interview was a serious
piece of business to the serious-minded realist [HG].
To Field, at the time and for months after, it was a huge
and memorable joke" (II, 260).

C381. Thorp, Willard. *American Writing in the 20th Century.* Cambridge, Mass.: Harvard U Press, 1960. P. 156 and
passim as indexed.
HG was the first novelist "to domesticate literary
naturalism in America, but he went only a short distance
towards the naturalism of Norris and Dreiser." He was
influenced by Herbert Spencer.

C382. ---. "Introduction," *Great Short Works of American Realism*, ed. Willard Thorp. N.Y.: Harper & Row, 1968. Pp. xiii-xxii.
HG is mentioned briefly on pp. xiii, xviii, and xxi. Thorp credits HG with being the first to attach the term "local color" to American regional realism.

C383. Tooker, L. Frank. *The Joys and Tribulations of an Editor.* N.Y.: Century, 1924. Pp. 159, 278.
Reminiscences of the editor of *Century* magazine include mention of HG's recording of a conversation with John Burroughs about John Muir and of the fact that *Century* published HG's *Mountain Lover.*

C384. Traubel, Horace. *With Walt Whitman in Camden.* 4 vols. Vol. I, Boston: Small, Maynard, 1906; Vol. II, N.Y.: Appleton Century, 1908; Vol. III, N.Y.: Mitchell Kennerley, 1914; Vol. IV, ed. Scudley Bradley. Philadelphia: U of Pennsylvania Press, 1953. Passim as indexed.
Volumes II, III, IV include letters from and to HG and numerous scattered mentions.

C385. *Twentieth Century Authors*, comp. and ed. Stanley J. Kunitz and Howard Haycraft. N.Y.: Wilson, 1942. Pp. 516-517.
Biographical sketch which includes HG's own brief summary of his life as contained in a letter he wrote to the editors of this volume a few months before his death.

C386. Vanderbilt, Kermit. *The Achievement of William Dean Howells/A Reinterpretation.* Princeton, N.J.: Princeton U Press, 1968. Pp. 129, 190, 198, 200, 203, 205.
Brief references to the HG-Howells relationship.

C387. Van Doren, Carl. *The American Novel 1789-1939.* N.Y.: Macmillan, 1940. Pp. 225-228 and passim as indexed.
HG was spokesman for dissenters against the "official type of realism favored by Howells." Whereas the "romancers had studied the progress of the frontier in the lives of its victors; G studied it in the lives of its victims...." HG stood closer to "the humane Millet than to the angry Zola."

C388. ---. "Argument," in *Contemporary American Novelists 1900-1920*. N.Y.: Macmillan, 1922. Pp. 38-47.
[Rptd in revised form from *Nation*, 113 (23 Nov 1921), 596-597. See under "Periodicals."]

C389. Vogel, Stanley M., and Ella M. Murphy. *An Outline of American Literature/From Civil War to Present Day*. 2 vols. Boston: Student Outlines, 1961. II, 14, 112-116.
HG "strove to give a completely realistic picture of rural life in the Middle West"; his story "Up the Coulee" is unforgettable for its "relentless, objective realism."

C390. Wagenknecht, Edward C. *Mark Twain/The Man and His Work*. Norman: U of Oklahoma Press, 1935; 1961. Pp. 57, 165.
Brief mention of HG's meetings with Twain.

C391. ---. "Towards Naturalism--2. HG: 'Veritism' and After," in *Cavalcade of the American Novel, From the Birth of the Nation to the Middle of the Twentieth Century*. N.Y.: Holt, Rinehart and Winston, 1952. Pp. 205-212 and passim as indexed.
HG embodied his critical theories in only one novel: *Rose*. All of his other novels deal with the romantic materials of the Far West. *Norsk* is the best of his early novels. *Rose* is the novel "which best exemplifies G's early ideals." As Howells one time indicated, *Money Magic* is the best of his later works. Commenting on HG's "decline," Wagenknecht says, "Writers do not usually turn away from their native material until they have exhausted the use they can make of it, and the truth of the matter is that, outside of *MTR*, G's strongest social and economic convictions had never directly inspired his best work." HG's "richest and most characteristic mood was achieved late, in *Son* and its successors."

C392. ---. *William Dean Howells/The Friendly Eye*. N.Y.: Oxford U Press, 1969. Pp. 48-49, 70, 89-90, 119-120, 273.
Brief references to the HG-Howells relationship, usually in the form of HG's estimates or memories of Howells or Howells' opinion of or advice to HG.

C393. Wagner, William Douglas. "The Short Stories of HG: *MTR* and *Folks*--A Critical Analysis." Unpublished dissertation. Bowling Green State U, 1972. [DAI, 33 (1972), 289A.]

Study employs "a mechanistic literary analysis" to examine G's "use of the traditional elements of the short story--character, plot and narrative method, setting, structure, and style." Conclusion is that, "drawing upon a single formula for effective composition and fired by strong emotion," G "produced some of the finest stories of American farm life ever written."

C394. Walcutt, Charles Child. "Adumbrations: Harold Frederic and HG," in *American Literary Naturalism, a Divided Stream*. Minneapolis: U of Minnesota Press, 1956. Pp. 45-65 and passim as indexed.

HG was one of the first writers to show traces of naturalism in his work but not as "a thoroughly formulated philosophy." What does appear in his work "is an infusion of vigorous new blood into the pale and attenuated Victorian forms then available to the American writer." *CI* was less hostile than it at first seemed. HG's realism was tempered considerably by Gilder and the genteel tradition and, as the happy ending of *Jason Edwards* shows, HG "was already yearning to abandon the hard life of a radical for the comfortable prestige of literary circles." HG, like Frederic, had trouble constructing plots, especially when he moved from sketches, which he did so well (*MTR*), to novels. His sketches present a determinism which is set off against a moral order and the plea for help in easing the burdens of Western man. Form and meaning are united artistically in HG's sketches, which are confining in themselves; they are tight and unmoving, and the "characters are trapped." However, when HG introduces movement into the sketches, as in "A Branch Road," he can't stop talking and must continue his protestations. His "determinism is pure protest." *Rose* shows the beginnings of naturalism in fiction and gives HG a place in the history of American literature.

C395. Walker, Franklin. *Frank Norris/A Biography*. Garden City,
N.Y.: Doubleday, Doran, 1932; rptd Russell & Russell,
1963. Passim as indexed.
In *MTR* and *Rose*, "HG, continuing in the footsteps
of Kirkland and Howe, began to apply continental
methods to the school of local color, coining for them
the name 'veritism' and defending them in *CI* (1894)"
(237).

C396. Walker, Warren S., comp. *Twentieth-Century Short Story
Explication/Interpretations, 1900-1966, Of Short Fiction
Since 1800*. 2d ed. Hamden, Conn: Shoe String, 1967.
Pp. 197-198.
Fourteen HG stories are listed.

C397. Wann, Louis. "HG," in *The Rise of Realism/American
Literature From 1860 to 1900*, ed. Louis Wann. Rev. ed.
N.Y.: Macmillan, 1949. Pp. 860-862.
Biographical sketch, followed by quite complete list-
ing of HG's books and selected works about him. Also
includes notes for three HG selections in the anthology:
"Under the Lion's Paw," "Literary Emancipation of the
the West" [from *CI*], and "A Visit to the West" [from
Son].

C398. Ward, A. C. *American Literature 1880-1930*. N.Y.: Dial,
1932. P. 255.
Mention of *Son* in discussion of the richness of early
20th-century American autobiography.

C399. Warfel, Harry R., and G. Harrison Orians, eds. "Introduction,"
American Local-Color Stories. N.Y.: American Book,
1941. Pp. xxii-xxiii, 598.
HG was a writer of Middle West "whose two volumes
of short stories exemplified the author's new literary
theory, veritism, which demonstrated that local color,
if not always realistic, is not opposed to realism."
Short biographical sketch (598).

C400. Wasserstrom, William. *Heiress of All the Ages/Sex and
Sentiment in the Genteel Tradition*. Minneapolis: U
of Minnesota Press, 1959. Pp. 80-81 and passim as indexed.

Examination of *Rose,* specifically the father-daughter
relationship, in discussion of the presentation of women
in American literature.

C401. Webb, Walter Prescott. *The Great Plains.* N.Y.: Ginn, 1931.
Pp. 453, 470-473, 483, 485.

HG's place in the literature of the Great Plains belongs
in the category of "The Literature of the Farm" as compared to the more romantic "Literature of the Frontier
and the Cattle Kingdom." An exponent of life on the
prairie farm, his interpretation of that life as unrelieved
ugliness suggests that he "caught the spirit of the agricultural prairie, but he did not catch the spirit of the
Plains."

C402. Weber, Harley Ronald. "Midwestern Farm Writing in the
Late Nineteenth Century: A Study in Changing Attitudes."
Unpublished dissertation. U of Minnesota, 1967. [DA,
28 (1968), 3160A-3161A.]

HG is one of three writers who are examined closely
in this study (Howe and Kirkland are the other two).
Conclusion reached is that "in their best work Howe,
Kirkland and G did indeed challenge the beliefs that
were their common inheritance; they did re-examine, and
in many respects find wanting, the ideology of the Jack-
sonian past. But their questioning never became a re-
pudiation; it remained tentative, qualified, incomplete,
a loosening of basic convictions and the beginnings of
intellectual change rather than transformation. In important ways the agrarian realists remained firmly plant-
ed in the beliefs of the past."

C403. West, Ray B., Jr. *The Short Story in America 1900-1950.*
Chicago: Regnery, 1952. Pp. 28-30 and passim as indexed.

HG, Crane, and Howells "mark the beginning of
naturalistic fiction in America" though they really belong to the nineteenth century. The main stream of
American naturalism runs from HG, through Norris and
Dreiser, to Farrell.

C404. Westbrook, Perry D. *Mary Wilkins Freeman*. N.Y.: Twayne, 1967. Pp. 69, 111, 120, 172.
Brief mention of HG, who "unintentionally" reduced the concept of local color to "absurdity when he branded as local color all literature that conveys a feeling for place or period." At a 1926 ceremony HG gave Mrs. Freeman the Howells Medal of the American Academy of Letters.

C405. Whipple, T. K. *Study Out the Land*. Berkeley and Los Angeles: U of California Press, 1943. Pp. 69-84.
[Rptd from *New Republic*, 90 (21 Apr 1937), 311-314. See under "Periodicals."]

C406. White, William Allen. *The Autobiography of William Allen White*. N.Y.: Macmillan, 1946. Pp. 217, 288-289.
White met HG on train going to Populist meeting in Kansas. Reminiscences of HG in Chicago at the turn of the century.

C407. ---. "Fiction of the Eighties and Nineties," in *American Writers on American Literature*, ed. John Macy. N.Y.: Liveright, 1931. Pp. xi, 389-399.
HG, a writer of the Middle West, protested against "the smugness of the pastoral writers who told of the delights of the rural scene" (390). HG sent a story to R. W. Gilder, who was upset with the "loose English anachronisms, vulgarisms" which HG used in his work.

C408. ---. *Selected Letters of William Allen White/1899-1943*, ed. Walter Johnson. N.Y.: Holt, 1947. P. 171.
In letter of 10 Oct 1916 to Norman Hapgood, White mentions that HG wanted him to sign a statement taking sides in the 1916 presidential campaign, but White refused.

C409. Williams, Blanche Colton. "HG," in *Our Short Story Writers*. N.Y.: Moffat, Yard, 1920. Pp. 182-199.
Detailed biographical sketch followed by more specific analyses. "Up the Coulé" is "the best example of unflinching realism produced in its decade" and, with *Son,*

illustrates "the approved method of the realist artist."
Howard in the story is "a composite of Hamlin and
Frank," and Grant represents HG's father. In "A
Day of Grace" Milton Jennings is modeled after HG's
friend Burton. Also discussed are the significance of
hands in HG's works, his use of the church setting, his
depiction of young men, and his occasional optimism.

C410. Williams, Stanley T. *American Literature.* Philadelphia:
Lippincott, 1933. Pp. 135, 160.
HG's "sometimes acrid" pictures of farm life contrast
with Howells' simple and serene stories (135).

C411. ---. *The American Spirit in Letters.* Vol. XI of The Pageant
of America Series. New Haven, Conn.: Yale U Press,
1926. P. 277.
HG, as realist, described his early life "with a bitterness that we can understand but not always condone."
He "softened" in his later works, but he became "too
ready to teach us something."

C412. ---, and Nelson F. Adkins, eds. *Courses of Reading in
American Literature with Bibliographies.* N.Y.: Harcourt, Brace, 1930. Pp. 133-134.
Listing of major HG works and of a few critical pieces
about him.

Wilson, Otilie Erickson. See Wilson, Rufus Rockwell, with
Otilie Erickson Wilson.

C413. Wilson, Rufus Rockwell, with Otilie Erickson Wilson. *New
York in Literature/The Story Told in the Landmarks of
Town and Country.* Elmira, N.Y.: Primavera Press,
1947. Pp. 103, 109, 111, 113, 120-121, 158-159, 178,
218-219, 277, 323.
Scattered mention of HG before he moved to California,
when he lived in New York. Many of these brief references are
quotations from HG's volumes of reminiscences relating
to experiences he had in New York and to his memories
of encounters with various other writers then living in
New York, including Crane, Edwin Markham, John Burroughs, Howells, and Kate Douglas Wiggin.

C414. Witham, W. Tasker. *The Adolescent in the American Novel.* N.Y.: Frederick Ungar, 1964. Pp. 185-186.

In speaking of the influence of communities on adolescents in the West, Witham points out that "the harshness of Midwest farm life which HG made famous in *MTR* (1891) appears in most twentieth-century novels as an occasional danger rather than a constant condition."

C415. ---. *Panorama of American Literature.* N.Y.: Stephen Daye, 1947. Pp. 196-198.

Brief summary of HG's career.

C416. Woodress, James. *Booth Tarkington/Gentleman from Indiana.* Philadelphia: Lippincott, 1955. Pp. 40, 74, and passim as indexed.

HG and Tarkington shared interest in spiritualism and admired each other's work.

C417. ---. *Dissertations in American Literature/1891-1966.* Rev. and enl. ed. Durham, N.C.: Duke U Press, 1968. Items 1040-1046.

In addition to the seven dissertations on HG which are listed, cross-references direct attention to five others which relate to him.

C418. *The World's Best Literature,* ed. John W. Cunliffe and Ashley H. Thorndike. N.Y.: Warner, 1917. X, 6195-6196.

Brief summary of HG's life and major works to date precedes reprinting of his poem "A Summer Mood" and the storm on Lake Michigan scene from *Rose.* "At times, carelessness of technique and lack of taste can be detected in his writings, but his strength and spirit make amends for these defects." *CI* is "a series of audacious papers...racy and stimulating in the extreme." *Songs* "contains many a stroke of imaginative beauty." *MTR* includes "work as striking as anything he has done." *Norsk* "possesses a fine romantic flavor." *Rose,* "decidedly his strongest full-length fiction," is "daringly unconventional, but strong, earnest."

C419. Wright, Austin McGiffert. *The American Short Story in the Twenties*. Chicago: U of Chicago Press, 1961. Pp. 26-28, 36-38, 43-44, 61-62, 202-203, 292-294, 378-379, 382-384, 398, and passim as indexed.

Considerable brief scattered mention of HG's stories under various of the divisions which Wright establishes: "The Individual in His Society" ("a prominent feature of the world of G is the co-operative community spirit, solidarity that is highly effective and beneficial to all"); "People and Places"; "Social Problems" ("most of the suffering in G's world is a result of the community's struggle with the 'land' "); and "Comedy and Romance." A scene from "Under the Lion's Paw" is excerpted as Appendix F and briefly analyzed.

C420. Wright, Lyle H. *American Fiction/1876-1900/A Contribution Toward a Bibliography*. San Marino, Calif.: Huntington Library, 1966. Pp. 214-215.

Lists twelve titles by HG, with brief descriptions in several instances, and indication of libraries owning copies of all titles listed.

C421. Wright, Nathalia. *American Novelists in Italy*. Philadelphia: U of Pennsylvania Press, 1965. P. 22.

HG was one of those novelists of the 20th century "who have visited but been little if at all inspired by Italy."

C422. Wykes, Alan. *A Concise Survey of American Literature*. N.Y.: Library Publishers, 1955. Pp. 101-102, 176.

HG and Howells foreshadowed Crane's naturalism. In *MTR* and *Folks* "is to be found no single concession to refinement or romanticism." Readers rejected HG's early work until "the literary climate had completely changed and naturalism was an accepted thing."

C423. Zardoya, Concha. *Historia De La Literatura Norteamericana*. Barcelona: Editorial Labor, 1956. Pp. 178-179.

Brief summary of HG's life and writing career.

C424. Ziff, Larzer. "Crushed Yet Complacent: HG and Henry Blake Fuller," in *The American 1890's/Life and Times of a Lost Generation.* N.Y.: Viking, 1966. Pp. 93-119 and passim as indexed.

Not very sympathetic to HG, Ziff presents a detailed biographical sketch and points out that he was not equipped for local-color stories because they demand "a tranquil and loving sense of region" and conscious literary development. HG was able, to some degree, with the assistance of Kirkland, to turn out local-color stories. However, his language is often weak, and he tends to state rather than dramatize. "When finally, in the mid-nineties, G settled into writing romances about life in the Rockies, this was not so much a betrayal of his promise as an acceptance of the themes for which his language was better suited." One reason for HG's retreat from realism was his desire for more popular appeal and his wish to reach larger audiences provided by a magazine like *McClure's.*

INDEX

This index is in three parts. The first is an index to the authors of the entries in the Garland Checklist. The second is an index to the subjects of the entries in the checklist, with the major exception of Hamlin Garland's own writings. The third section is an index to Garland's works as subjects of the entries in the checklist.

This index is largely the work of Mrs. Joanne Giza, to whom the compilers of the checklist owe an immense debt of gratitude.

I. Author Index

262

263

Hale, Edward E., Jr. A50

Halleck, Reuben Post C157

Halsey, Francis W. A124

Hamilton, Clayton B324

Hammond, Percy B135

Handlin, Oscar C167

Haney, John Louis C160

Hansen, Chadwick A456

Harbert, Earl N. C330

Harkins, Edward F. C161

Harlow, Alvin F. C162

Harris, Elbert Leroy C163

Harrison, Stanley R. B425

Hart, James D. C164, C165

Harte, Walter Blackburn A5,
 B73, B80

Hartwick, Harry C166

Harwick, Robert B387

Hatcher, Harlan C168

Hatton, Frederic B129

Hawthorne, Hildegarde A315,
 A322

Haycraft, Howard C385

Hayes, Marion D. A352, A390

Haynie, Henry A203

Hazard, Lucy Lockwood C169,
 C170

Henson, Clyde C171

Henson, Clyde E. B350

Herne, James A. C172

Herne, Mrs. James A. C172

Herne, Julia A. C114, C172

Herron, Ima Honaker C173, C174

Hewlett, Maurice A327

Hicks, Granville A393, C175

Hicks, John D. C176, C177

Higgins, John E. B401

Higginson, Thomas Wentworth
 C178

Hilfer, Anthony Channell C179

Hill, E. B. B175

Hill, Eldon C. B232, B325, C180,
 C181

Hippensteel, H. S. C182

Hoeltje, Hubert H. B212

Hoffman, Daniel G. C183

Hoffman, Frederick J. C184, C185

Hofstadter, Richard C186, C187

Holaday, Clayton A. C188

Holloway, Jean C189, C190, C191

Holman, C. Hugh C192

Holsinger, Paul M. B416

Hopkins, Mary Alden A279

Hopkins, Frederick M. B175

Hornberger, Theodore B339, C35

Horton, Rod W. C193

Horwill, Herbert W. A221

Hough, Robert L. C194

Howard, Leon C195

Howe, M. A. De Wolfe C22

Howe, Will D. C6

Howell, Eleanor R. B101

Howells, Mildred C196

Howells, William Dean A7, A66,
 A291, B137, C159, C197, C198

Hubbell, Jay B. A402, C199, C200

Hughes, Hatcher B185

Hurd, Charles E. B30

Hutton, Graham C201

Inge, M. Thomas C202

Inkersly, Arthur B85

Irsfeld, John H. B429

Irwin, Grace Luce A119

Izzo, Carlo C204

Jackson, Anne Wakely A374

James, Henry B93

Jensen, Merrill C358

Johnson, Jane C205

Johnson, Merle B175, C206

Johnson, Thomas H. C239

Johnson, Walter C408

Jones, Arthur E., Jr. B346

Jones, Howard Mumford C207, C208, C209

Jones, Joseph C7

Jones, Richard Foster A317

Jordan-Smith, Paul C22

Kaplan, Justin C210

Karolides, Nicholas J. C211

Katz, Joseph B421

Kazin, Alfred A442, C212

Keiser, Albert C213

Kelly, Florence Finch A300

Kern, Alexander C. C90

Kilmer, Joyce B147

Kindilien, Carlin T. C214

Kirk, Clara M. B413

Kirk, Rudolf C216

Knight, Grant C. C217, C218, C219

Knowlton, Kent A355

Koerner, James D. B358

Kolb, Harold H., Jr. C220

Kramer, Dale C221

Kranendonk, A. G. Van C223

Krause, Sydney J. C224

Kuhig, Verna K. A451

Kunitz, Stanley J. C240, C385

Labrie, Rodrique Edward C225

Lake, Ivan Clyde B182

Lanier, Sidney C367

Lapham, J. A. B195

Latham, Harold S. C22

Lawrence, Josephine C22

Lawton, William Cranston C226

Lazenby, Walter B400

Leary, Lewis C227, C228

Lee, Guy Carleton A146, A160

Leighton, George R. B263

Leisy, Ernest E. C229, C230

Lenehan, William T. C231

Leonard, Neil B411

Lewis, Lloyd C232

Lewis, Sinclair C233

Lewisohn, Ludwig C234

Lieberman, Elias C236

Lillard, Richard G. C80

Linson, Corwin R. C237

Liptzin, Sol C238

Little, Richard Henry B141

Loggins, Vernon C241

Long, E. Hudson C45

Lord, Isabel Garland C22

Loveman, Amy A391, B302

Lovett, Robert Morss A326,
  B111, C242

Lowe, Orton C243

Lowry, Robert C22

Luccock, Halford E. C244

Ludeke, Henry C245

Ludwig, Richard M. C246

Lyon, Peter C247

Mabie, Hamilton Wright A123,
  B70

MacArthur, James A179

MacDonald, William A404,
  A418

Macy, John C407

Maillard, Denyse C257

Mane, Robert B402, C22,
  C258

Mann, Arthur C259

Mann, Charles W., Jr. A452

Mantle, Burns B123

Marble, Annie Russell C260

Marchand, Ernest C261

Marchand, J. A264

Markham, Edwin A253, C159

Marsh, Philip C262

Martin, Jay C263

Martinec, Barbara B428

Marx, Leo A454

Masefield, John C22

Matthews, Brander A12

Matthiessen, F. O. C265, C266

Matusow, Allen J. B395

Maule, Harry E. C233

Maurice, Arthur A366

May, Henry F. C267

McAleer, John J. C248

McComb, E. H. Kemper C249

McDowell, Frederick P. W. C250

McElderry, Bruce R., Jr. B351,
  B365, B378, C22, C251, C252,
  C253

McGall, Edith C254

McKeehan, Irene Pettit C255

McMurray, William C256

Mencken, H. L. A371, C268,
  C269

Mendum, E. Bedloe A97

Meriwether, Lee B326

Metcalf, John Calvin C271

Metzger, Charles R. C311

Metzger, Walter C51

Meyer, Roy W. B418, C272

Michaud, Regis C273

Miers, Earl Schenck C208

Millard, Bailey B243

Miller, Charles T. B412

Miller, James McDonald C274

Millgate, Michael C275

269

Wagner, William Douglas C393
Walcutt, Charles Child C394
Walker, Franklin C395
Walker, Robert H. B391
Walker, Warren S. C396
Wann, Louis C397
Ward, A. C. C398
Warfel, Harry R. C399
Wasserstrom, William C400
Weaver, James B. B146
Webb, Walter Prescott C401
Weber, Harley Ronald C402
Weiss, Irving R. C6
Wertheim, Stanley B417, B422
West, Ray B., Jr. C403
Westbrook, Perry D. C404
Whipple, T. K. B253, C405
White, William Allen A377,
  A388, B221, C406, C407, C408
Whitford, Kathryn B389, B406,
  B419
Wiggin, Marian A449

Williams, Blanche Colton C409
Williams, John Joseph B410
Williams, Stanley T. C410, C411,
  C412
Williams, Talbott A83
Wilson, Edmund B426
Wilson, Otilie Erickson C413
Wilson, Rufus Rockwell C413
Wingate, Charles E. L. B20, B25,
  B33, B46
Witham, W. Tasker C414, C415
Woodress, James C8, C9, C10,
  C11, C12, C416, C417
Woods, Katherine A368
Woods, Mary Katherine B134
Wright, Austin McGiffert C419
Wright, Lyle H. C420
Wright, Nathalia C421
Wulling, Emerson B385
Wykes, Alan C422
Zardoya, Concha C423
Ziff, Larzer C424

II. Subject Index

Adams, Henry C339

"Addolorata's Intervention"
B426

Age of Innocence C242

Aldrich, Thomas Bailey B378,
C134

Alice in Wonderland A371

An American Tragedy C275

Babcock, Burton B407

Badger, Retta B233

Barrie, Sir James M. B196

Beadle C370

Bellamy, Edward C120

Bennett, Horace C134

Bentzon, Th. B100, B368, C19

Bierce, Ambrose C207

"Black Riders" B396

Booth, Edwin B372

The Border Legion A288

Boyesen, H. H. C119

Bromfield, Louis A337

Burlingame, Roger C88

Burroughs, John B170, C383,
C413

Butler, Samuel C1

Cable, George Washington
B78, B79, B399, C120, C210,
C265

Caldwell, Erskine B302

Canby, Henry Seidel C342

Carpenter, Frank G. B91

Cary, Alice C299

Cather, Willa B169, B232, B284,
B362, C40, C57, C233, C321

Catherwood, Mary Hartwell B63,
B340, B379, C97, C344

The Chicago Renaissance in American Letters B364

Clavernook C299

The Confident Years C58

Conrad, Joseph A350

Conway, Moncure C200

Cooper, James Fenimore A329,
C316

Cozzens, James Gould C275

Crane, Cora C149

Crane, Stephen A379, B104, B186,
B213, B228, B347, B361, B373,
B386, B396, B402, B403, B406,
B417, B422, B423, C17, C29,
C32, C34, C47, C56, C62, C71,
C79, C146, C148, C149, C183,
C207, C225, C231, C237, C281,
C298, C308, C310, C330, C340,
C353, C354, C360, C361, C364,
C365, C403, C413

Criticism and Fiction C215, C218

Cross, Milton B209

272

274

275

III. Works by Hamlin Garland

A99, A103, A456, A457,
A458, B198, B378, C33,
C134, C167, C203, C251,
C252, C263

"A Branch Road" A54, B31,
B414, C37, C125, C236, C341,
C394

The Captain of the Gray-Horse
Troop A120, A121, A122,
A123, A124, A125, A126,
A127, A128, A129, A130,
A161, A167, A179, A207,
A318, A326, B198, B418,
C60, C80, C167, C213, C217,
C260

Cavanaugh A252, A253,
A254, A255, A256, A257,
A258, A259, A260, A261,
A266, B198, C80, C307,
C322

"Color in the Wheat" C126

Companions On The Trail A387,
A388, A389, A390, A391,
A392, A393, A394, A395,
A396, A397, A399, A400,
A401, A402, B226, C150

Crumbling Idols A45, A47,
A48, A49, A50, A51, A52,
A54, A452, A453, A454,
A455, B82, B87, B314,
B338, B340, B346, B349,
B360, B373, B411, B427,

C4, C27, C35, C85, C105, C119,
C140, C151, C153, C166, C205,
C212, C218, C222, C267, C273,
C296, C315, C322, C332, C358,
C361, C362, C394, C395, C397,
C418

"Current Fiction Heroes" B181

A Daughter of the Middle Border
A311, A312, A313, A314, A315,
A316, A317, A318, A319, A321,
A328, A403, B162, B163, B198,
B353, C49, C51, C159, C207,
C260

"A Day of Grace" A264, C409

"A Day's Pleasure" B248

"Delmar of Pima" C334

"The Development of American
Literature" B83

"The Drift of the Drama" B83

"Drifting Crane" C91

The Eagle's Heart A104, A106,
A108, A109, A110, A111, B103,
C53, C303

"Ebb-Tide in Realism" B63

"Elder Pill" A267

"The Evolution of American
Thought" B370, B397

"The Farmer's Wife" A46

The Forester's Daughter A273,
A274, A275, A276, A277, A278,
A279, A280, C269

Fortunate Exiles B333, B335

279